Second Language Research Methods

Herbert W Seliger
Elana Shohamy

Oxford University Press 1989

Oxford University Press
Walton Street, Oxford OX2 6DP

Oxford New York Toronto
Delhi Bombay Calcutta Madras Karachi
Petaling Jaya Singapore Hong Kong Tokyo
Nairobi Dar es Salaam Cape Town
Melbourne Auckland

and associated companies in
· Berlin Ibadan

Oxford, *Oxford English*, and the *Oxford English* logo are trade marks of
Oxford University Press

ISBN 0 19 437067 4

Typeset in 10 on 12 Sabon
by Hope Services (Abingdon) Ltd
Printed in Hong Kong

Contents

Acknowledgments

We wish to thank our respective families for suffering through the birth pangs of this book. We hope they will regard the result as worth the effort.

We would also like to thank our students, who have responded to much of this material and who have taught us much about the problems encountered in the first stages of carrying out research. Finally, we wish to acknowledge the contribution of our fellow second language researchers. May we all continue to learn from each other.

Introduction

What this book is about

It is evident to anyone reading research in second language acquisition, that the field is *inter-disciplinary*. The study of second language acquisition can be linguistic, psycholinguistic, sociolinguistic, sociological, psychological, and educational. That is, it draws on a wide number of perspectives about the phenomena of second language as well as the research methodology associated with these different disciplines.

We have tried to give equal focus to a variety of approaches to research in this book but realize that we could not hope to describe all the possible methods or all of the possible types of research. We have, therefore, tried to describe what could be considered paradigmatic types and principles of second language research. The possible designs of research in second language are only limited by the ingenuity of the researcher and the conditions under which the research is being conducted.

The purpose of this book is to introduce the process of carrying out research in second language acquisition and bilingualism. The book is aimed at those who are new to second language research, or who may have done some research without guidance. It is intended for graduate and undergraduate students in courses in research methods and design, specifically in second language acquisition, bilingualism, and applied linguistics.

As the reader of this text gains experience in the process of conducting second language research, he or she will discover that such research is conducted in a wide variety of environments, natural and formal, with subjects of different ages and with a wide variety of goals and underlying theories.

The text discusses second language research from the conception of research questions through the development of research designs, data-gathering procedures and data analysis. However, we have not provided recipes for carrying out research but have taken the approach that if the reader understands the *principles* involved in the unique and varied conditions of second language research, he or she will be able to analyze a research problem and develop an appropriate methodology and design.

As will be evident from a review of the table of contents, this book does not deal with statistics except in a very limited way in Chapter 9. Statistical procedures should not be confused with the thought that must go into research method and design. We felt at the outset that what is not needed is another book on statistics. Several good texts on statistics are already in existence and we have given a reference list of some of them in the Appendix. Chapter 9 gives an overview of some of the more common data-analysis procedures which are used in second language acquisition but we strongly recommend that anyone intending to pursue second language research acquire a more in-depth knowledge of statistical procedures for research.

The table of contents reveals that we have focused on the preparatory stages of conducting research, since we feel that it is only with careful and fastidious preparation that good research can be carried out. It has been our experience both as active researchers in second language and as members of thesis and dissertation committees, that the first stages of exploring the ideas for research and developing the structure of the actual study are, without doubt, the most important. To paraphrase the Buddha's teachings: if the builder of a house finishes his work with the finest roof but the house rests on a poorly constructed foundation, the roof and all that is under it will collapse.

The research cycle

A common thread which unifies this text is the idea that research is *cyclical*. It is an ongoing activity which is never totally completed because each piece of research raises additional questions for more research. Either the results lead the investigator on to related questions or the original question or hypothesis with which the research began cannot be answered or confirmed and the investigation must begin again but with a gain in knowledge and experience.

We have tried to give expression to the essentially cyclical nature of research in the way we have structured this book. It has been organized so as to reflect the cyclical nature of the research process itself.

The research cycle and the organization of the book

> What is research?   (Chapter 1)
>
> A paradigm for second language research   (Chapter 2)
>
> The preparatory stages of research – developing questions and hypotheses for research   (Chapter 3)
>
> Contextualization of research – reading the literature (Chapter 4)
>
> The components of research – taking account of variables; internal and external validity   (Chapter 5)
>
> Research design – qualitative, descriptive, and experimental approaches   (Chapters 6 and 7)
>
> Data collection procedures   (Chapter 8)
>
> Analyzing the data   (Chapter 9)
>
> Putting it all together – drawing conclusions and developing new questions and hypotheses   (Chapter 10)

The parameters of second language research

The conceptual foundation of this book is found in Chapter 2, where we describe a research framework consisting of four parameters that encompass the unique features of research in second language. These parameters describe different aspects of second language investigation and constitute a useful taxonomy for categorizing, describing, and evaluating second language research. Throughout the text, we refer back to these four parameters because they enable us to view research design and method from a more unifying and coherent perspective.

How to use the book

Each chapter contains a set of *activities* based on the content of the chapter and intended to concretize some of the main ideas of that chapter. Carrying out second language research requires thinking *and* doing. In this sense, the chapters, with their accompanying activities, are meant to complement each other so that the text becomes both a discussion of second language research and a 'field manual' for research-like activities. Some of these activities require the reader or student-researcher to consult other texts and journals. Still others require a 'hands on' approach to constructing designs, developing instruments, and so on. These activities are intended to supplement the content of the chapters in which they occur, and to help the reader to think and experience rather than simply read and go on to the next chapter.

1 What is research?

> Race made a slight grimace. 'I'm used to that. It often seems to me that's all detective work is, wiping out your false starts and beginning again.' 'Yes, it is very true that. And it is just what some people will not do. They conceive a certain theory, and everything has to fit into that theory. If one little fact will not fit it, they throw it aside. But it is always the facts that will not fit in that are significant. . .'
>
> (Agatha Christie: *Death on the Nile* 1938)

Introduction

One might say that knowing how to look at research problems and how to carry out research is related to the state of mind of the researcher. The state of mind of the researcher reflects, to some extent, the world in which he or she lives. What researchers believe, what they accept as forms of knowledge, is often a reflection of their social and cultural context. While we would like to think that research is objective and always seeks to show the 'truth' or the 'facts' about some phenomenon which is being investigated, we are not always conscious of the influences around us.

We are living in what we think is a period of scientific objectivity. However, Aristotle, Ptolemy, Galileo, Copernicus, and Einstein all felt this way about their own times and accepted as scientific facts things which later generations would disprove or criticize.

This chapter will be concerned with establishing some ways of thinking about research in general and about second language research in particular, by discussing the following questions:
- How is research similar to and different from naturally occurring cognitive processes involved in learning?
- What are the differences between conclusions reached on the basis of 'common sense' and intuition on the one hand, and scientific procedures on the other?
- And, finally, when we have reached our conclusions, how do we know if they are reliable? That is, how do we know when we really know something?

Research as a natural process

Research and reality

Many of us have images of the researcher dressed in a white smock, spending hours in a laboratory or facing a blackboard filled with arcane mathematical notation, suddenly crying out with great emotion, 'Eureka!' and making a discovery that will forever make his or her name remembered down through the generations. What is closer to the truth is that, as part of natural human activity, we all carry out activities that have the basic characteristics and elements of research.

Not all research is carried out in laboratories or involves complicated statistics. In fact, 'research' is so common that it surrounds us on a daily basis. Every day, we carry out activities that have the same basic components as academic research. We carry out these activities because we seek answers to questions about phenomena that occur in our daily lives.

Let us imagine the following scene: An infant is in a playpen, fenced in from the surrounding world, not yet in control of the language that will enable him to communicate with those around him. The child's parents are sitting in the same room and the child sees an object on the other side of the room. The child wants the object but cannot get out of the playpen. Nor is he able to say, 'Mom, please hand me the ball.' The child views the object and attempts to voice a sound he has come to associate with it. 'Baa,' he calls. No response. 'Baa,' he calls again. This time one of the parents notices the child. 'What is he saying?' asks the parent. The mother suggests to the father that the child is hungry. 'No, I don't think so,' answers the father, 'he has just eaten.' 'Maybe he needs to be changed,' offers the mother. 'Didn't you just change him after he ate?' asks the father.

After many guesses (or *hypotheses*) about what the child is trying to express and the rejection of these possibilities for various reasons, the parents guess that the child wants something. The child's word 'baa' resembles something in the room, a brightly colored ball. The mother develops a new hypothesis. Perhaps the child wants the ball. She crosses the room, picks up the ball, holds it out to the child and says with rising intonation, 'Ball?' The child indicates that this is what he has been trying to say by responding with a smile and a squeal of excitement.

The basic components of research in the real world

We note that this everyday experience contains the following components:

1 There is some form of behavior that is not clearly understood: the child vocalized.
2 The behavior is observed and found to be special for some reason. Questions are raised regarding the reasons for the behavior: why did the child, who had previously been quiet, begin to vocalize?
3 Several possible explanations for the unusual behavior are sought and related in some way to previous knowledge or past events: the baby's unique behavior is related to experiences that he had just had, such as eating or being changed.
4 One of the possible explanations is considered to be the one that most probably explains the behavior. This becomes the parents' 'hypothesis' about the behavior, based on both observed facts and previous knowledge. The other hypotheses are rejected.
5 To test this hypothesis or answer the research question, more data need to be collected about the baby's behavior in other instances of vocalization. In this case, the parents' experiment seems to indicate that the child was indeed vocalizing the word *ball.*

Another way to be certain that the baby was saying the word for 'ball' would be to wait for a second occurrence of the sound 'baa' and pick up another object in the room to check the baby's reaction. Several repetitions of this procedure would lead to the confirmation or rejection of the hypothesis.

Notice also that the parents' hypothesis was formed on the basis of an observed language phenomenon that occurred naturally. Another way of testing the hypothesis would be for the parents to try to elicit a vocalization from the child. They might decide to see whether the baby responds differently when shown different objects and whether he responds consistently with the sound 'baa' when shown the ball. For example, if the parent held up the ball and the child responded with some other word, the parents would have to revise their thinking about the baby's language development. They might conclude that:

1 The hypothesis about the relationship between the vocalization

'baa' and the ball is premature. That is, the parents were imputing to the child linguistic abilities that did not really exist.
2　The child is at a stage in his language development in which he sometimes uses the appropriate word for the object and at other times says whatever comes to mind. In other words, it may be that the child is experimenting with his language ability.

The above demonstrates that research questions can be investigated from many different perspectives by using different procedures such as *observation, questioning, experimentation,* and *elicitation*. Once hypotheses have been formed, tested, and confirmed or rejected, it may be necessary to repeat the experiment or reconfirm the conclusions by researching the question using different means. As we shall see in Chapter 2, each of these different perspectives affects the way the research is carried out.

Research might also be conducted internally in what Einstein referred to as 'mind experiments'. In this case, questions are raised and answers found by using reason and logic. A second language learner may listen to others using the language he or she is trying to acquire and think about the way native speakers use the language. It has long been accepted that the process underlying the acquisition of a second language grammar is hypothesis testing. The following is an actual example of an internal experiment carried out by an eight-year-old second language learner and later reported to her parents.

The child was in the process of acquiring Hebrew as a second language. One day, she was playing with her Hebrew-speaking friends as they were climbing up a rocky hillside. The second language learner heard her Hebrew-speaking friends using the same expression again and again. They were saying *eze kef, eze kef*. At first, she thought that they were saying, 'Oh what rocks, oh what rocks!' But then, she reported, she reasoned to herself, 'Why would they be laughing and talking so much about rocks?' She theorized that they must be saying something that expressed their excitement about the climbing. She concluded that they must be saying something like the English, 'Oh, what fun!' Subsequently, she approached a friend who knew both English and Hebrew and confirmed her interpretation.

These examples demonstrate that research in the broader sense of observing, and forming and testing hypotheses is a process that can take place unconsciously as well as consciously, externally as well as internally and is a basic learning mechanism from infancy through adulthood. As will be seen in this chapter and the following chapters, these same processes are also part of formal or scientific research. Scientific research is what is usually associated with the word 'research' and while we do not usually think of the child acquiring a first or second language as carrying out research, the same basic components are present in scientific research as well as in child language acquisition and in other everyday activities.

However, even though the processes identified with research are also part of normal learning activity, it does not mean that research is simply a matter of doing what comes naturally or acting on the basis of intuition. In order to conduct formal research, it is important to be aware of some important differences between conclusions reached on the basis of natural intuitive learning processes and those arrived at through systematic scientific investigation. It is also important to recognize when we really have reached a reliable conclusion about something and when we have not, that is, when we really know something and when that conclusion may be false. The following two sections will deal with these two important issues.

Scientific research and common sense

While we have said that the basic components of research are found in everyday experience, there are some important differences that should be kept in mind between research and everyday activities. If research is so simple and so natural, why read a book on research methods and design? Why not simply rely on our intuitions and common sense to reach conclusions about the language phenomena that we observe?

People who do not do research but have intuitions about language learning and teaching typically react to second language research by regarding it as a confirmation of their common sense. ('I knew that.' 'That doesn't make sense.' 'According to my experience. . .')

While common sense, intuition, and introspection about experience are useful, they are of limited value unless used appropriately. It has been cynically suggested that a guiding rule for common sense is that new ideas should look like old ones. That is, new ideas should confirm what we already know or believe. Some feel that the purpose of science and scientific research is to confirm the beliefs of common sense. If this were the case, science would be involved in supporting superstition and prejudice as well as 'good' common sense. For many years, it was believed that children learn a first language by simply imitating their parents. We now know, after many years of scientific research, that what appears to be a common sense conclusion about language acquisition is not true and that language acquisition is much more complicated.

The conclusions of common sense might become the starting point for scientific research but should not become the end point. Science might begin with the question: Do children really learn a language by imitation, as seems to be suggested by common sense? In this section, we will explore some important differences between a scientific approach to such a question and one based on common sense. One of the functions of scientific research can be to provide empirical or factual support for common sense or to disprove what has become accepted as common sense. Of course, methods and knowledge that masquerade as science have been used to support prejudices and superstitition – as we have witnessed in our own century – and the scientist must be alert to the misuse of science.

The differences between knowledge arrived at through common sense and intuition on the one hand, and scientific research on the other, can be expressed by concepts such as 'organized', 'structured', 'methodical', 'systematic', 'testable', and especially by the notion of *disciplined inquiry*.

Scientific research is conducted systematically

Common sense conclusions are reached on the basis of superstition, superficial responses to problems, and unexamined beliefs. Recently, one of the authors asked a foreign language teacher why he had the children in a fourth grade class memorize all of the intricate rules of grammar and spent little or no time on having them use the language for communication. His reply was that he could not see how they could be expected to use the language before they had committed to memory what he considered to be the 'grammar rules' of the language. When he was told that native speakers of the language no longer observed some of these rules, he replied, 'That's even more of a reason to learn the rules. Native speakers shouldn't be our standard.'

A scientist might begin with the question: Can children utilize explicitly taught formal grammar in the acquisition of a second language? This same scientist would then systematically observe children learning second languages in natural contexts; try to discover the role of grammar learning for children in a school context; and then plan a program of research to see how children fared under foreign language teaching methodologies employing grammar teaching and under those which did not.

Science builds theories by systematically testing an interrelated body of hypotheses

Common sense conclusions are often based on superficial evidence which supports something which someone wants to believe. Laymen test the theories held about the world in a selective and subjective way. While it may be said that scientific research is also selective – all possible hypotheses cannot be tested at once – a scientist selects hypotheses for research in a systematic way. The layman often ignores or explains away any disconfirming evidence. In the example above, the foreign language teacher believed that languages are learned by first committing prescriptive grammar to memory. The supporting evidence for this teacher's belief may have been his own limited experience as an adult. It might also be based on a belief that the body of prescriptive grammar rules is the language itself. That might have been the way he was taught, which led him to believe that it must be a good method. He may not have taken the time to consider all the failures that have resulted from this particular approach to language teaching.

Theories and hypotheses which are used in research are formulated so that they can be tested by the researcher and others who wish to replicate the research. We say that hypotheses must be *falsifiable*. They must be amenable to some kind of test which might ultimately disprove them.

In our example, it would not be enough to say that children learn a language better without grammatical explanation because we believe it to be so. If we say that children learn foreign languages more effectively without an emphasis on formal grammar, we would have to formulate this idea in a manner which would allow us to gather evidence confirming or rejecting it as a hypothesis. The research on this question would have to be carried out so that others who might wish to test our hypothesis under slightly different conditions (with, say, older or younger subjects) would be able to follow our procedures.

Scientific research seeks to describe, identify, and control relationships among phenomena in order to study them

In the previous section, we noted that it is a very natural response to look for and notice relationships among the phenomena we see around us. Parents do this when they try to interpret what their children are saying. Unfortunately, we sometimes arrive at conclusions which appeal to our common sense but which may be incorrect. We observe that children sometimes imitate words and phrases which they hear from other speakers before they understand what these words mean. From there, it is only a short step to pointing to imitation as the primary manner in which children acquire the whole language system. And since common sense tells us that this is how first languages are learned, it is only another short step to concluding that second languages may also be learned by imitation and repetition of sentences in the second language even though the learner may not fully understand them.

Research, on the other hand, seeks to identify relationships and reach conclusions about them after ruling out alternative explanations. It might be concluded on the basis of observation that there is a relationship between successful language learning and being willing to make guesses about how to say something in a second language. However, it is not good enough to state that good language learners are good guessers. It is necessary first to define what is meant by a 'good language learner' and what is meant by a 'guess' and even a 'good guess' before the phenomenon can be explored in a systematic way. Secondly, it is necessary to control for other possible causes of successful language learning, such as motivation, before drawing any conclusions about the role of guessing.

If it can be assumed that research involves planned and systematic inquiry, an additional problem confronting the researcher is knowing when the inquiry has reached a conclusion. A conclusion in research is another way of stating that we know something we did not know before we began the investigation. The conclusion may even be that we do not know something we thought was a fact. It may be that what we know is in the form of a theory that still remains to be tested or examined. However, in all of these forms of research, the final objective is to arrive at some form of knowledge that we did not possess before the investigation began. In the next section, we shall examine the kinds of knowledge brought to light in second language research. It is important for the researcher and the consumer of research to distinguish between these different forms of knowledge.

Finding answers: How do we know something?

An important dilemma which research must deal with is how we know when we have found the answer to a question. As we shall see, there are different methods which research can use to answer the questions which it poses. How do we know when either we or another researcher have found an answer to a question posed about second language?

Research findings in second language studies and bilingualism may be categorized according to four types of knowledge which these findings represent. It is often a good idea for a reader of research to ask what kind of knowledge is represented by different claims made in a study. Not all conclusions are necessarily reached on the basis of the same kind of knowledge. Thus, the conclusions of a study might be based partially on belief (Type 1) and partially on a description of a language phenomenon or the results of an experiment (Type 3 or 4).

Four types of knowledge found in second language research

Type 1: *Knowledge as belief*

When we know something on the basis of belief, it may mean we want to believe something to be true but have never submitted it to an empirical test. Many of the conclusions reached through 'common sense' may be put into this category.

Weinreich (1953) presents these 'scientific' conclusions reached by researchers on bilingualism:

> Reis (1910) writing about the trilingualism of those who live in Luxembourg stated, 'The temperament of the Luxembourger is rather phlegmatic. . . We have none of the German sentimentalism or the French vivacity. . . Our bilingual electicism prevents us from consolidating our conception of the world and from becoming strong personalities.'

Gali (no date) suggested that bilingual persons may be morally depraved because they do not receive effective religious instruction in their mother tongue in childhood.

Beliefs die hard because people want to believe them. Consumers of research must remember to ask for the source of a researcher's statements. Sometimes, the beliefs of the researcher are presented as the research when, in fact, they may represent the musings of the researcher rather than facts based on actual research. If beliefs are presented as research, then the research should be treated with circumspection and seriously questioned. Conclusions which are based on belief should be regarded as possible hypotheses for research rather than as established knowledge about second language.

Type 2: *Knowledge as authority*

This form of knowledge is similar to Type 1 because it comes from a source which is accepted at face value. This source may be another scientist who has achieved a reputation and whose opinions about phenomena in his field of research are accepted either as proven facts or as educated judgments from a respected researcher. Unfortunately, the source of this kind of knowledge is often forgotten and it achieves the same status as knowledge arrived at through careful research.

A common example of knowledge that derives from authority rather than from research is the status achieved by many of the language teaching methods which achieve popularity. One need only mention the Silent Way, Suggestopedia, and Community Language Learning as methods which were accepted on the basis of authority rather than after controlled testing of the efficacy of the methods.

We may have to use authorities in developing research, and may appeal to knowledge derived from authorities to support a hypothesis. There is intrinsically nothing wrong with this as long as this form of knowledge is not presented as proven fact, as the following example illustrates. Notice that the use of the verb 'claims' indicates that the citation may be regarded as a hypothesis to be examined rather than as an established fact.

> Long (1981) claims that such activities promote optimal conditions for students to adjust their input to each other's level of comprehension . . . and thereby facilitate their second language acquisition.

> (Doughty and Pica 1986)

The following statement could be regarded as combining belief and authority as sources of knowledge. An authority is given and then the beliefs of that authority are stated, thus giving more weight to a view that has not been empirically demonstrated.

Referring to those studies which found that informal contact does contribute to differences in proficiency, Krashen (1981) points out that 'these subjects were highly likely to have engaged in real communicative use of language.'

(Spada 1986)

Type 3: *A priori knowledge*

We arrive at this type of knowledge by starting with a set of axioms about some phenomenon and then developing our knowledge of it by using reason and logic working within the system defined by the axioms. Type 3 knowledge resembles beliefs. However, this form of knowledge is usually founded on some previous systematic empirical work or observation, as this example:

In keeping with second language acquisition theory, such modified interaction is claimed to make input comprehensible to learners and to lead ultimately to successful classroom acquisition.

(Doughty and Pica 1986)

Modern linguistic theory as manifested by the transformational-generative school is an example of the *a priori* method of arriving at knowing something. We arrive at a description of the underlying abilities of a language speaker by developing a description of the abstract rules of language. This is done by first formulating a theory of language knowledge which constitutes the axiomatic foundation for developing linguistic descriptions within this framework.

In second language research, we often begin with *a priori* knowledge. For example, we might begin by accepting the idea that there are universals of language acquisition and then investigate to see how extensive a particular universal might be. A linguistic universal might be that all languages conform to a set of rules for forming relative clause sentences. We might then hypothesize that this set predicted, in some way, the order by which second language learners acquired the rules for forming relative clauses in the second language. In order to test this prediction, we would have to carry out an experiment. In this example, we began with Type 3 knowledge, which led us to Type 4 knowledge.

Type 4: *Empirical knowledge*

In this type, we arrive at knowing something through the processes of observation and/or experimentation. Empirical knowledge is obtained by interacting with the real world, observing phenomena, and drawing conclusions from experience. In this method of arriving at knowing something we might begin with one of the types of knowledge described above but appeal to some process which will allow us to examine the question by externalizing it.

When a method for seeking knowledge is externalized, it is opened up to a system of checks and balances by others. This approach is sometimes mistakenly referred to as the 'scientific method' even though science does not always involve interacting with the real world. A theoretician, for example, might develop a theory in a systematic way without experimenting with it in a laboratory. Externalizing a research question allows us to control for the effects of various extraneous factors, to propose alternative methods of investigation, and to submit the results to public inspection. It is also more objective because it appeals to evidence available to others and outside the researcher himself.

Empirical knowledge about second language can be obtained through careful observation and description or through experimentation in which a single factor may be isolated for study. Whichever approach is used, it will be characterized by the fact that data are collected from people actually involved in some aspect of second language and these data will be carefully analyzed in some way. The methods used for obtaining empirical knowledge will be carefully documented by the researcher in order to permit others to attempt validation and replication of the findings. The following example summarizes the findings of an experiment in sentence interpretation:

> For all constructions tested, dative constructions, simple NVN sentences, and relative clauses, it was found that with increasing exposure, cue usage in the second language gradually shifts from that appropriate to the first language to that appropriate to the second.
>
> (McDonald 1987)

In summary, research in second language will bring the researcher into contact with all of the kinds of knowledge we have discussed above. Unfortunately, knowledge which is based on belief or authority is sometimes given the status of empirical knowledge or knowledge which has been demonstrated. When reading second language research, the reader should be aware of the basis for conclusions or claims made by the writer. Throughout this book, the assumption will be that we are concerned with Type 4 knowledge. In many cases, the researcher will necessarily have recourse to Type 3 knowledge as a stimulus for research or may begin a study because of a commonly held, but never validated, view (Type 1 or 2) about what takes place in second language acquisition.

Basic, applied, and practical research

In second language research, a useful distinction can be made between three different kinds of research. Each kind of research contributes to our further understanding and knowledge of second language phenomena. The three kinds are *basic* or *theoretical*, *applied*, and *practical* research. This division is useful because second language research covers such a wide variety of possible topics and questions, from constructing theoretical models to explain second language acquisition, to investigating the applications of theoretical constructs in linguistics to actual language acquisition contexts, to the practical utilization of theoretical and applied findings in language teaching methodologies and classroom language learning.

Each category of research often contributes to revision of the content and structure of the other categories. For example, findings in applied research may lead to a revision of theories in basic research. Thus, the relationship between basic, applied, and practical research is not unidirectional. (See Figure 1.1.)

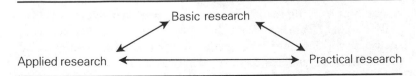

Figure 1.1   Kinds of second language research and their relationship

While the borderlines between these categories of research are not always clear-cut, the division is useful when considering the field of language. Consider the following example: A linguist (A) holds the theoretical position that different languages share universal features (Type 3 knowledge). He is interested in understanding what the languages of the world have in common in terms of the rules necessary to form relative clause sentences. He examines many different languages and concludes (Type 4 knowledge) that all the languages he has investigated have grammatical devices for forming such relative clauses. Now he would like to see the degree to which these rules are shared by different languages. For example, are the rules for forming relative clauses the same for such disparate languages as Persian, English, and Chinese? How are they similar and how are they different? What abstract principles can be arrived at which will describe all the rules necessary to form relative clauses for any of the world's languages, and yet also contain within these principles some mechanism for showing how these languages are different in some way?

Now let us consider a further development of this example. Another linguist (B) is interested in seeing whether the description provided by linguist (A) has any validity in predicting the order in which the rules of relativization in English are acquired by a speaker of another language such as Persian (Type 4 method of knowing). Do the rules which are described conform to what people actually do when they learn a language? Do the rules predict an order of acquisition or the difficulty experienced by learners from different first languages? Does the description of linguist (A) predict the errors that will be made by language learners in the research conducted by linguist (B)?

Finally, let us consider researcher (C). Researcher (C) is not a linguist but is involved in language education, specifically in using linguistic description as the basis for developing better and more effective textbook materials for teaching English as a second or foreign language. Linguistics is not necessarily the only field that a textbook writer would consult. He would also take into consideration research in learning theory, pragmatics, and other relevant fields.

Researcher (C) may consult the work of linguist (A) to see what such descriptions consist of, devoid of any real world context, and then consult linguist (B) to see to what extent the work of linguist (A) reflects what actual learners do when learning another language, particularly when learning how to form relative clauses in this language. Based on the work of both linguists, researcher (C) may conclude any of the following:

1 The research of linguist (A) is too complex to form the basis for textbook materials.
2 The work of linguist (B) shows that the description of (A) does not reflect the psychological reality of what language learners actually do, and therefore is of little use for the development of curriculum materials.

3 The work of (B) demonstrates that (A)'s description is valid and can be used as the basis for instructional materials. (C) may then construct a study in which materials based on (B) are compared with other materials to see if the insights provided by basic and applied research provide a superior foundation for the development of second language materials.

The above describes three stages and three kinds of research that may be conducted in second language. (See Figure 1.2.) Linguist (A) dealt with *basic* or *theoretical* research and was concerned with developing an abstract linguistic description within a particular theory of language knowledge. Linguist (B) was not concerned with developing an independent theory of relative clauses but rather with *applying* the product of (A) to a specific problem – the processes by which learners acquire the knowledge described by (A), when they are acquiring that knowledge in a second language context.

Type	Example
1 Basic	Universals of relative clauses
2 Applied	Order of acquisition
3 Practical	Materials development

Figure 1.2   Kinds of research

Finally, (C) was interested in the *practical* aspects of relative clauses. What can be done with insights gained from (A) and (B) for the language classroom or language learning materials? (C) may also be described as a researcher because, in a real sense, he must carry out research which will have practical implications. It will not be enough for him to review and evaluate the work of (A) and (B). It will probably be necessary for him to develop experimental curriculum materials which will then be tried out in a classroom context and evaluated comparatively with materials based on a different linguistic format.

The example above is, of course, an idealization of the division of types of research, because even practical research can have theoretical implications, so that the borderlines are often not clear. Ideally, for example, applied and practical research should influence the construction and revision of theories and hypotheses developed in basic research. The relationship between the types of research should be *bidirectional*.

This division is useful in helping us to understand the limitations of the research product itself. Not all research is meant to be applied or to have practical uses. Sometimes practical applications for basic research are premature if theories are not tested under the conditions in which they will be applied. In Chapter 5, we will refer to this as a problem of *external validity*.

Summary

Research is the formalization of natural processes we all carry out from birth in dealing with the environment. It involves curiosity about some phenomenon and the posing of testable questions about relationships among observed phenomena.

Research differs from common sense because it is *planned*, *systematic* investigation. Its theories are testable and falsifiable and it attempts to study phenomena through careful description and identification, sometimes controlling and manipulating phenomena in order to study them in isolation.

Research concerns obtaining knowledge. Knowledge can come from four different sources: belief, authority, *a priori* hypotheses or theories, and empirical evidence. Scientific research is concerned with discovering knowledge from the last two sources.

Research can be divided into three types: basic or theoretical, applied, and practical. While each of these types of research may be carried on independently of the others, there is often an interaction between these types, with findings in one category influencing research in the others.

Activities

1 Select three articles from journals on second language acquisition research. Categorize, with examples, the types of knowledge represented in these studies. Are these types of knowledge clearly labeled?

2 Consider the relationship between basic, applied, and practical research. Can you think how linguistic theory might be influenced by language teaching research?

3 As a parent, you have the opportunity to choose bilingual or monolingual education for your child. How might you make

your decision? What kind of research would help you decide? What kinds of questions would you pose and seek answers to in the research? Which kind of research – basic, applied, or practical – would be most useful in helping you reach your decision?

References

Doughty, C. and Pica, T. 1986. '"Information gap" tasks: Do they facilitate second language?' *TESOL Quarterly* 20:2.

McDonald, J. L. 1987. 'Sentence interpretation in bilingual speakers of English and Dutch.' *Applied Psycholinguistics* 8/4:379–414.

Medawar, P. 1982. *Pluto's Republic.* Oxford: Oxford University Press.

Spada, N. 1986. 'The interaction between type of contact and type of instruction: Some effects on the L2 proficiency of adult learners.' *Studies in Second Language Acquisition* 8:181–200.

Weinreich, U. 1953. *Languages in Contact.* The Hague: Mouton.

2 A paradigm for second language research

The language I have learnt these forty years,
My native English, now I must forgo,
And now my tongue's use is to me no more
Than an unstringed viol or harp.
Or like a cunning instrument cas'd up –
Or being open put into his hands
That knows no touch to tune the harmony.
Within my mouth you have engaol'd my tongue,
Doubly portcullis'd with my teeth and lips,
And dull unfeeling barren ignorance
Is made my gaoler to attend on me.
I am too old to fawn upon a nurse,
Too far in years to be a pupil now.

(Shakespeare: *Richard II*, Act 1, Scene 3)

Research and the phenomena of second language

The words above are spoken by Thomas Mowbray, Duke of
Norfolk, in Shakespeare's play *Richard II*, after King Richard has
banished him from England to France. In Mowbray's speech we
find the common fears experienced by someone who must leave his
native language and culture, adjust to new surroundings, and
acquire a new language. Because of his age, Mowbray feels that he
will never again be able to express himself in a new language to the
same degree that he was able in his native tongue.

Mowbray's problem is a universal one. Second language learning
occurs all over the world for a variety of reasons such as
immigration, the demands of commerce and science, and the
requirements of education. Learning another language may be the
most ubiquitous of human intellectual activities after the acquisition
of the mother tongue. It is therefore not surprising that research in
this field has become one of the exciting frontiers of cognitive
science.

Because of the complexity of second language acquisition, it is
not possible to investigate it from any single perspective. Research
in second language varies according to:
– the *circumstances* under which the research is conducted.

Circumstances vary firstly in relation to the context in which second language acquisition is taking place. Research on language acquisition taking place in natural environments will be different from that conducted in the classroom. Secondly, the circumstances will also vary depending on whether the language being learned is a second or a foreign language. Thirdly, they may vary according to the age and other characteristics of the learners.

– the *methodology* used in the research. There is no one preferred research approach for the study of all second language acquisition phenomena. Research methodologies may be determined by such factors as the philosophy of the researcher, the theory motivating the research, and objective factors such as the conditions under which the research is being conducted and the question being investigated.

– the *tools* used to study second language. Information on second language acquisition may be gathered through a variety of means such as observation, testing, interviews, and instrumentation. Here too, the manner in which data are gathered will vary.

The study of the phenomena associated with second language learning must necessarily be multifaceted and multidisciplinary, taking account of knowledge and research methodologies from areas such as linguistics, anthropology, psychology, sociology, education, and others. Each of these disciplines can contribute further insights into the phenomenology of second language acquisition. Furthermore, each of these areas provides the researcher with different perspectives, goals, and tools for studying the phenomena of second language learning. These different disciplines and the wide range of research methodologies represented in these areas can provide a more complete picture of second language acquisition.

Because of the complexity of second language acquisition itself and the variety of ways in which it may be studied, it would be useful to have a coherent and consistent set of characteristics with which to categorize the possible approaches, objectives, designs, and data-gathering methods used in this field. In this chapter and in succeeding chapters, we will develop an approach to research which reflects the unique characteristics and complexity of second language acquisition.

The framework discussed in this chapter is an attempt to capture in four interrelated and interdependent research parameters, the salient features of second language research. These parameters will furnish a useful framework within which to consider problems inherent in carrying out research and discussing and comparing research studies.

Four parameters for second language research

Our framework for examining second language research will evolve from four questions which will provide the metatheoretical basis upon which research methods can be developed. The first two questions are concerned with the level at which research is *conceptualized* and entails decisions about the general *approach* to the research problem and the *purpose* for which the research is intended. The remaining two questions relate to the level at which conceptual decisions about the approach and purpose of the research are concretized or put into *operation* in the form of research *design* and *data-gathering and analysis*.

At the conceptual level

1   What special *conditions* does the phenomenology of second language impose on how we approach research questions? Here we will discuss different ways of dealing with the complexity of second language as a composite of many elements, each of which can be studied separately, or as a whole of interacting parts.

2   What is the overall objective or purpose of the research? Is it to gather information about a second language phenomenon in order to *describe* it or to *discover* possible patterns and relationships among the factors that comprise it? Or is it to *test* a particular hypothesis which predicts relationships among second language phenomena? To what degree do these different purposes complement each other? Here we will discuss the differences between research which *describes* and/or *generates* hypotheses and research which *tests* hypotheses.

At the operational level

3   What must be considered in the *control* and *manipulation* of different factors in second language research? Within this parameter, we will discuss approaches which impose little or no control and those which attempt to control identifiable factors.

4   How are data *defined*, *collected*, and *analyzed* within different second language research contexts? What are the different procedures

for data collection and how are they affected by the approach, purpose, and design of the research?

Each of these questions defines one of four parameters which we will use to characterize second language research. In the following pages we will describe each parameter, referring back to them at appropriate places in future chapters. While it is the purpose of the parameters to provide a useful framework for the discussion and conduct of second language research, it should be recognized that research does not always conform to the distinctions implied by the parameters.

Parameter 1: Synthetic and analytic approaches

An examination of any single situation in which second language is studied will reveal many different interacting factors. Each of these factors can represent a separate area of study in itself. This is what is meant by the 'phenomenology' of second language. One can study the effects of the first language on second language acquisition (SLA), the role of personality variables of different kinds of learners, the role of the social environment and the interaction of the individual with environments such as the foreign or second language classroom, and the physiology and biology of human language learning and the part they play in second language acquisition. No matter how comprehensive a list we would assemble here, it would be difficult to list all of the factors involved in second language acquisition.

However, we might simplify the complexity somewhat by taking a systems approach. This is, we might group all of the factors involved in second language learning under some set of unifying categories. This enables us to deal more easily with the complexity and to talk about 'biological factors', 'linguistic factors', 'affective variables', etc. A number of language related systems, such as the biological, psychological, or syntactic systems, have traditionally been identified as relating to or affecting second language acquisition. Each of these systems will have within it other subsystems. The syntactic system or the phonological system, for example, contain smaller systems, such as the complementizer system or the vowel system.

It should be remembered that while we talk about these systems as realities, they are constructs representing the way we have come to look at language acquisition and language. While we may speak of the roles of the psychological or biological systems of the learner or of the phonological or syntactic systems of the first or the second language, discussing language in this way is really a convenient convention developed by linguists and applied linguists to allow us to examine the very complex factors involved in second language acquisition.

For example, even though we may refer to the acquisition of second language phonology, it should be kept in mind that this does not take place in a vacuum. Other forms of acquisition are taking place at the same time and may affect it. In studying the acquisition of phonology, we might focus on the acquisition of the vowel system, the effects of syllable structure on acquisition, and the role of sociolinguistic variation in second language phonology. (See Ioup and Weinberger (1987) for examples of research in these areas.) That is, the study of second language acquisition may be viewed as sets of nested and intersecting circles, each larger circle containing sets of other circles within it. (See Figure 2.1.) Each circle can be regarded as its own self-contained system and studied separately or as part of a larger system (or circle), or as containing subsystems (or smaller systems) within itself.

Viewing second language learning as a super-system of interacting systems allows us to grasp the enormous complexity involved in carrying out research in this area, while at the same time understanding how at any level we can approach research either by looking at the larger picture or any of its parts.

There are two ways to approach the study of a field with many component parts: either we attempt to grasp the whole or large parts of it in order to get a clearer idea of the possible interrelationships among the components, or we identify small parts of the whole for careful and close study, attempting to fit the small pieces into a coherent picture of the whole at a later stage. If we take the example of second language phonology above, we might study the problem of age and foreign accent at a general level or target a very specific aspect of phonology such as the acquisition of the stress system for learners of a particular age group.

The well-known story of the five blind men describing an elephant is an appropriate metaphor for these two approaches to the investigation of second language. Each blind man described the small part of the elephant that he was able to grasp and tried to infer a picture of the whole animal from that small part. In the case of second language research, it would be helpful to have a sixth blind man who could feel the whole animal, however inadequately, before trying to fit all of the descriptions of the small parts together.

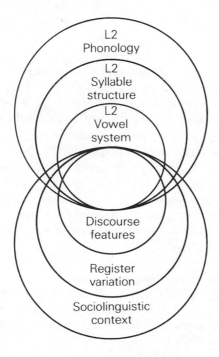

Figure 2.1   A systems view of second language acquisition

The point at issue here is that research in second language can be approached from a *synthetic/holistic* perspective, which emphasizes the interdependence of the parts of the field, or from an *analytic/ constituent* perspective, which focuses on the role of the constituent parts that make up the total phenomenon. By 'synthetic' or 'holistic', we mean an approach to second language phenomena that allows us to view the separate parts as a *coherent whole*. By 'analytic', we mean an approach that will identify and investigate a single factor or a cluster of factors which at some level are constituents of one of the major systems. (See Figure 2.2.) While

Synthetic/Holistic ⟵――――――――――⟶ Analytic/Constituent

*Figure 2.2   Parameter 1: Approaches to the study of second
language phenomena*

each type of research has legitimate purposes or value by itself, *synthetic/holistic* research and *analytic/constituent* research may be seen as complementing each other.

Let us assume that we have decided to investigate the relationship between one constituent of the biological system, *age*, and one constituent of the language system, *phonology*. This interaction of the two systems might be approached from a *holistic* or *synthetic* perspective, namely, by investigating the relationship between the biological factor (age), and the acquisition of the second language sound system as expressed in the *general sense* of foreign accent. While we realize that a particular concept in language acquisition is a synthesis or composite of many other factors, we may choose not to analyze it into its component parts and study each of these parts separately, but rather to approach it in a holistic way. For example, we might decide to study the effects of age on foreign accent without trying to specify at this point in the research what characterizes the specific linguistic features of a foreign accent.

The *synthetic/holistic* view of a language phenomenon may be the more valid one in some instances because analyzing a second language variable into its component parts may result in a distortion of the phenomenon. For example, a study of the turn-taking behavior of children acquiring a second language in a classroom might benefit more from an approach that examines turn-taking for all the learners and the teacher at the same time. Focusing on only one group of learners or a particular kind of turn-taking may not give a valid picture.

In the case of 'foreign accent', the relationship between the biological component and the language component can be further analyzed so that we might investigate a specific *constituent* of the notion 'foreign accent'. It might be decided that one aspect of foreign accent is related to the vowel quality of the learner's performance in the second language. We might decide to limit the investigation to adult learners from the same first language who are above the age of thirty, and to study the acquisition of the vowel phonemes of English. Note that the investigative process now involves *analysis* of the phenomenon into its sub-parts.

The *analytic* process can be extended to more specific levels of investigation. In our example, the acquisition of vowels might be studied by a panel of judges who would employ a subjective evaluation in order to arrive at a conclusion, focusing only on specific vowels. Alternatively, in order to limit the effect of the subjectivity of the judges, it might be decided to analyze vowel phonemes on a spectrograph, which would give us a picture of the vowel phonemes of the non-native speaker for comparison with the spectrographs of native speakers. That is, the evaluations of the judges would be supplemented, and perhaps validated, by the spectrographic analysis. In this example, a *synthetic/holistic* approach would be supplemented by one which is *analytic/constituent*.

Parameter 2: Heuristic and deductive objectives

The second general parameter is concerned with the objective or the purpose of the research. Research may have as a *heuristic* objective the *discovery* or *description* of the patterns or relationships yet to be identified in some aspect(s) of second language, or its aim may be to *test* a specific hypothesis about second language. In the former case, the objective may be to describe what happens or to gather data and *generate hypotheses* about the phenomena studied. In the latter case, the aim is to *test hypotheses* in order to develop a theory about the phenomena in question.

Heuristic or hypothesis-generating research

If the aim of the research is heuristic, the investigator observes and records some aspect or context of second language. There may be no complete theories or models to guide the researcher or to stimulate specific research questions at this point. Data are collected in an attempt to include as much of the contextual information as possible. These data may then be categorized or analyzed or written up descriptively. Often the result of such research may be the formulations of hypotheses.

Example

A study is interested in finding out why some second language learners are more successful than others. It is decided to observe language learners in classroom environments and to record as much information as possible about the learning process in that context. The aim is to observe as many factors as possible which might be related to successful second language acquisition (learners raising hands to participate, writing in notebooks, talking to themselves and to their peers, etc.).

We may have some general ideas, based on the work of other researchers as to why some learners achieve more than others. We may nonetheless choose to approach the question with as few preconceptions as possible. In the process of analyzing the data, we may find ourselves with lists of a great many observed behaviors. We may then decide to look at all of the different behaviors and try to categorize them into the patterns which seem to emerge from what has been observed. For example, our observations may reveal that verbal and non-verbal behavior should be considered as separate categories. The verbal interactions of teachers with learners may also reveal patterns which are different from those of the learners with each other.

Note that when the aim of the research is heuristic, an effort is made to avoid preconceptions about what good language learners do. We proceed from the data, the actual behavior or unprocessed observations, to patterns which are suggested by the data themselves. This process is considered to be heuristic because of its *inductive* nature. This inductive character often allows the research situation and the data to define the shape and the flow of the investigation. Having a *heuristic* objective to the research enables us to discover patterns, behaviors, explanations, and to form questions or actual hypotheses for further research.

Deductive or hypothesis-testing research

In this type of research, the investigator may begin with hypotheses which are based on observations suggested by heuristic research, or hypotheses found in second language acquisition theory or in other areas which appear to have relevance to second language. The *deductive* approach, as distinct from the *heuristic* approach, begins with a preconceived notion or expectation about the second language phenomena to be investigated. In this sense, it may be said that *deductive* research is *hypothesis-driven*. That is, the research begins with a question or a theory which narrows the focus of the research and allows the second language phenomenon to be investigated systematically. The question or hypothesis may relate diverse second language factors to each other or show that one causes another. Deductive research in second language might also be driven by theories or questions developed in other fields. It might be hypothesized that a theory developed in another field has explanatory value for understanding a given second language phenomenon.

Example

In cognitive psychology, the constructs or notions of 'field independence' and 'field dependence' were developed. This theoretical construct claims that some subjects are able to perceive a geometric figure embedded in a background pattern while others cannot. That is, subjects can be categorized as either dependent on the field or background upon which the pattern appears ('field dependent') or independent of that field or background ('field independent'). This construct is thought to apply generally as a characteristic of learning style.

The first thing to notice in this example is that we begin with a possible idea about how to categorize learners and, rather than discovering a category for learners, we begin with an assumption or hypothesis that this categorization may apply to second language learning as well. If we apply this concept to second language learning, we may hypothesize that good language learners may be 'field independent', allowing them to extract language rules from the language data in which the rules are embedded, while poor language learners are 'field dependent', which would explain their difficulty in learning a language from natural language data. The concept of field dependence can thus become the source of hypotheses about second language acquisition.

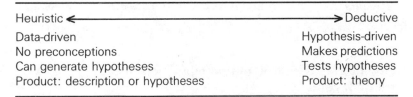

Figure 2.3 summarizes the end points and differences discussed above between the *heuristic* and *deductive* research objectives. Between each of these end points there are possible research formats which may combine attributes from both sides. The type of question asked in the research will determine what the objective or purpose of the research will be. In Chapter 6 we shall discuss forms of descriptive research the purpose of which is both heuristic and deductive, in that it gathers data and tests hypotheses formed on the basis of the data.

Parameters relating to the operational level of research design and methodology

Whereas parameters 1 and 2 were concerned with describing the approaches and objectives of second language research, parameters 3 and 4 describe characteristics at the operational level of *design* and *methodology*, once the approach and objective have been defined. These operational-level parameters are the result of decisions made at the conceptual level of planning the approach and purpose of the research. Figure 2.4 summarizes the implicational relationship between the different parameters.

Parameter 1	Synthetic	or	Analytic
Parameter 2	Heuristic	or	Deductive
Parameter 3	Degree of control/manipulation		
Parameter 4	Data collection/analysis		

*Figure 2.4   Implicational relationship between the different.
parameters*

Parameter 3: Control and manipulation of the research context

All forms of research imply some kind of control or manipulation of factors in the research context, even if that control expresses itself in the selection of the behaviors to be observed or of the data for further analysis. Thus, at one end of this parameter are designs which intentionally exert little control, manipulation, or restriction on the research context. At the other extreme are research designs which methodically manipulate and control various components in the research context, such as experimental treatment, the type and number of subjects who will participate, and when and how the subjects in the study will perform. This parameter should be viewed as a continuum on which there are intermediate positions which combine characteristics from both polarities. The possible types of research which can occur on this continuum will be discussed in detail in Chapters 6 and 7. It is also important for the second language researcher to realize that the degree of control and manipulation affects the kind of data which will be gathered

(Chapter 8), the analysis of research results (Chapter 9), and the ability to interpret and generalize these results outside the immediate research context (Chapter 10). Below, we will examine factors which affect the degree of control and manipulation of second language research design.

Four factors related to the degree of control and manipulation

Each of the four factors discussed below may also be described in terms of the relative degree (low to high) to which they apply to the research design. (See Figure 2.5.) While these four factors may be discussed independently, they are implicationally related in the sense that a high degree of one will imply a high or low degree of another. Thus, for example, a high degree of restriction in the focus of the study implies that there must be a concomitantly high degree of control of variables but a low degree of researcher subjectivity in the interpretation of the data.

Restriction of scope/focus:	Low	to	high
Control of variables:	Low	to	high
Attention to form:	Low	to	high
Researcher subjectivity:	High	to	low

Figure 2.5   Factors related to the degree of control of the research context

1 *Restriction of scope/focus*

In any study, decisions must be made as to whether and how to set limits on the scope or focus of the investigation. These decisions tend to affect the kinds of designs and methods which will be used in the research. Low levels of restriction on scope or focus will mean that it will be more difficult to control for the effects of different factors or variables in the research context. However, this may be a conscious decision on the part of the researcher who wishes to pursue a *heuristic* approach to the research question and who may fear that restriction or control may distort the study of the second language phenomenon under consideration. A decision to restrict the research to a narrower scope or focus will facilitate the control of variables and the use of deductive hypothesis-testing methods. In general, the more restricted the scope, the more the research context will have to be manipulated since restriction implies the selection of some aspect within the research context for closer study.

Let us take as an example the study of children's acquisition of a second language in the classrom. Adopting a *synthetic* approach, it may be decided to conduct a study in which the scope is as unrestricted as possible. This would mean that the investigation would try to record anything and everything of note without deciding which observed phenomena were of significance and which were not.

On the other hand, adopting an *analytic* approach to such a study would require us to narrow the scope, and it might be decided to investigate the relationship between the development of the children's metalinguistic abilities (as in a phoneme segmentation task in the second language) and the acquisition of reading skills. In order to carry out this study, it would be necessary to limit the focus of the research to very specific aspects of language and reading, to develop appropriate tests to evaluate children's metalinguistic abilities, and to use methods which would make it clear that the relationship between reading and metalinguistic ability is not due to some other unidentified factor. This kind of study would narrow the focus to a particular kind of data, such as reading test scores and the performance of the subjects on metalinguistic tests.

2 Control of variables

Research may be characterized by the degree of control exercised by the research design and methodology over the variables, identified and unidentified, in the research context. While Chapter 5 will be devoted to a discussion of different kinds of variables, at this point it is sufficient to think of variables as those different factors which play a role in a study such as *language, the characteristics of the subjects or learners,* or the specific factors being studied, such as a *metalinguistic ability.*

It is clear that restrictions on the scope of the phenomena to be investigated and the control of variables are interrelated. The more the investigation is limited in scope, the more it is necessary to control for the effects of factors which may confuse the interpretation of the results. That is, in order for findings to be clear, the investigator must be able to say that the results are due to the particular factors studied and not to anything else, identified or unidentified, that may have been present at the time the research was conducted.

We have already discussed two possible examples of research on children's second language acquisition in the classroom. In the first, few variables are controlled because it may not be clear what the variables are and the researcher may feel that it is preferable to describe what occurs naturally without changing the context. In fact, the purpose of the study might be to describe what the possible factors are. In the second example, the study of reading and metalinguistic ability, it is assumed that the primary factors that could affect the outcome of the study have been identified and that those which are not relevant to the central research question can be controlled through various measures, such as the way the research is designed and the way data are collected.

3 *Attention to form/subject awareness*

One of the unique aspects of research involving language is that language can be studied as a medium for communication as well as an object in itself. When we use language as a tool for communication, we usually pay more attention to the content we wish to communicate and less to the form of language itself. If the object of research is to examine the form of language such as syntax rather than its content, many possibilities are open to the researcher. For example, the performance of second language learners using the language in a natural setting could be analyzed. Alternatively, a specific task could be developed to constrain the learners to produce the form which is the focus of the study.

In the case of investigating language acquisition in a natural setting, we might collect samples of language in an interview or a role-play situation in which the speakers are focused on the content of language and not on its form. Ideally, in order to obtain data which are truly representative of this naturalistic use of language, the subject should be unaware that data are being recorded at all. If the object of the research is a specific form, learners might be asked to imitate sentences, to transform sentences into questions, or to judge the acceptability of sentences presented to them by the researcher.

In general, it may be stated that the more the focus is narrowed, the more it may be necessary to manipulate the research context and the more likely it is that the learners/subjects will become aware of being involved in a study. While narrowing the focus and manipulating the context is necessary for certain kinds of studies, the concomitant effect may be to sensitize the subjects to the very act of research. Because they know that they are participating in research, there is a possibility that their performance will not be the same as it would be if they were performing the same task in a natural environment. The subjects may now shift their conscious attention to that aspect of language performance under observation, and change or edit it in some way. (See Ellis 1986, for a discussion of 'variability in interlanguage'.)

In research in which the focus is not clear to the subjects, it is more likely that the data collected will be representative of what learners normally do. Tarone (1979, 1982) has referred to this difference in learner performance as the difference between colloquial and superordinate forms. The former is thought to be more natural, with little attention to form, while the latter is carefully edited with a high level of attention to form.

In studies which are more controlled and manipulated, there should be a concern for the validity and representativeness of the findings. The question of the degree to which data collected from second language learners in a research environment are representative of what they normally do will be discussed under issues dealing with problems of external validity in Chapter 5.

4 Researcher subjectivity

Often, the less controlled and focused a research study is, the more the interpretative abilities of the researcher are called into play. Limiting the role of subjectivity in the interpretation or description of second language phenomena may therefore be seen as a function of the degree of manipulation and control exerted over the research environment. The more focused the object of the investigation, the more likely it is that researchers will have to use tools outside of or in addition to their own interpretative powers.

For example, research which is both *synthetic* and *heuristic* and places fewer restrictions on the scope of the phenomena to be studied, must depend more on judgments made by the investigators as to what will be recorded and what will be ignored. When data collected in this kind of research are reviewed, they are placed into categories established by the researchers, who impose a structure on the data which was not there before. The nature of that structure depends to a great extent on their perception of the data. The broader the scope and focus of the research, the more some form of selectivity and inferencing must inevitably be involved. This does not mean of course that selectivity is not involved in *analytic* and *deductive* research. The primary difference is that while researcher subjectivity may be involved in the *selection* of the design, etc., the research itself may be more easily replicated since its procedures are more objective. Procedures which have been developed in research to control for researcher subjectivity, such as reliability measures, will be discussed in Chapters 6, 7, and 8.

Parameter 4: Data and data collection

Low explicitness ← — — — — — — — — — — — — — — — — — → High explicitness

Figure 2.6   Parameter 4: Degrees of explicitness of data collection procedures

There is an interdependency in second language research between the approach (*synthetic* or *analytic*), the purpose (*heuristic* or *deductive*), the degree of focus and control in the design of the research, and data collection. All of these parameters are interrelated and interdependent. However, Parameter 4 is perhaps the most concrete manifestation of this relationship between the *conceptual* and the *operational* levels of research discussed earlier in this chapter. The approach, objective, and design of the research will be expressed both in *what* data will be regarded as important and the *manner* in which those data will be collected and analyzed.

The procedures used to collect data will be affected by factors such as the kind of discipline (linguistics, sociology, psychology) within which the researcher is working and whether the research is *synthetic* and *heuristic* or *analytic* and *deductive*. For example, linguistic theory today defines data in accordance with certain axioms about the nature of language. A study of second language acquisition within this framework would therefore use procedures which would elicit one kind of data but ignore another. Because second language research cuts across many disciplines, the discipline within which the research is conducted will affect what are defined as data and how they are obtained. Second language data will be different within a linguistic, educational, or sociological context. This has become an important issue in second language research and can lead to different conclusions about the significance or meaning of different kinds of data (Seliger 1983, Cohen 1984).

Two important questions in connection with data collection are:

1 What constitute the data for second language investigation?
2 How are data collected and analyzed?

1 *What are data?*

As noted above, there is a reciprocal relationship between the kind of questions asked, the design of the investigation, and kind of data to be collected. Data might include *all behaviors observable* by the researcher in a second language event such as a language lesson, *sentences* of a specific type that learners utter in response to stimuli controlled by the investigator, or *subjects' opinions* about speakers of the second language. A review of second language research reveals that the term 'data' covers a wide variety of phenomena.

As an example of the problem of defining 'data' in second language research, linguistic theory distinguishes between competence, or underlying knowledge, and performance, that language which we actually produce or comprehend. This dichotomy becomes more complicated when discussing second language acquisition. Is all performance produced by second language learners indicative of their underlying grammatical knowledge? Is the distinction between competence and performance valid for second language acquisition? If the distinction is valid, how is it reflected in the manner in which data are collected?

Let us take the investigation of language learner strategies as a further example of the problem of defining data. In addition to defining a strategy, it will have to be decided what constitutes evidence for a strategy in the behavior of the learner. Since only external behavior is available for observation, which behaviors will be considered examples of strategies and which will not? These questions become important not only in the development of data collection procedures and instruments but also in the control of variables and the interpretation of research results, as will be shown in Chapter 5. We cannot decide *how* data will be collected and interpreted until it has been decided *what* will be collected. This in turn must be considered at the conceptual levels (Parameters 1 and 2) as well as at the operational levels (Parameters 3 and 4).

2 *How are data collected?*

The *manner* in which data are collected involves other considerations, such as the approach and the objectives of the research. There is a wide variety of procedures and methods available for the collection of data in second language research. In general, data collection procedures in second language research will vary in terms of the degree of *explicitness* with which the procedure focuses on the data which are sought. (See Figure 2.6.) Data collection procedures may define data more narrowly and focus more or less directly on the data sought, whether that be a language form or a response to a motivation questionnaire. (See also the discussion of this point in Chapter 8.)

The degree to which the procedures used to collect data focus explicitly on the data being sought and draw attention to them will also result in the subjects or producers of the data becoming more aware of the procedure itself. Some procedures are more likely to draw the attention of the subject to the data sought and thus affect the quality of the data. For example, asking a subject to decide whether an isolated sentence is grammatical draws attention to the metalinguistic activity of judging the form of the sentence, something that would not happen if the same sentence were embedded in a meaningful context with other sentences.

In a study investigating the strategies learners use in writing in the second language, samples of writing are analyzed and subjects are asked to describe or explain how they arrived at a particular formulation. The subjects verbalize the processes which led them to produce the sentences in their writing sample. These verbalizations become the data and are the result of the learners' attention having been drawn *explicitly* to certain language forms. (See Cohen and Hosenfeld 1981, for a more detailed discussion of these procedures.) It is clear that this type of data presents problems of interpretation. We can see from this example that there is a danger that such data could be the result of a description of what the learners really did, a description of what the learners thought they did, or a description of what the learners thought the investigator wished to hear. In Chapters 6 and 8, we will discuss some ways of increasing the reliability of this kind of data.

The problems demonstrated by this example also exist in situations where metalinguistic tests are used to elicit data consisting of judgments of grammaticality. In this case, where the focus is on sentences or other isolated parts of language, the manner in which the test is administered, and even the amount of time allowed for the judgments may affect the subjects' responses.

What all of this demonstrates is that no data collection procedure is foolproof and that the investigator must be aware of the consequences of using any procedure. In second language research, the data may become an artifact of the procedures themselves. Observation or taping of natural conversations is less likely to draw the subjects' attention to the particular kind of data being sought, although the act of observing or taping may affect the subject's behavior, while an instrument such as an attitude questionnaire or a metalinguistic test may make the subject aware of what the investigator is seeking. As we have already discussed, this awareness on the part of the subject may or may not affect the validity of the data.

Summary

This chapter has discussed the major characteristics of second language research within a framework of four parameters. (See Figure 2.7.) These parameters serve to describe second language research at two different levels: the *conceptual* and the *operational*.

At the conceptual level, the researcher must address questions dealing with the *approach* which will be taken with respect to the study of second language phenomena, and the *objective* or *purpose* of the research. Will the investigation approach the study of second language from a *synthetic* perspective, which attempts to capture the whole phenomenon, or will it approach the study *analytically* by investigating one of the *constituent* parts of the phenomenon (Parameter 1)? The researcher must also consider the objective or purpose of the research. Is it *heuristic* or descriptive, or is it *deductive* and aiming to test a predetermined theory or hypothesis (Parameter 2)?

At the operational level, the researcher must decide the *degree of control* which will be imposed on the research context and how this degree of control will affect the outcomes of the investigation (Parameter 3). Once approach, objective, and degree of control have been established, consideration must be given to deciding *what data* are of importance for the investigation and *how* those data will be collected (Parameter 4).

It is evident from the discussion in this chapter that while the four parameters describe different aspects of second language research, they are *interdependent* and that decisions at the conceptual level have important implications for parameters at the operational level. It is also evident that decisions about the degree of control of the research or the manner in which data will be collected cannot be made before decisions have been made at the conceptual level to determine the approach of the research and the purposes it is expected to serve.

Parameter 1:	Synthetic and analytic approaches to the phenomena
Parameter 2:	Heuristic and deductive objectives
Parameter 3:	The degree of control and manipulation of the research context
Parameter 4:	Data and data collection

Figure 2.7   Summary table of second language research parameters

It is useful to investigate second language from the perspective of these parameters because they capture the unique characteristics of second language research. Second language acquisition is an area of investigation which draws on many other fields such as linguistic theory, education, first language acquisition, psychology, and others. It cannot adopt the research paradigm of any one of these related fields but must develop research methodologies of its own which allow for a variety of approaches and flexibility in investigating research questions.

Each of these parameters is a continuum, often with many intermediate positions which combine some of the characteristics of each of the end points. Our discussion has primarily focused on the extreme positions of the parameters for the purpose of demonstrating the paradigm. Future chapters will discuss variations along these continua. Chapter 3 will describe how research questions or hypotheses can be designed within this framework. Chapter 5 will discuss questions of variables and validity in second language research. Chapters 6 and 7 will describe different approaches to design in accordance with the parameters, while Chapters 8 and 9 will discuss data collection and analysis. Chapter 10 will be concerned with putting all the parts of the study together and reporting the research.

Activities

1 Consider some of the differences between first language acquisition and adult second language acquisition (age, learning environment, psychological development, etc.). How might these differences affect research design and methodology in the two areas?·

2 What are some of the different social settings in which second language acquisition can take place? In a general sense, how

might research be different in these different settings? What are some problems you might foresee?

3 Assume that language competence is an internal representation of what people know when they know a language. What are some problems created by this view, particularly for second language research? How might they be overcome?

4 Consider an aspect of the speech act system such as the ability to make a *request*. How might the acquisition of *requests* be studied from the two perspectives of Parameter 1?

5 Compare two studies on the same research question in second language in terms of the four factors affecting degree of control discussed under Parameter 3.

6 Analyze the instruments of two second language acquisition studies purportedly examining the same question. To what degree do you think the findings of the studies are comparable, given the manner in which data were collected in each study?

7 Select a topic of research. Show how that topic can lead to different research plans according to the different parameters. Keep your plan in outline form.

References

Cohen, A. and Hosenfeld, C. 1981. 'Some uses of mentalistic data in second language research.' *Language Learning* 31/2:285–314.

Cohen, A. 1984. 'Studying second language learning strategies: How do we get the information?' *Applied Linguistics* 5/2:101–112.

Ellis, R. 1985. *Understanding Second Language Acquisition*. Oxford: Oxford University Press.

Ioup, G. and Weinberger, S. H. 1987. *Interlanguage Phonology: The Acquisition of a Second Language Sound System*. Cambridge, Mass.: Newbury House.

Seliger, H. 1983. 'The language learner as linguist: Of metaphors and realities.' *Applied Linguistics* 4/3:179–191.

Tarone, E. 1982. 'Simplicity and attention in interlanguage.' *Language Learning* 31/1:69–84.

Tarone, E. 1979. 'Interlanguage as chameleon.' *Language Learning* 29/1:181–191.

3 The preparatory stages of research

'Have you guessed the riddle yet?' the Hatter said turning to Alice
again.
'No, I give it up,' Alice replied, 'what's the answer?'
'I haven't the slightest idea,' said the Hatter.
'Nor I,' said the March Hare. Alice sighed wearily. 'I think you
might do something better with time,' she said, 'than waste it asking
riddles with no answers.'

(Lewis Carroll: *Alice in Wonderland*)

Introduction

In Chapter 2, we developed a set of parameters which help to define
the conceptual and operational dimensions of second language
research. In this chapter we shall be concerned with the beginning
stages of setting up actual research from the general conception of
the research idea to the formulation of a research plan or
hypothesis. That is, the idea of research will be approached as a
disciplined form of scientific inquiry. Implicit in this concept of
research is the need to develop a careful plan for carrying out
research.

A problem which novice researchers in second language acquisition
may have is selecting a topic for research. Sometimes the researcher
does not know how or where to begin the creative act of starting a
new research endeavor. Sometimes the topic chosen is trivial or
impractical or there is a leap from the conception of an idea to a
full-blown experiment with no consideration of other alternatives
or obstacles which may arise. All of this makes it very important to
consider carefully the *preparatory stages* to research, which are
discussed in this chapter.

A word of caution is necessary at this point. Conceiving and
carrying out research is as much a creative process as it is a scientific
one. The procedures described in this chapter are an attempt to
formalize the beginning steps in the research process. We recognize
that there are many pathways which may be followed in developing
and conducting research. The preparatory steps described in this
chapter attempt to provide a sense of logical progression which, in

the case of the experienced researcher, is often intuitive. We recognize the danger in over-formalizing an activity that contains an element of 'art'. We feel, however, that novice researchers especially will benefit from following these preparatory steps.

While much of this chapter implies a more analytic-deductive hypothesis-testing approach to research, most of the discussion will also be suitable for the development of synthetic-heuristic hypothesis-generating research as well. Throughout the chapter, we will indicate the differences where appropriate. However, no matter what the orientation, no aspect of the development of a research project or study is more important than the initial steps in which research questions and hypotheses are considered and developed.

In contrast to the riddle which the Mad Hatter posed to Alice, part of the problem of doing research is formulating questions that *can* be answered within the framework of the research. As we shall see, there is an integral relationship between the development of good research questions and the execution of the research itself. If the questions are inaccurately or vaguely posed, the total structure of the research and its significance will be affected. A skill to be acquired by every researcher is the ability to formulate good questions. It is the formulation and fine-tuning of the research question that will contribute to reliable, valid, and significant results.

In the following sections of this chapter, we shall move through the progression of stages implicit in the development of research. This, of course, does not mean that all experienced researchers go through these steps in a deliberate manner. However, it is suggested that the novice researcher in second language try to follow this progression in order to avoid pitfalls which will only become apparent at later stages.

Where do research questions come from?

The novice researcher is often perplexed about how to begin the process of research. Students carrying out their first research project involving collecting data or conducting an experiment are bewildered about how to begin, how to control the various aspects of their study, and how to carry out the study so that the results are both specific and meaningful.

It is useful to conceive of the preparation for research as an evolutionary process consisting of *phases*, with each successive phase being a refinement of the preceding one. That is, the preparatory steps of research are cyclical in nature with each phase encompassing a narrower, more focused vision of the preceding step. In the case of any particular research, there must be preparatory steps before the actual research can be carried out.

These preparatory steps can best be described as the phases that researchers go through initially before reaching the point of conducting an experiment, carrying out observations in the field, or collecting data in some way. These preparatory steps should precede any actual research such as observations and data collection or putting into operation a concrete experimental design. The research study or design is itself the end product of a process of careful preparation.

Figure 3.1 illustrates *four phases* in the development of a research project, in the form of a flow chart. Research may take different forms depending on a number of factors, the most important being the type of question being investigated and the research format most appropriate for the investigation. In Chapter 2, we described the various parameters of second language research. These parameters become concretized in the process of developing the research question. At different points in the development of a research project, decisions such as whether the research should be approached *synthetically* or *analytically* and whether the research objective is to describe or test a hypothesis about a second language phenomenon will affect future steps in the development of the research.

Phase 1: The general question

Sources for questions:
    Experience and interests
    Other research
    Sources outside second language

In Chapter 1, we stressed that good scientists are observant of phenomena around them. Their state of curiosity derives from a lack of understanding of something. In the field of second language studies, curiosity and the resultant questioning can arise from a number of sources. These *sources* provide the stimuli for questioning the phenomena associated with second language. We shall discuss below some of the sources from which research questions might be derived.

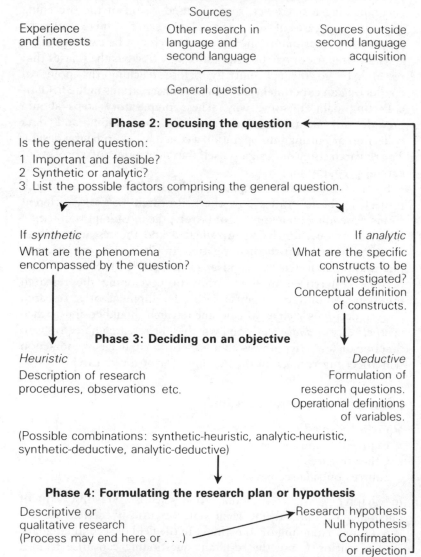

Phase 1: Formulating the general question

Sources

| Experience and interests | Other research in language and second language | Sources outside second language acquisition |

General question

Phase 2: Focusing the question ←

Is the general question:
1 Important and feasible?
2 Synthetic or analytic?
3 List the possible factors comprising the general question.

If *synthetic*
What are the phenomena encompassed by the question?

If *analytic*
What are the specific constructs to be investigated?
Conceptual definition of constructs.

Phase 3: Deciding on an objective

Heuristic
Description of research procedures, observations etc.

Deductive
Formulation of research questions.
Operational definitions of variables.

(Possible combinations: synthetic-heuristic, analytic-heuristic, synthetic-deductive, analytic-deductive)

Phase 4: Formulating the research plan or hypothesis

Descriptive or qualitative research
(Process may end here or . . .)

Research hypothesis
Null hypothesis
Confirmation or rejection

Figure 3.1   Preparatory phases of research

1 Experience and interests

Questions for research can derive from everyday experience with language learning. Curiosity can be aroused by something observed in a personal language learning experience which leads to further questioning and perhaps to the development of original research from this questioning.

You may come to the field of second language acquisition with questions from other areas in which you have an interest and which can be related to research in this field. For example, the theories and methodologies of the field of reading may hold implications for research in second language acquisition. To what degree is learning to read in a second language the same as learning to read a first language? Does the ability to read in the first language facilitate learning to read in a second? Do the metalinguistic abilities related to reading in a first language help or hinder learning to read in a second? How does the ability to read in a language with a different orthographic system affect learning to read the target language?

With the development of research in metacognitive processes, there has been renewed interest in language learners keeping diaries documenting their experiences and conscious thought processes while in the language class or other second language learning contexts. Such diaries might include the author's feelings during the actual language lesson but recorded after class, attitudes to language learning, attitudes toward the teacher, self-analysis of the methods used for practising the language and so on. While these diary reports are subjective in terms of what is reported and recalled, they can raise interesting questions for further controlled research. In other words, they may be a place to begin.

Bailey (1983) recorded in a diary her own experiences of learning French as a foreign language. She noticed evidence of competitiveness and anxiety in her writing, which raised questions in her mind about whether such feelings were facilitative or not. She then related these experiences to other literature dealing with competitiveness and anxiety in second language learning. Teachers, similarly, may wish to keep diaries of things observed in a language lesson or of any student behaviors that seem to have some effect on language learning.

In the examples above, which are drawn from everyday experience, there is no preconceived or *deductive* notion of what we should observe or record. Instead, a diary of experiences is kept, without focusing on any particular aspect or question. By sifting through diary entries or informal observations, it may be found that a number of factors are of interest for further research. The evaluation or description of these factors can become a later stage of the research or a single factor may be isolated for more controlled study.

2 Reading other research in language and second language

Involvement in a professional field requires researchers to read research conducted by others in order to keep up with developments, innovations, and new insights. However, reading research in a field such as second language learning and teaching can itself become a source for further questioning and curiosity about claims made by a theory or the way a study was conducted.

A theory which claims that learners monitor output in terms of grammatical rules learned in the classroom (Krashen 1978) can lead to research on how grammatical rules are learned and used by learners, and whether such rules can make a difference in the learners' performance (Seliger 1979).

Research useful for stimulating ideas for further investigation can be found in two categories:

a) Research of a theoretical nature, which presents a theory, a synthesis of other theories, or the discussion of implications for second language research of a theory outside of second language. In this category, we find research in theoretical linguistics, research discussing the relevance of theoretical linguistics for second language research, research which reviews or surveys other research around a central issue but which contains no original empirical research itself, and so on.

As an example of this, linguistics in recent years has been concerned with the theory of universal grammar and how it pertains to language acquisition (Chomsky 1981). Some have seen this theory as having potential for explicating issues in second language acquisition and have explored this (Cook 1985). Some journals, such as *Applied Linguistics*, specialize in articles which contain discussions of theoretical issues. This book will not be concerned with how to conduct this kind of research which is, in a sense, research about research. For our purposes, it is sufficient to observe that theoretical research may be considered *hypothesis-generating* because of the questions which it intentionally raises.

b) Empirical research, which may be *heuristic* or *deductive* and may or may not be based on a particular theory or hypothesis, but is assumed to be based on data collected from second language learners. To continue with the previous example above, if the theory of government and binding, part of universal grammar, is taken as a potential explanation for second language acquisition, it should be able to predict the kinds of errors learners will make. If that is the case, the theory will have important implications for predicting the order of acquisition of grammar rules in the second language, defining what rules will likely be transferred from the first language, and what rules are likely to be learned independently of the first language. Many researchers have already begun exploring this theory with these questions in mind (Flynn 1987, Mazurkewich 1984, White 1985).

While reading research in second language acquisition and other fields, readers should ask themselves a number of questions to stimulate their own thinking about possible original research, such as:

1 Does this research test or generate hypotheses?
2 If the research is descriptive, where do the data come from?
3 If the data are gathered from other studies or sources, how reliable do the data seem to be?
4 What is the hypothesis or theory being tested?
5 Is the design or methodology appropriate for the kind of research?
6 Does the research really test the hypothesis or theory?
7 How are the conclusions reached by the research supported by the research and the data?
8 Are theoretical claims made by the research supported? How?
9 Does the research make a clear distinction between the results of the study based on data and extrapolations which may go beyond the data?
10 Are hypotheses which still remain to be tested presented as conclusions or results?
11 Are there good alternative explanations to those given by the author?

These and similar questions will be discussed more extensively in Chapter 4, which deals with reviewing literature once the research topic has been selected. The questions above are primarily to stimulate thinking while reading research. Not only is it more productive for comprehension to read research with a questioning mind, but it can also lead the reader to the eventual development of researchable questions.

3 Sources outside second language acquisition

While the examples above are taken from linguistics, similar research of a theoretical and empirical nature is found in psychology, sociology, and education. Here too, questions and hypotheses for research in second language can be found. In fact, it appears that most of the more interesting theories about second language acquisition have derived from these other fields and have become tools for investigation within second language research.

General questions which may be developed into research can come from a field not normally associated with language or language acquisition. For example, the concept of *anomie* is concerned with the social psychological orientation of the individual in society. The concept is concerned with relative feelings of social rootlessness and was first proposed by Durkheim in 1897. Six decades passed before researchers used this concept to describe the psychological trauma experienced by bilinguals as they become more integrated into the second language social group and begin to feel alienation toward their L1 group. The application of this concept gave rise to instruments for measuring anomie among second language learners. The relative degrees of anomie measured by these instruments became a correlate of the instrumental or integrative orientation of the language learner (Lambert and Gardner 1959). The type of orientation was then used to predict success in various aspects of second language acquisition.

Exposure to sources of knowledge such as everyday experience, reading other research in linguistics and second language in related fields such as psychology, social psychology, and education arouses curiosity and questioning. As Pasteur noted long ago, 'Le hasard ne favorise que les esprits préparés.' That is, research questions are not the result of chance or wild guesses but develop naturally in 'prepared minds', that is, minds occupied with ideas and concepts and sensitized to observation.

Once questions have been raised in the mind of the researcher as a result of *curiosity, observation,* and *reading,* these questions must be formulated in a general sense. Referring back to Figure 3.1, we can see that before entering into Phase 2 or Phase 3, the question must be stated in a form which will allow it to be further narrowed. For the researcher, this is often a difficult stage because it requires the careful analysis of the general question in order to reduce it to a level where it may be considered researchable.

Let us take an observation discussed above as an example to see how we might move through the steps in Phase 1:

Observation
Learners acquire language at different rates.

Curiosity
Are different rates of acquisition due to characteristics of learners or teachers?
Are different rates of acquisition due to some aspect of method or material?

As we consider this observation, we arrive at a general question about the phenomenon of different rates of acquisition.
General question: Why do learners of a second language progress at different rates?

The problem with this general question is that it is too broad and too inclusive. In its current formulation we do not know whether we are speaking of children or adults, learning in a classroom or in nature, learning all skills or a specific skill such as reading, learning a foreign language, or a second language, and so on. In other words, before we can decide whether to approach this question on a *synthetic* or *analytic* basis, there are many other questions which must first be asked. This brings us to Phase 2.

Phase 2: Focusing the question

Is the general question feasible? Should it be approached synthetically or analytically? If synthetically, what are the phenomena encompassed by the question? If analytically, what are the specific factors to be investigated?

Having arrived at a general question, it is now necessary to consider whether it is possible or feasible to do research on such a question. If it is feasible, the next step is to decide what basic approach (in terms of Parameter 1), *synthetic* or *analytic* (Chapter 2), would be best for this kind of research. Sometimes the decision about the basic approach to the research question can only be made at a later stage after more consideration is given to the factors or variables which make up the question.

Feasibility

While it may be fairly easy to agree that the general question is important, it is more difficult to decide if it is feasible. Another way of asking whether there is an answer to the general question is to ask whether the question can be investigated given the researcher's or the world's state of knowledge, the intellectual, academic, and research tools available, and the conditions under which the research would have to be conducted. In brief, we are asking, 'Is finding an answer to the general question feasible?'

The question of feasibility may be divided into several subparts which we shall now discuss. The question must be formulated so that any investigation may be carried out within the limitations of the resources available for the research.

If the researcher is able to test the general question for feasibility before progressing to more advanced phases of developing the research, much waste of time and energy can be avoided. Below are some of the questions relating to feasibility which should be raised at this stage in the development of the research project. It is best to ask these questions at this stage in order to avoid aborting a study at a later stage because of some unforeseen problems.

1 How can the answer to the general question be found? What does it entail? Will finding the answer necessitate setting up an experiment? Will it require the development of a test or a survey questionnaire?

2 Does the researcher have the prerequisite background knowledge to investigate the question? Is a knowledge of linguistics or sociolinguistics necessary? How much statistical analysis appears to be involved? Will someone with more expertise be required? If the study is to be related to other peripheral areas, how much research should be done before proceeding to the next phase?

3 Are the terms and concepts used in the formulation of the general question defined clearly and consistently? Are the concepts and terms used in a way that is consistent with how other researchers have used them?

4 What logistical and practical problems can be anticipated? If the general question asks about the language acquisition of children or adults, will the researcher have access to the number of subjects required to investigate the question? Who will collect the data? Is it necessary to train assistants? If computer analysis of data is necessary, will there be access to computer time and assistance? Will the researcher need to be trained in the use of computer statistical analysis such as SPSS or SAS?

Researchers should try to avoid proceeding directly to the stage of the research itself without considering the theoretical and practical implications of the general question, because this inevitably leads to false starts or problems with the design and methodology of the research. Even experienced researchers sometimes have to discontinue efforts because of unforeseen or unavoidable obstacles. However, the more experienced researchers become, the more they learn to ask questions about feasibility and to predict possible areas of difficulty. It is not unusual to abandon research ideas at the general question stage because of infeasibility.

Let us now apply these questions of feasibility to the general question, *Why do learners of a second language progress at different rates?*

1 *How?*

In the case of this general question, there are several possibilities. The research could be conducted in a school setting or in a natural setting by studying individuals in the process of second language acquisition. It could be studied *synthetically*, by observing groups of learners and describing their activities, or *analytically*, by focusing on some specific aspect of language acquisition such as the acquisition of a syntactic form or a discourse strategy associated with acquisition. It might be possible to select learners who have already been identified as learning at different rates and test them for various characteristics that have been related to successful language learning. In other words, there are many possible ways to investigate this question and it would be wise, before beginning, to explore them for possible advantages and disadvantages.

2 *Prerequisite knowledge*

Investigating this general question would require different kinds of knowledge depending on the direction which the researcher decides to take. If the goal is to observe the social processes involved in second language acquisition, then it is necessary to acquire background knowledge in areas such as group behavior, language interaction patterns in groups, and theories relating to the role of the social environment in language acquisition.

If, however, the focus of the research is on the linguistic factors involved in the development of language competence by good and poor language learners, then the research will require familiarity with linguistic theories pertaining to second language acquisition, methods for analyzing linguistic data, and methods for collecting such data.

3 *The consistent definition of concepts and terms*

In the case of the general question under consideration, the definition of terms such as *language learner, language learning, rate of learning,* will have to be narrowed considerably in order to be useful for Phase 2 (Figure 3.1), in which the general question will become more focused.

It is clear that in a study concerned with rates of acquisition, a consistent definition of *language learning* or *acquisition* is crucial. Will acquisition be defined in terms of scores on a test? Will a functional measure of acquisition be used, such as the ability to perform specified discourse functions? This does not mean that definitions of terms used must be universally accepted. If the research carefully defines how terms will be used for the purposes of the particular study, problems of ambiguity and inconsistency will be avoided.

4 Logistical and practical problems

This aspect of feasibility includes factors bearing on the logistics of the investigation. Do we have direct access to groups of subjects? How much time will be required to study this question? Will the subjects be available throughout the duration of the study? Will special equipment such as tape recorders, video, or body microphones be required? Will the procedures used to collect data be intrusive to the ongoing routines of the class? How does the research schedule fit in with the school schedule of the classes being studied?

Under the heading of practical problems, no detail should be left unexamined. If it is decided to develop data from video tapes of the subjects performing a language task or interacting in a language lesson, additional judges may be necessary in order to record and agree upon what is being observed. However, this means that these judges will have to be trained in methods of observation; coding instruments which can be used in a consistent manner will have to be developed.

Which approach: synthetic or analytic?

Having considered the level of feasibility of the general question, it is now necessary to decide which approach, *synthetic* or *analytic*, is the most suitable.

Chapter 2 discussed the difference between the two approaches and how it is possible to view second language phenomena from either perspective. A synthetic approach would view the research holistically, as a composite of factors which might not be easily or validly analyzable into separate parts. An *analytic* approach would select one or several factors which make up the phenomenon for close analysis, perhaps in a controlled study. Either perspective has implications for research design and method.

It is useful, before deciding which approach to take to the general question, *Why do learners of a second language progress at different rates?*, to think about the factors which might be involved in determining different rates of language acquisition. Some of these factors might be more suitable for an analytic approach, others for a synthetic approach. There are also factors involved in rate of acquisition which could be investigated by either approach:

1 The learner's previous language learning experience.
2 The learner's attitude toward the language class, the teacher, or the materials.
3 The learner's aptitude for language.
4 The learner's first language.
5 The learner's sex.
6 The amount of practice which the learner engages in both in and out of the language class.
7 The kind of practice which the learner experiences – drill versus communicative use of the target language.
8 Personality characteristics of the learner.
9 Cognitive characteristics of the learner. (This list is extensive but not necessarily exhaustive.)

The synthetic approach

It may be decided to approach the research from a synthetic perspective. This may be because of the nature of the factor or factors to be studied, or because it is felt that a particular phenomenon is best studied from a holistic point of view and that taking an analytic approach will distort the nature of the phenomenon. For example, if it is felt that something related to the manner or amount of *practice* in the language class is responsible for different rates of acquisition, it may be decided to look at all or many aspects of classroom practice such as practice in drills, group practice, individual practice, controlled practice, spontaneous practice, or practice in pairs. All of these forms of practice are part of the total phenomenon which we refer to as 'practice' and to isolate one form from the others may distort its role, while taking a synthetic approach may allow us to evaluate the *relative* contribution that each form of practice makes to the overall process of acquisition.

At this stage, then, the decision would be concerned with what phenomena would be included in the *composite* concept of 'practice'. That is, because we may not have a clear idea of what kind of practice or how much practice plays a part in varying rates of acquisition, we would decide to look at a whole range of types of practice and how they *interrelate and interact* as they naturally occur in the language class.

The analytic approach

As discussed in Chapter 2, taking an *analytic* approach means that the second language phenomenon is analyzed into its constituent parts and one or a cluster of these constituent parts is examined in greater detail to the exclusion of other factors. When an analytic approach is taken, it usually means that the investigation will benefit from looking at some aspect of the second language problem in isolation; that a constituent approach to the phenomenon is possible and will not distort the nature of the phenomenon itself; and that enough is known about the constituent factor chosen for it to be studied in isolation.

Returning to the particular factor of *practice*, let us suppose that we had grounds for believing that some aspect of individual practice was responsible for differing rates of acquisition. In an analytic approach, a single factor or cluster of factors relating to individual practice in the language classroom would be isolated for further study. For example, we might decide to study individual practice in formal settings, such as drills, or combine a study of individual practice in formal and communicative settings.

For an *analytic* approach, it is necessary to define the terms used in the general question more precisely. At this stage, we are concerned with arriving at a conceptual rather than an operational definition. That is, in addition to defining what is meant by terms such as 'rate', 'learning', and 'different rates', we must also define conceptually what we mean by 'practice', 'formal practice', 'communicative practice', and other related terms. An important problem that arises in much research is the lack of clear and consistent definitions of the terms which later become the focus of the research. Note that the process we are describing consists of a gradual narrowing of the focus of the study. Having a clear and agreed conceptual definition of the terms will facilitate operationalizing them in Phase 3.

Phase 3: Deciding on an objective or purpose

Once an approach has been decided, the objective of the research must be considered. Is the purpose to discover or describe or is it to test a hypothesis that is based on previous work? The reader is referred to the discussion of Parameter 2 in Chapter 2.

Heuristic	Deductive
Description of research proce-dures, observations; some operational definition of terms	Operational defintion of terms or factors; formulation of research question or hypothesis

Table 3.1   Phase 3: Deciding on an objective or purpose

Heuristic research

It will be recalled from Chapter 2 that *heuristic* research was characterized by its *inductive* and *descriptive* nature. The researcher may begin with a general notion about some aspect of second language learning and gather data in various ways to learn more about the phenomenon under study. Descriptions or hypotheses may then be developed from these data. Other forms of heuristic research may describe specific aspects of second language acquisition in order to see if they correlate with other factors. If the decision is made to pursue the research question through *heuristic* research methods, this last phase will consist of developing the plans or procedures which the research will follow.

Research might have a heuristic purpose or goal but be combined with either a *synthetic* or an *analytic* approach to the research problem so that we might have *synthetic-heuristic* or *analytic-heuristic* research depending on the approach to the second language phenomenon and the goals of the research. For example, in the case of *analytic-heuristic* research, if we suspected that a specific factor involved in classroom language learning played a part, but were not certain what that part was, or had no theory or hypothesis, we might conduct a heuristic study focused on that particular constituent of classroom language learning. The case of *synthetic-heuristic* research is perhaps the more common. This combination might be decided upon if it was felt that the research should be as inclusive as possible without any predispositions for assigning more importance to one factor or another.

As was noted in Chapter 2, *heuristic* research does not necessarily begin with preconceived hypotheses. However, some awareness of the factors involved in the phenomenon may help decide what research strategies to follow. If the purpose of our research on the question of rates of acquisition is to *discover* what factors most affect it, we do not begin with a hypothesis to be confirmed or rejected. Rather we might begin with only a vague idea about what factors affect different rates of acquisition or with a suspicion that some factors, such as those listed on page 55, may be more important than others.

Deductive research

Any of the nine factors listed under Phase 2 could serve as the basis for more focused research questions. In Chapter 2, we noted that research with a *deductive* objective or purpose begins with a preconceived notion about what may be found. This preconceived notion is then formulated as a *prediction* or *hypothesis* to be confirmed or rejected. The hypothesis is usually grounded in a theory which attempts to explain the behavior in question.

As in the previous discussion of heuristic research, deductive research can be combined with either a synthetic or an analytic approach. An example of *synthetic-deductive* research would be an investigation in which a relationship is predicted between a large number of related variables or factors on the one hand and a language ability on the other. However, because the group of factors is seen as interdependent in some way, they are first treated synthetically as a composite whole to see whether in combination they correlate with language ability. In a study of factors which predict a second language learner's ability to acquire accurate pronunciation, Purcell and Suter (1980) first examined a battery of twenty variables which they hypothesized would predict accuracy in pronunciation. Gradually, through statistical procedures, the authors limited the size of the group of factors, first to a set of twelve and finally to a set of two factors which best predict pronunciation accuracy.

In our discussion of *deductive* research, we will limit ourselves to a single factor, number 6, from the set of nine which we previously listed. What we have done is to break down or analyze the cluster of factors which we associate with rate of acquisition and attempt to study a single factor because we have some *deductive* basis or theory for believing that this factor can predict rate of acquisition.

The process we have followed is *analytic* because we have broken down the *synthesis* of factors into *constituent* factors, and *deductive* because we have analyzed one of these as being most likely to be related to rate of acquisition. This kind of research can be characterized as *analytic-deductive*. We now try to reformulate this isolated factor in the form of a *focused question* about the relationship between practice and rates of acquisition:

– 6 Does the amount of practice affect the learner's rate of acquisition?

The focused question allows us to look at specific factors that intuitively relate practice and rate of acquisition. In this case, within the focused question, there are terms which, for the purposes of research, will have to be defined more precisely. The degree of definition will later facilitate the design and methodology of the research whether it be experimental, observational, or descriptive. The description and definition of these factors subsumed under the focused question may best be arrived at through a questioning process as before:

– 6A How is 'language practice' to be defined? How will it be measured?

– 6B How is 'acquisition' to be defined? Will it be defined in terms of grammatical competence, communicative competence, or a combination of the two? How will it be measured?

– 6C What kind(s) of practice are thought to affect rate of acquisition?

– 6D How is the amount of practice thought to affect rate of acquisition?

– 6E How will measures of language practice be related to measures of language acquisition?

It is at this point, in answering these questions, that the researcher is forced to confront the crucial problem of translating *conceptual definitions* into *operational definitions*, defining the terms or constructs which will be studied. Methodological issues are also addressed at this stage, such as whether the research can be carried out with a small number of subjects by conducting in-depth case studies of a few learners, or whether the research requires many subjects in order to test the hypothesis.

Let us continue our hypothetical example for the purposes of demonstration. It may be that after our review of the literature, we will find two competing definitions of 'language practice', one relating to the frequency of repetitions of a sentence pattern (6A) and another relating to the meaningful use of language in a communicative context (6A'). Let us also assume that we will define language acquisition as the learner's ability to function with language in meaningful or real-life situations (6B). That is, successful communication will be considered a measure of language acquisition. At this point, we will not discuss the more complex questions of how we could measure successful communication. Chapter 8 will discuss the development of instruments to measure various constructs.

Exploring the implications of the questions raised under 6A and 6B leaves us with more focused questions about the relationships between practice and acquisition. (See Figure 3.2.)

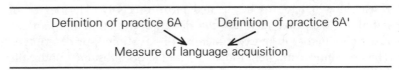

Figure 3.2   The relationship between practice and acquisition

Questions 6D and 6E put the theoretical construct *language practice* into more concrete or operational form. They require us to consider how the behavior we are researching can be quantified and what quantification might mean for the underlying research question. What, for example, can be considered a unit of 'practice'? What will be considered 'acquisition'? How will these units be measured and interpreted?

However, it should be emphasized that constructs cannot be translated into concrete or operational form in an actual study or experiment until there are clear answers to the questions 6A and 6B. If the construct 'practice' is not clearly defined, it would be foolish to design and carry out research measuring this ill-defined idea. We might define 'practice' as the number of times a subject repeats a sentence from a language laboratory tape or as the number of self-generated sentences that a subject produces in a face-to-face communicative context. Each definition will produce different outcomes and different interpretations about the role of practice.

Phase 4: Formulating the research plan or the hypothesis

If the study is to be some form of heuristic research, this last phase will consist of deciding on appropriate procedures and designing methods for collecting data relating to a single factor or a synthesis of factors which may affect the rate of acquisition. In Chapter 6, we will discuss in detail the procedures for conducting various kinds of heuristic research.

If the study is to be deductive, the procedures are more complex. This is because deductive research requires the demonstration of a clear relationship between the factor or variable which is thought to be closely related to or responsible for the rate of acquisition. In Chapter 1, it was stated that the requirements for a scientific hypothesis are that it be testable or falsifiable. A hypothesis, contrary to popular belief, is not supposed to lead to conclusions which cannot be tested further. Confirming or rejecting a research hypothesis is always conditional or qualified since it must always be open to falsification, rejection, or revision. New evidence may present itself or other relevant research may cast new light on the object of research. It is part of the 'game' of science to view research as the best possible 'guess' at a particular point in our state of knowledge. As new insights and knowledge are gathered and new theories present different ways of viewing the same phenomenon, hypotheses will necessarily be revised or rejected.

Qualitative or descriptive research   ↗ Research hypothesis
(The process may end here or . . .)

↓

Null hypothesis

↓

[Confirmation or rejection]

The research hypothesis and the null hypothesis

Question 6 above asked: Does the amount of practice affect the learner's rate of acquisition? Let us assume that we have arrived at satisfactory conceptual and operational definitions of all of the terms which are found in the question. The next step is to convert this question into a research hypothesis.

The research hypotheses in this example might take one of the following forms:
- H1 Learners who exhibit high levels of practice will acquire at a faster rate than those who do not.
- H2 Learners who exhibit high levels of practice will acquire at a slower rate than learners who do not.

– H3 Learners who exhibit high levels of practice will acquire at the same rate as those who do not.

Note that the first two hypotheses are 'directional'. That is, they make a prediction about the direction of the possible outcome of the research. The only problem with directional hypotheses is that it is very difficult to argue unambiguously for a specific factor causing the directional effect. The results may be due to high levels of practice. Unfortunately, the results may be due to other factors as well. (Chapters 5 and 7 will discuss this problem in greater detail.)

Because it is difficult to 'prove' a directional hypothesis conclusively, the research hypothesis is usually stated in the form of a *null hypothesis*. The third hypothesis above, H3, is the null hypothesis and states that no differences exist between the rates of acquisition of high level practicers and low level practicers. There are statistical tests which may then be applied to the data to show whether there is or is not a significant difference between the two groups. If the null hypothesis cannot be rejected at a statistically significant level, that is, it cannot be shown that the high and low level practicers are *not* different in rates of acquisition, then the *research hypotheses* (H1 and H2) are automatically rejected.

It is usually the hope of the researcher to reject the null hypothesis. If this hypothesis is rejected, it is interpreted as meaning that one of the other research hypotheses is supported. Since it is unlikely that high levels of practice will lead to slower rates of acquisition, the rejection of H3 is assumed to provide indirect support for H1. That is, in actual practice, the *research hypothesis*, while the focus of the research itself, is not the hypothesis that is tested. Rather, for the purposes of the research itself, a *null hypothesis* is formulated. The null hypothesis is usually a statement of what the research really hopes to *disprove*. That is, the null hypothesis is stated so that its *falsification* or *rejection* will lead to *acceptance* of one of the research hypotheses.

Confirmation or rejection of the hypothesis is not, of course, the end of the research process. In Figure 3.1, we have shown an arrow returning to Phase 2. This is intended to show that the outcome of the research is recycled back to the theory or hypothesis from which it emanated, either requiring an adjustment in the original theory or a rethinking of the original hypothesis for the purposes of continued research.

Summary

Chapter 3 has traced the preparatory stages in the development of a research project from the stage of an observation to the decision about the general approach. The phases of this process are summarized below. All scientific research does not necessarily follow the progression through the four phases which we have described here. However, we have followed these stages in order to describe the logic involved in developing a research idea in second language.

The four phases in the development of research were:

Phase 1: The general question
Phase 2: Focusing the question
Phase 3: Deciding on an objective or purpose
Phase 4: Formulating the research plan or the hypothesis

Activities

1 If you are a language teacher, keep a diary of your teaching experience for a week. At the end of the week, review your diary. What research questions are suggested in your diary about second or foreign language learners? About teaching? About teacher-learner interaction?

2 Select a study from a second language journal. (See Chapter 4 for suggestions.) What additional questions are suggested by the research that were not investigated by the researcher?

3 Select a research journal in an area such as cognitive psychology, sociology, or education. Find an article which raises a theoretical issue and discuss how this issue might have relevance for second language research.

4 Select two topics for a research project. Discuss:
   a) The source of the topic.
   b) Why it is important to investigate.
   c) Problems of feasibility.

5 Select a topic in second language research, such as the relationship of age to second language acquisition. Follow this topic through the steps outlined in Figure 3.1 along each of its branches, developing research plans for both heuristic and deductive research.

References

Bailey, K. M. 1983. 'Competitiveness and anxiety in adult second language learning: Looking *at* and *through* the diary studies' in H. W. Seliger and M. H. Long (eds.): *Classroom Oriented Research in Second Language Acquisition*. Rowley, Mass.: Newbury House.

Chomsky, N. 1981. *Lectures on Government and Binding*. Dordrecht: Foris.

Cook, V. J. 1985. 'Chomsky's universal grammar and second language learning.' *Applied Linguistics* 6/1: 2–18.

Durkheim, E. 1897. *Le Suicide*. Paris: G. Alcan.

Flynn, S. 1987. *A Parameter Setting Model for L2 Acquisition*. Dordrecht: D. Reidel.

Krashen, S. D. 1978. 'Individual variation in the use of the monitor' in W. C. Ritchie (ed.): *Second Language Acquisition Research*. New York: Academic Press.

Lambert, W. E. and Gardner, R. C. 1959. 'Motivational variables in second language learning.' *Canadian Journal of Psychology* 13.

Mazurkewich, I. 1984. 'Dative questions and markedness' in F. R. Eckman, H. Bell, and D. Nelson (eds.): *Universals of Second Language Acquisition*. Rowley, Mass.: Newbury House.

Purcell, E. T. and Suter, R. W. 1980. 'Predictors of pronunciation accuracy: A reexamination.' *Language Learning* 30/2: 271–287.

Seliger, H. W. 1979. 'On the nature and function of language rules in language teaching.' *TESOL Quarterly* 13:359–369.

White, L. 1985. 'The acquisition of parameterized grammars: subjacency in second language acquisition.' *Second Language Research* 1/1: 1–17.

4 Contextualization of research

> The excavator should be familiar with the work of his precursors
> and his contemporaries; he should know where to fit his new data
> into the total picture. . .
>
> (W. F. Albright: *The Archeology of Palestine*)

The what and why of contextualization

Once the area, topic, or problem of the research has been chosen
and defined, the research needs to be placed in a broader context by
reviewing the related literature. This will be referred to as
contextualizing the research.

There are a number of reasons for contextualizing the research.
On the one hand, it helps the researcher broaden the view and
perspective of the research; on the other it helps him or her narrow
down the topic and arrive at a focused research question. These
two purposes, which seem to be contradictory are actually
complementary, because in research there is a need to both *expand*
the perspective and to *narrow* it down in order to arrive at a
workable research question.

Therefore a review of the literature should take place a number
of times during the research process. In the preparatory phase it
helps the researcher *select* an area, topic, or problem; this process
was described in Chapter 3. In the second stage, once the topic has
been selected, a thorough and systematic review of the literature is
necessary to *broaden* the perspective of the research and to
familiarize the researcher with the theoretical framework underlying
the selected topic. Finally, the literature is reviewed once more
when the researcher needs to *narrow down* the topic in preparation
for the actual administration of the research. It should be noted,
however, that in carrying out actual research these different
purposes are not pursued in strict sequence.

We will now describe these stages through a hypothetical
example of researchers who are about to conduct research in the
area of age and second language acquisition.

Selecting the research topic

Consider the example of researchers who have a general interest in the effect of age on second language acquisition. While this interest may have evolved from observations of their personal experiences (arriving in a country as immigrants and having difficulties in learning the new language – unlike their children, who seem to have learned the language much faster, with no observed difficulties) they begin reviewing the literature, searching for research articles and other materials which address this topic. They obtain initial references on the topic from bibliography lists given by the lecturers at the second language acquisition course they may be attending at the time. In the process of reviewing these sources they locate additional references and materials from the bibliography lists included in these articles. While reading the material they realize that although there is ample research on the topic there are also many unanswered questions. For example, there are conflicting findings as to the effect of age on second language acquisition in different learning contexts (formal or informal). There also seem to be differences in the effect of age on the acquisition of certain aspects of language. Research studies show, though not consistently, that age is correlated positively with the learning of grammar (the older people are, the better they acquire grammar), but that younger children seem to have an advantage in acquiring phonology. They then discover that while there are a large number of studies on age and second language acquisition in informal contexts, there is very little research on the phenomenon of age and language learning in the school context. This issue, they believe, is very important since it may have implications for curriculum planning, teaching methodologies, and educational policies. The researchers therefore decide to carry out their research on the effect of age on the acquisition of phonology in formal versus informal contexts.

This is still a *general* topic of research that is not immediately researchable, since there are many aspects which need to be worked on before the researchers are ready to begin the study. They will have to go through a number of phases (outlined in Chapter 3), in order to examine the feasibility of this research topic. Then, in order to arrive at better-defined and more focused questions or hypotheses, the researchers will have to make decisions about the specific age of the subjects and the type of formal instruction they receive. The specific context of informal learning will have to be decided and the topic will be researched either by designing an experiment where learners of a certain age get a specific type of instruction in school, or it will be studied by observing different types of learners in a variety of learning contexts without conducting an experiment.

By reviewing the literature and examining other research studies in the same field, the researchers will be able to decide on the details of the research topic, making it more specific and focused.

Broadening the perspective and narrowing the question

Once the researchers have selected the topic, they need to expand it, mainly by investigating prevailing theories relating to it. Thus, during this stage the researchers will conduct a more thorough and systematic review of the literature by examining and reviewing current theories in a number of related disciplines such as applied linguistics, linguistics, psychology, neurolinguistics, sociology, and education. They will want to familiarize themselves with the theories these disciplines provide on various aspects of the research topic. In the above example, these will include current theories on the acquisition of phonology, on age-related differences in ability to acquire certain aspects of a second language, and on the effect of the learning context (formal versus informal) on learners of different ages. Notice that the researchers focus also on related disciplines, beyond applied linguistics. Clearly at this stage the researchers cannot simply rely on the bibliography list obtained in a university course, but will need to collect references from other sources as well. Indices such as *Resources in Education* and *Language and Language Behavior Abstracts* are likely to include references to additional articles not encountered in the earlier literature review. The researchers may also wish to conduct a *computer search*, to generate updated references on the topic and thus obtain a larger pool of references. A description of such sources and the procedures for obtaining them will be described in the next section of this chapter.

In reviewing the literature, the researchers will have to make a decision as to which references are most relevant and most useful, by reading the abstracts that precede most articles. They are likely to begin by reviewing articles which relate most directly to the research topic, such as those which focus on differences in the acquisition of phonology by learners of different ages in different learning contexts. They will be likely to review first the most recent ones and then work backwards towards less recent research.

Following this, they will explore other relevant areas in the literature, such as studies on differences in the learning of other school subjects in formal versus informal contexts, work on the relationship between age and learning, focusing on cognitive, affective, and neurological aspects of child development, and possibly research on the rate of language acquisition of monolingual and bilingual learners of different ages. Readings in such areas will provide a better understanding of how different aspects of language are acquired at different stages of development in a variety of learning contexts.

In reviewing the literature the researchers may also encounter research studies similar to the ones which they are planning to conduct. These will provide useful ideas on how to design their own research.

Focusing on the relevant information

In reading the literature the researchers will focus on a number of things. They may, for example, be interested in finding out why, where, and by whom the research was conducted, what the underlying assumptions of the studies were, and which procedures and methodologies were used for collecting the data. They will focus on the major findings of such research, and most importantly, how such studies added to the body of knowledge on the topic.

By acquainting themselves with the relevant literature, the researchers obtain a comprehensive and broad understanding of the topic, and are thus able to arrive at a clear and well defined question for conducting the research. For example, if much of the surveyed research focuses on the acquisition of phonology in informal contexts, it may provide a framework, or a rationale for conducting research on the effect of age on the acquisition of phonology in a formal context. The findings obtained in informal contexts are useful for creating hypotheses about another setting. If the literature review reveals that there are conflicting findings about the topic, this can provide a rationale for examining the same question from a different point of view, possibly with improved methodology, so as to offer more convincing findings and more clearly defined hypotheses. For example, if studies show that there is no direct relationship between age and the acquisition of phonology in informal contexts, the researcher could hypothesize that no direct relationship will be found in formal contexts either. Or if, in reviewing the literature on age, the researchers learn about the significance of the critical period in acquiring phonology in informal contexts, they may pose a research question which relates to the effect of age on children's learning ability before or after that period. The fact that the phases of development are different in boys and girls, for instance, may lead the researchers to examine differences between the sexes, or other variables such as personality, learning styles, and motivations.

While reading, the researchers will summarize and keep records of all the above information. They may use index cards or store the information on a computer database and thus compile a bibliography list which they are likely to use at a later stage for writing the literature review.

To sum up, the process of contextualization helps the researchers to *generate* and *select* a research topic, *expand* their understanding, and *broaden* their knowledge and perspective of that topic, and at the same time *arrive* at a researchable and *well-defined* question for the research. The literature review helps them realize that the problem they are interested in is part of a larger body of knowledge. The review will also indicate whether there have already been important findings within this research area, whether there are still areas to be investigated, and whether the research that is about to be conducted is likely to add new information to that body of knowledge.

Now that the purposes of contextualizing the research and the phases in the research process have been discussed, we will locate the sources for the literature review. We will then return to a more detailed description of the process involved in reading the literature and in organizing and reporting the literature review.

Locating the sources for the literature review

As has been mentioned, material for the literature review can be located within the second language acquisition discipline and in adjacent areas such as linguistics, education, psychology, sociology, or any other discipline considered relevant to the specific research topic. In describing the sources there is a need to differentiate between sources used for *reference* such as indices, computer searches, bibliography lists, and so on, and the *actual* and specific material, such as journal articles, reviews, etc. In the following section we provide a description of both sources. In the category of references we will discuss indices, computer searches, bibliographies, professional conferences, and the 'underground' press. Under the actual material we will discuss sources such as journal articles, edited collections, reviews, and books.

1 Indices

Indices are publications which provide large numbers of references on a variety of topics, and are therefore instrumental in pointing the researcher to existing material in the field. They are the most commonly used source for obtaining references to the literature. The references are listed according to author's name and subject. Listings include various types of information, such as the year of publication, the place where the material was first published or presented, where and how it can be obtained, and the form in which it was published (paper, article, or report). Most indices also include abstracts or other types of descriptions which summarize the content of the material and are therefore useful for indicating to the researchers the relevance of the material to their research topic. Different indices are published quarterly, monthly, bi-annually, or annually. Figure 4.1 is an example of material from the index *Resources in Education*, with a description of the different types of information it provides.

When searching for references on a given topic, the researchers will first make use of the *Thesaurus of Descriptors* which lists key words or *descriptors*, to assist them in finding references related to their topic. For example, in a search for references related to the topic of age and second language acquisition, the relevant descriptors in the *Thesaurus* are likely to be age, second language learning, informal learning, bilingualism, school learning, and cognition. Figure 4.2 is a sample page from the *Thesaurus of ERIC Descriptors*, compiled by Educational Resources Information Clearinghouse (ERIC).

The indices which are most useful for second language learning research are those of work in linguistics, applied linguistics, education, sociology, and psychology. Descriptions of these indices are provided below:

Language and Language Behavior Abstracts (LLBA) is published quarterly by Sociological Abstracts. It summarizes the contents of periodicals, papers, monographs, and transactions published in over thirty languages, and covers the areas of anthropology, speech, applied linguistics, rhetoric, psycholinguistics, education, and communication. This index includes abstracts, subject index, source index, and author index, and is invaluable for locating references in second language acquisition.

SAMPLE RESUME

ERIC Accession Number – identification number sequentially assigned to documents as they are processed.

Author(s).

Title.

Organization where document originated.

Date Published.

Contract or Grant Number.

Alternate source for obtaining document.

Language of Document – documents written entirely in English are not designated, although 'English' is carried in their computerized records.

Publication Type – broad categories indicating the form or organization of the document, as contrasted to its subject matter. The category name is followed by the category code.

ERIC Document Reproduction Service (EDRS) Availability – 'MF' means microfiche; 'PC' means reproduced paper copy. When described as 'Document Not Available from EDRS,' alternate sources are cited above. Prices are subject to change; for latest price code schedule see section on 'How to Order ERIC Documents.' in the most recent issue of RIE.

Clearinghouse Accession Number.

Sponsoring Agency – agency responsible for initiating, funding, and managing the research project.

Report Number – assigned by originator.

Descriptive Note (pagination first).

Descriptors – subject terms found in the *Thesaurus of ERIC Descriptors* that characterize substantive content. Only the major terms, preceded by an asterisk, are printed in the subject index.

Identifiers – additional identifying terms not found in the *Thesaurus*. Only the major terms, preceded by an asterisk are printed in the subject index.

Informative Abstract.

Abstractor's Initials.

ED 654 321   CE 123 456
Smith, John D.   Johnson, Jane
Career Planning for Women.
Central Univ., Chicago, Il..
Spons Agency – National Inst. of Education (ED).
  Washington, DC.
Report No. – CU–2081–S
Pub Date – May 83
Contract – NIE–C–83–0001
Note – 129p.; Paper presented at the National
  Conference on Career Education (3rd, Chicago,
  Il., May 15–17, 1983).
Available from – Campus Bookstore, 123 College
  Ave., Chicago, Il. 60690 ($3.25).
Language – English, French
Pub Type – Speeches/Meeting Papers (150)
EDRS Price – MF01/PC06 Plus Postage.
Descriptors – Career Guidance,* Career Planning,
  Careers, *Demand Occupations, *Employed
  Women, *Employment Opportunities, Females,
  Labor Force, Labor Market, *Labor Needs,
  Occupational Aspiration, Occupations
Identifiers – Consortium of States, * National
  Occupational Competency Testing Institute
  Women's opportunities for employment will be
directly related to their level of skill and experience
and also to the labor market demands through the
remainder of the decade. The number of workers
needed for all major occupational categories is
expected to increase by about one-fifth between
1980 and 1990, but the growth rate will vary
by occupational group. Professional and technical
workers are expected to have the highest predicted
rate (39 percent), followed by service workers
(35 percent), clerical workers (26 percent), sales
workers (24 percent), craft workers and supervisors
(20 percent), managers and administrators (15 percent), and operatives (11 percent). This publication
contains a brief discussion and employment information concerning occupations for professional and
technical workers, managers and administrators,
skilled trades, sales workers, clerical workers, and
service workers. In order for women to take
advantage of increased labor market demands,
employer attitudes toward working women need to
change and women must: (1) receive better career
planning and counseling, (2) change their career
aspirations, and (3) fully utilize the sources of legal
protection and assistance that are available to them.
(SB)

Note: ERIC stands for Educational Resources Information Clearinghouse, published by *Resources in Education*

Figure 4.1   Sample résumé from Resources in Education

134/LANGUAGE ROLE

Speech Communication
Speech Habits
Speech Skills
Written Language

LANGUAGE ROLE *Jul. 1966*
CIJE: 528   RIE: 498   GC: 450
RT Cultural Influences
Language
Language Attitudes
Language Maintenance
Language Research
Social Dialects
Social Influences
Sociolinguistics

LANGUAGE SKILLS *Jul. 1966*
CIJE: 1,627   RIE: 2,405   GC: 450
NT Audiolingual Skills
Communicative Competence
(Languages)
Reading Skills
Vocabulary Skills
Writing Skills
BT Skills
RT Basic Skills
Cloze Procedure
Communication Skills
English (Second Language)
Error Analysis (Language)
Expressive Language
Interpreters
Interpretive Skills
Language
Language Acquisition
Language Aptitude
Language Arts
Language Dominance
Language Fluency
Language Processing
Language Proficiency
Languages
Language Tests
Linguistic Competence
Linguistic Performance
Listening Comprehension
Monolingualism
Psycholinguistics
Receptive Language
Second Language Learning
Sentence Combining
Speech Skills
Translation
Verbal Ability
Word Study Skills

LANGUAGE STANDARDIZATION
Jul. 1966
CIJE: 141   RIE: 135   GC: 450
SN The official acceptance by at least some
groups within a speech community of
certain general patterns of pronunciation,
grammar, orthography, and/or vocabulary
BT Language Planning
RT Dialects
Diglossia
Languages
National Norms
National Programs
Native Language Instruction
Official Languages
Romanization
Sociolinguistics
Standard Spoken Usage

LANGUAGE STYLES *Jul. 1966*
CIJE: 562   RIE: 554 GC: 450
SN Optional variants in sounds, structures,
and vocabulary of a language which are
characteristic of different users,
situations, or literary types
UF Linguistic Styles
BT Language Usage
Language Variation

RT Cliches
Editing
Expressive Language
Language
Language Classification
Language Patterns
Language Rhythm
Literary Devices
Native Speakers
Speech Skills
Standard Spoken Usage
Writing Skills

Language Tapes
USE AUDIOTAPE RECORDINGS

LANGUAGE TEACHERS *Jul. 1966*
CIJE: 545   RIE: 614   GC: 360
UF Fles Teachers (1967 1980) #
Foreign Language Teachers
Second Language Teachers
BT Teachers
RT English Instruction
Languages
Native Language Instruction
Second Language Instruction

LANGUAGE TESTS *Jul. 1966*
CIJE: 640   RIE: 909   GC: 830
SN Tests to measure proficiency, diagnose
strengths and weaknesses, or predict
future performance in a native or foreign
language (note: for foreign language
tests, coordinate this term with 'second
language learning,' and, when
appropriate, the language)
BT Verbal Tests
RT Achievement Tests
Cloze Procedure
Language
Language Dominance
Language Proficiency
Languages
Language Skills
Listening Comprehension Tests
Reading Tests
Second Language Learning
Speech Tests
Writing Evaluation
Writing Skills

LANGUAGE TYPOLOGY *Jul. 1966*
CIJE: 62   RIE: 97   GC: 450
SN Classification of languages on the basis
of similarities and differences in their
structural features – phonology,
grammar, and vocabulary, including
semantic meaning in specific contexts
BT Language Classification
RT Contrastive Linguistics
Descriptive Linguistics
Etymology
Language Patterns
Language Universals
Morphology (Languages)
Phonemes
Phonology
Syntax
Tone Languages

LANGUAGE UNIVERSALS *Aug. 1968*
CIJE: 188   RIE: 232   GC: 450
SN Characteristics assumed to be common
to all languages
UF Linguistic Universals
BT Language
RT Artificial Languages
Behavioral Science Research
Case (Grammar)
Diachronic Linguistics
Distinctive Features (Language)
Language
Language Acquisition
Language Patterns
Language Research
Languages

Language Typology
Linguistic Difficulty (Inherent)
Linguistic Theory
Negative Forms (Language)
Structural Analysis (Linguistics)

LANGUAGE USAGE *Jul. 1966*
CIJE: 1,808   RIE: 1,608   GC: 450
UF Sexist Language #
NT Language Styles
Standard Spoken Usage
RT Business English
Code Switching (Language)
Cohesion (Written Composition)
Dialects
Error Analysis (Language)
Grammatical Acceptability
Language
Language Attitudes
Language Dominance
Language Maintenance
Language Of Instruction
Language Patterns
Language Planning
Language Processing
Languages
Language Variation
Linguistic Borrowing
Linguistics
Miscue Analysis
Native Language Instruction
Native Speakers
North American English
Pragmatics
Sociolinguistics
Speech Habits
Urban Language
Written Language

LANGUAGE VARIATION *Jun. 1975*
CIJE: 368   RIE: 410   GC: 450
SN Differences in systems of a language
that result from historical, geographic,
social, or functional changes
NT Creoles
Dialects
Language Styles
Linguistic Borrowing
Pidgins
BT Sociolinguistics
RT Code Switching (Language)
Contrastive Linguistics
Diachronic Linguistics
Dialect Studies
Diglossia
Grammatical Acceptability
Language
Language Usage
Urban Language

LANGUAGES *Jul. 1966*
CIJE: 106   RIE: 283   GC: 440
SN (note: use a more specific term if
possible)
NT African Languages
Afro Asiatic Languages
American Indian Languages
Australian Aboriginal Languages
Austro Asiatic Languages
Basque
Burushaski
Caucasian Languages
Classical Languages
Creoles
Dialects
Dravidian Languages
Eskimo Aleut Languages
Indo European Languages
Japanese
Korean
Malayo Polynesian Languages
Modern Languages
Pidgins
Sino Tibetan Languages
Uralic Altaic Languages
Vietnamese

RT Bilingualism
Conversational Language Courses
Etymology
Fles
Foreign Language Books
Foreign Language Films
Foreign Language Periodicals
Giottochronology
Idioms
Intensive Language Courses
Language
Language Classification
Language Dominance
Language Enrichment
Language Enrollment
Language Fluency
Language Laboratories
Language Maintenance
Language Of Instruction
Language Patterns
Language Planning
Language Proficiency
Language Research
Languages for Special Purposes
Language Skills
Language Standardization
Language Teachers
Language Tests
Language Universals
Language Usage
Middle English
Monolingualism
Multilingualism
Mutual Intelligibility
Notional Functional Syllabi
Old English
Second Language Instruction
Word Frequency

LANGUAGES FOR SPECIAL PURPOSES
Apr 1975
CIJE: 114   RIE: 113   GC: 440
SN Languages taught to or learned by non-
native speakers who need a certain
specialized foreign language capability in
their studies, profession, or trade
NT English For Special Purposes
BT Language
RT Languages
Second Language Instruction
Second Language Learning

LAO *Jul. 1966*
CIJE: 0   RIE: 21   GC: 440
UF Laotian
BT Sino Tibetan Languages

Laotian
USE LAO

Laotian Americans
USE ASIAN AMERICANS; LAOTIANS

LAOTIANS *Mar. 1980*
CIJE: 3   RIE: 15   GC: 560
UF Laotian Americans #
BT Indochinese
RT Asian Americans
Cambodians
Vietnamese People

Laps
USE LEARNING MODULES

Large Cities
USE URBAN AREAS

LARGE GROUP INSTRUCTION
Jul. 1966
CIJE: 65   RIE: 79   GC: 310
SN Teaching of students in large classroom
situations (note: do not confuse with
'mass instruction')
BT Group Instruction
RT Mass Instruction
Small Group Instruction
Teaching Methods

Figure 4.2   *Sample page from the Thesaurus of ERIC Descriptors*

Language Teaching (previously titled *Language Teaching and Linguistics Abstracts*), is a quarterly which lists references to journal articles, books, and reports in linguistics and applied linguistics. It is a good source for European references not included in other indices. It also publishes survey articles on given topics in language learning.

Resources in Education (RIE) (previously titled *Research in Education*), is published monthly by ERIC. (See Figure 4.1.) It includes a large number of references and résumés on topics in first and second language learning and is generally available in most libraries in the U.S. and Europe. It contains references to articles, abstracts of reports, conference presentations, and other studies. Entries are arranged numerically. Each monthly issue contains subject and author indices from which bi-annual and annual cumulative indices are compiled. Subject headings used are from the *Thesaurus of ERIC Descriptors*. The information available in this index is often not found in other indices. In many libraries it is also possible to obtain microfiches of the actual documents.

Current Index to Journals in Education (CIJE) is also published by ERIC and is a monthly publication which indexes articles related to education appearing in approximately seven hundred and eighty journals, giving titles, authors, and abstracts of the documents. It includes a large number of references on different aspects of first and second language learning. Subject headings used are from the *Thesaurus of ERIC Descriptors*.

The last two indices are the printed equivalent of the ERIC computer database, described in 2 below.

Dissertation Abstracts International is published monthly in the U.S. by University Microfilms Inc. (Ann Arbor, Michigan). A special European issue is published quarterly. It lists abstracts of doctoral dissertations completed in the current year, and abstracts of dissertations accepted for other degrees from more than four hundred institutions in the U.S. and Europe. It is a useful source of material not yet published in journals.

Psychological Abstracts and *Sociological Abstracts* are comprehensive indices which review a large number of journals in psychology and sociology and provide good sources for language learning topics related to these disciplines.

2 Computer search

A computer search is the procedure by which references on certain topics are generated from available computer databases. It is a quick, efficient way to obtain references to articles, reports and papers available in specific databases. Many institutions therefore require research students to run a computer search before the research study is conducted.

The most important database in second language acquisition is the one by ERIC, which includes a large number of documents on different topics related to education. ERIC has a number of clearinghouses in different areas. Those which compile language references are Language and Linguistics and Bilingual Education. Items can be generated from the database after the researcher has identified descriptors from the *Thesaurus of ERIC Descriptors*. These descriptors are then used to scan the database and a list of relevant references can be printed out, beginning with the most recent ones. Each item listed includes the title, name of author, date, place of publication, where it can be obtained, and an abstract of the content of the document. Figure 4.3 displays a sample item obtained from a computer search using the ERIC database in the area of Cognitive Styles in Foreign Languages.

The first code number in the sample refers to the reference number in the database; following it are the title of the article, the author's name, place and date of publication, where the document can be obtained, the language in which it appeared, and the type of document.

Computer searches using the ERIC system can be conducted for a small fee in many libraries or through the ERIC Clearinghouse on Language and Linguistics (Center for Applied Linguistics, 1118 22nd Street, NW, Washington, D.C. 20037).

3 Bibliographies

These are a useful source for obtaining lists of literature references. *Annotated* bibliographies are reference lists which focus on specific topics, and are usually put out by research centres such as the ERIC Clearinghouse on Language and Linguistics and on Bilingual Education. One example is the annotated bibliography on language testing, compiled by Clifford and Lange and published in 1981. The Modern Language Association (MLA) publishes an annual annotated

EJ:68450   FL514691
Student-Teacher Cognitive Styles and Foreign
Language Achievement: A Preliminary Study.
Mansen, Jacqueline; Stansfield, Charles
Modern Language Journal, V.66, N.3, P.263–73,
Fall, 1982
Available from: Reprint: UMI
Language: English
Document Type: JOURNALS ARTICLE (080):
RESEARCH REPORT (143): NON-CLASSROOM MATERIAL
(055)
Journal Announcement: CIJJAN83
In terms of second-language learning, examines:
(1) What is the significance, educational and statistical, of
the performance difference between field-dependent and
field-independent students? and (2) Does the learner's
cognitive style interact with other factors in the learning
situation, such as the teacher's cognitive style, to affect
differentially? (EKN)
Descriptors: *Cognitive Style: College Students;
Language Aptitude; Performance Factors; *Second Language
Learning; *Success; *Teaching Styles
Identifiers: *Field Dependence Independence

*Figure 4.3   A sample item obtained from a computer search
(using the ERIC system)*

bibliography which includes references to a large number of books
and articles on a variety of language topics.

The bibliographies which accompany articles, reviews, or books
also provide accessible sources for obtaining useful references
which can often lead to additional references. However, it should
be noted that bibliographies can be selective and may overlook
relevant material. Since they are usually based on published
material, they do not always represent the most up-to-date
references.

4 Professional conferences

Research reports and papers presented at conferences also provide
valuable sources for locating references. The published conference
programs which list (and often describe) the papers presented are a
good source for finding out about unpublished ongoing and newly-

completed research. Included in such programs are the names of the presenters and their affiliations, titles of the papers, and often abstracts as well. Programs obtained from smaller meetings will also include proceedings of the actual papers presented. Many conference papers are listed and published in the *Resources in Education* index and are available on microfiche. It is also possible to write to the presenter to request copies of the paper.

5 The 'underground' press

This refers to the circulation of papers and other material among colleagues, often before the material is published in journals or books. Specifically, it relates to research which authors may have recently completed and not yet submitted to journals for publication; to research still in progress; to reports for limited circulation; and to students' theses and dissertations.

The underground press is a useful and important source for obtaining up-to-date references. It should be noted here that published material may be based on work completed some time previously, owing to the one-to-three years' delay between completion of the research and publication. Access to 'the underground' can best be gained through personal communication with researchers working in the related areas of research.

6 Journal articles

Journals (or periodicals) are collections of articles which are published regularly. Research published in journals follows a standard format, in that it addresses the research problem or question, reviews the related literature, describes the methods and procedures used for collecting and analyzing the data, and reports the results, conclusions, and implications of the research.

Different journals serve different readers. In second language acquisition, some journals are geared towards researchers. Others that include practical implications of the research findings are more oriented towards practitioners. Some journals address both types of audiences.

A list of journals in second language acquisition and in the related areas of linguistics, education, psychology, and sociology is given in the Appendix.

7 Edited collections and reviews

These have a thematic approach to presenting research. *Edited collections* are books which contain a number of research articles on given themes. The editor, by adding descriptions and discussions of the contribution of each research article to the topic and theme of the collection, is attempting to create a conceptual framework for the different studies. Edited collections are sometimes based on papers presented at small symposia, conferences, or meetings devoted to specific themes. For example, *Language Transfer in Language Learning* (Gass and Selinker 1983) is based on a meeting devoted to that topic. *Georgetown University Round Table on Language and Linguistics* publishes issues consisting of collections of the papers presented at their annual meetings, which have a different theme each year. Journals will occasionally publish thematic issues as well. For example, *Applied Linguistics* has published issues on the themes of lexicography, comprehension, and discourse analysis.

There are also specific *reviews* which survey and review trends of research in given areas. They can be in the form of *annual volumes* such as the *Annual Review of Applied Linguistics* in which each issue consists of a collection of papers relating to topics which vary from year to year, or in the form of review *journals* such as the *Review of Educational Research* or *Educational Review*.

Another source for thematic reviews are *meta-analysis studies*. Meta-analysis takes the results obtained from a large number of research studies on one problem, synthesizes, summarizes, and combines them in order to arrive at more conclusive answers about the problem (Hedges and Olkins 1985). For example, in the area of second language acquisition research there is a meta-analysis study on the effectiveness of bilingual education. (Willig 1985, Baker 1987, Willig 1987, Secada 1987). Meta-analysis studies provide the researcher with a useful source for obtaining comprehensive information on a given topic.

It should be noted that edited collections, reviews, and meta-analysis studies are often based on research that has already appeared in regular journals, and therefore they do not always represent the most up-to-date research; still, they are very worthwhile sources for obtaining a theoretical framework and a comprehensive view of research topics, and are therefore very useful for the literature review.

In summary, in this section we have described a variety of sources for locating references to the literature as well as for obtaining actual literature material. These different sources are listed in Table 4.1. Once the literature material is obtained the researcher needs to review and organize it. Ways of doing it will be discussed in the next section.

Sources

---

1 Indices
2 Computer searches
3 Bibliographies
4 Professional conferences
5 'Underground' press
6 Journal articles
7 Edited collections, reviews, books

Table 4.1   Sources for locating the literature material

Reading the literature

Once researchers have located the material, they need to sift through it to determine its relevance to their specific research topic. It is important to decide at this point how much reviewing should be done, which references should get more emphasis, and which aspects the researcher should focus on so that the material becomes meaningful for the contextualization of the research. Once the researchers have read the material they must decide how the material should be organized, presented, and reported in the literature review section of the research.

Determining the relevance of the material

Many of the sources which researchers find emerge during the process of enquiry. It thus becomes difficult to define the scope of the literature review before reading. One fairly common situation is that the literature review becomes an unending path and the researchers find it difficult to decide when to stop. If the scope of the readings is too broad, the researchers may be discouraged and may lose the right perspective on the research; if it is too narrow, on the other hand, they may overlook studies which contain important and relevant information. However, while the literature review never really ends, since the researchers will go on reading before, during, and even after the study is finished, it is important to set some boundaries. These can be determined by the *relevance* of the material to the study.

The initial decision is to determine whether or not the content of the report which the researcher reads is relevant to the research problem under study. If it is not relevant, it can be deleted; if it is relevant, the information it contains must be summarized or somehow put into a usable form so it will be retrievable again when the researcher needs it later.

The most useful way for researchers to determine whether certain material is relevant or not, is through reading the *abstracts* which appear in most indices and which accompany articles in most journals. The descriptions in the abstracts provide useful information on various aspects of the material.

One criterion for determining relevance is the degree to which the content of the article is *directly related* to the topic of the research. Another criterion is the *source* of the report. Material taken from journals aimed at researchers is likely to be more relevant than material from sources aimed at practitioners; well known and highly valued sources are preferable for most material, and material which comes from primary sources, such as the research article itself, as reported by the researcher, is usually more relevant than material which comes from secondary sources such as the report of another author on the research. Secondary sources are often less reliable and should only be used to obtain access to primary sources. Another criterion of relevance is the *recency* of the publication of the material; the more recent research is usually more relevant.

Compiling and summarizing the information

Once the researcher has selected the relevant materials and deleted the irrelevant ones, each report needs to be compiled and organized. This phase includes a) compiling a bibliography list and b) writing an abstract which contains the most important information of the report.

The bibliography list should be arranged alphabetically and each entry should contain the name(s) of the author(s), the title of the report, facts about publication, page numbers, and so on. If it is a journal article it should include the name of the journal, volume, and inclusive page numbers. If it is a book, it should include information about the publisher, and place and date of publication.

The abstract of each report should include the most important information of the report as well as criticism. It should be written in such a way as to be easily retrievable when the researcher has to write the literature review, which is usually arranged in alphabetical order and/or according to different subheadings related to the research topic. It is recommended that each abstract be entered on a 3 × 5 card or preferably in the database of a computer. Most word processor programs today have facilities for compiling bibliography lists in databases according to a number of different categories.

The information in the abstract should consist of a description of the most important points of the study, and the researcher should focus on points such as the reasons for conducting the research, the underlying assumptions of the study, the procedures and methodologies used for collecting the data, the major findings of the research, the specific new information which the study added to the research area, and a critical perspective of the research.

Table 4.2 provides a list of questions which researchers may find helpful in reading, summarizing, and criticizing research reports. The abstract should be brief, yet as accessible as possible when needed later in writing the literature report.

Table 4.2   Questions for reading, summarizing, and criticizing research

---

A About the research topic

1 What is the main research area?
2 What is the research problem?
3 What are the major research questions or hypotheses?

B About the research context

1 What other research studies were conducted in the same area?
2 What were their main findings?
3 What is the rationale of the research?
4 Why was it important to conduct the research?

C About the research method

1 What are the main variables of the study?
2 Which research design was used? (experimental, correlational, descriptive, multivariate, ethnographic?)
3 Description of the population, sample, and selection procedures
4 The data collection procedures – information about their development, reliability, validity, pilot study
5 Description of the data collected

Table 4.2 cont.

D About the data analysis
1 What are the specific data analysis procedures used?
2 Were they quantitative or qualitative, or both?

E About the findings
1 What were the main findings?
2 What does the researcher conclude from them?
3 How do the findings relate to the research context and to the underlying theories?
4 What are the implications of the findings?
5 What recommendations does the researcher make based on the findings?
6 What recommendations are drawn from the results?

F Criticism of the research
Consideration of A–E above and specifically:
1 the statement of the problem
2 the identification of the hypotheses
3 the description and definition of the variables
4 the appropriacy of the design of the study
5 the appropriacy of the instruments
6 the appropriacy of the data analysis procedures
7 the consistency of the results with the analysis
8 whether the conclusion, implications, and recommendations are warranted by the results.

Note: not all questions are applicable to all research reports

Organizing and reporting the review of the literature

Once the material for the review has been collected, reviewed, and summarized, the researchers need to synthesize it and write the review of the literature, to decide how to organize the information, and to compile the abstracts in the literature report.

Often the nature of the research problem will determine the organization of the literature review. The review can be organized according to the amount of information bearing directly on the research problem, that is, each question or hypothesis of the research is substantiated by the relevant literature. For example, in the study on the relationship between age and second language learning which includes hypotheses about age and the sex of the learner, age and the language learning context, and age and learning style, each of these hypotheses could be preceded by a review of the relevant literature.

Alternatively, the review can be organized according to the specific *variables* of the study. Thus in the same example, variables such as age (of children and adults) or context (formal and informal) are addressed separately. All the variables are eventually integrated and lead to the final set of variables of the study, that of the relationship between age and second language learning in a formal context.

Another approach is to present the literature *chronologically* or *historically*. The researchers either begin by reviewing the least recent literature on the topic and move towards the more current research in the field, or present the most current research first and work back to the less recent material. For controversial research topics, the literature review can be reported in a way that represents the different points of view or different schools of thought, focusing on specific research studies which represent each of these groups.

Reporting the literature review

However the material is organized, it is synthesized in a special section of the research article or thesis usually entitled the *literature review*. (See also the discussion in Chapter 10 on reporting research.)

The literature review is generally preceded by a section relating to the *context of the problem*. In that section the researchers provide general background to the research problem, the major theories as well as the controversies related to it, to familiarize the reader with the main issues of the research. In the literature review which follows, the researchers *describe* and *synthesize* the major research studies related to the topic of the research as they were recorded and organized in the abstracts. In doing this they focus briefly on the major findings of these studies, and when and by whom they were conducted. Studies directly related to the research will be reported in more detail, including information about the methodological approaches used and the data collection procedures and analysis.

The description and synthesis of a number of research studies then leads to a final statement regarding the *rationale* for the study. Specifically,. a rationale is a justification for the research, an explanation as to why and how the proposed study should be conducted, and what the current study will do that other studies did not. The researchers argue the case that there is a need for this study and that it will provide meaningful, significant, and new information in the research area. The review is often followed by a statement of the purpose and general plan for the proposed research.

In putting together the literature review then, we recommend that the researchers focus on the following points:

- the prevailing and current theories which underlie the research problem
- the main controversies about the issue, and about the problem
- the major findings in the area, by whom, and when
- the studies which can be considered the better ones, and why
- description of the types of research studies which can provide the basis for the current theories and controversies
- criticism of the work in the area
- the rationale and purpose of the proposed study.

The length of the review will vary according to the type of research report being prepared. (See Chapter 10 on this issue.) In an article for a professional journal the review is often limited to two or three pages. It essentially sets the research problem in context and may contain only five to ten references. On the other hand, for theses and dissertations an extensive review and reference to many more sources and reports is needed. In fact the review of the literature is one of the major parts of the work. It will therefore include more headings and subheadings, and more detailed information about each article.

Regardless of the number of references listed in the review, it is very important that they should be up to date.

We will conclude this chapter with two examples of reviews of literature reports taken from journal articles:

Example 1
In a study on the use of recall tasks (Lee 1986) the researcher first contextualizes the topic by describing the extensive use of recall tasks in second language acquisition research, and the types of task used. He then reviews the literature by reporting on a number of studies which resulted in variations in the results. The description of the extensive use of recalling in second language research and the variations that exist in the use of recalling tasks, provide the author with the rationale and purpose for conducting his study: 'Given the difference across research designs, the present study was intended to investigage the effect of certain variations in design. The following factors were tested: (1) planned versus unplanned recalls; and (2) recalling in L1 versus recalling in L2. To date, no direct comparison of recalls done in L1 versus L2 has been made. No such study has been conducted for L2 reading.' (p. 204)

Example 2
A researcher (Dunkel 1988) conducted research on the relationship between the content of L1 and L2 students' lecture notes and test performance. She contextualizes the research by describing the facilitative effects of taking notes in learning, the numerous programs to teach these skills, the limited empirical knowledge as to the relationship between the content of the subjects' notes and their test performance, and the lack of information as to what constitute 'good notes'.

She then continues with the literature review where she reports on a number of studies which investigated some of these issues.

The literature review is organized according to different topics: studies which examined the relationship between the content of notes and test performance, studies which attempted to determine how 'quality of notes' relates to the post-lecture recognition or recall performance, those which examined notes taken by college students and their grades in certain courses, and those studies which investigated student variables related to lecture notes.

The literature report, and especially the finding regarding gender differences between note-takers, leads the researcher to the rationale for her own study: 'If gender differences between note-takers exist, it is possible that there may be other differences attributable to ethno-cultural background or language proficiency among note-takers from different regions.' 'Such differences might provide important information concerning the note-taking strategies employed by these students as well as the relationship between the content of L1 and L2 students' notes and their comprehension and retention of English language lecture material. . . . Thus in light of the dearth of research concerning cross-cultural differences in students' notes, the complete lack of research on the content of L2 students' notes, and the increased pedagogical focus placed on training L2 students to develop listening and note-taking skill in English, a study was conducted to . . .' (p. 263). Here she continues with a description of the purpose and plan of her own study.

Thus, the researcher began by contextualizing her research problem. She then reviewed and reported on the relevant literature, organized according to different topics, and this led her to the rationale and purpose of her own study. More specific research questions followed, leading in turn to a description of the design of her research and the procedure used in conducting it.

These aspects of design and procedure will be discussed in the following chapters of the book.

Summary

In this chapter we first discussed the functions of contextualizing the research: to help select a research problem, to broaden the perspective of the research, to acquaint the researcher with existing literature on the topic, to create a rationale for the study, and to help the researcher narrow down the research question in preparation for conducting the research.

We then described the different sources for locating the literature: references to existing material, such as indices, computer searches, and bibliographies, and the actual material such as journal articles and reviews. We ended the chapter with a description of criteria for determining the relevance of the material to the research topic, guidance on procedures for reading the literature in preparation for conducting the research, and suggestions on ways of organizing and reporting the literature review.

Activities

1 Locate six references from indices on the topic of the role and use of strategies in reading comprehension. Two of the references should be from language indices, two from educational indices, and two from psychological and/or sociological indices. Which descriptors did you find to be most helpful in locating the references?

2 Choose a hypothetical research topic in your field of interest. Locate ten articles on that topic through a survey of the different sources (indices, annotated bibliographies). Try to obtain items from a variety of sources (journals, books, edited collections, reviews, papers presented at meetings of professional bodies).

3 Now determine which items are most relevant to the research topic. What criteria did you use to make that decision?

4 Summarize the relevant items in a way that will lead to a research question or a hypothesis.

References

Aiken, E. G., Thomas, G. S., and Shennum, W. A. 1975. 'Memory for a lecture: Effects of notes, lecture rate, and information density.' *Journal of Educational Psychology* 67:439–444.

Baker, K. 1987. 'Comments on Willig's "A meta-analysis of selected studies on the effectiveness of bilingual education."' *Review of Educational Research* 57/3:351–362.

Baker, L. and Lombardi, B. R. 1985. 'Students' lecture notes and their relation to test performance.' *Teaching of Psychology* 12:28–32.

Gass, S. and Selinker, L. 1983. *Language Transfer in Language Learning.* Rowley, Mass.: Newbury House.

Dunkel, P. 1988. 'The content of L1 and L2 students' lecture notes and its relation to test performance.' *TESOL Quarterly* 22/2:259–281.

Hedges, L. V. and Olkin, I. 1985. *Statistical Methods for Meta-analysis.* Orlando, FA.: Academic Press.

Lee, J. 1986. 'On the use of recall task to measure L2 reading comprehension.' *Studies in Second Language Acquisition* 8/2:201–212.

Secada, W. G. 'This is 1987, not 1980: A comment on a comment.' *Review of Educational Research* 57/3:377–384.

Willig, A. C. 1985. 'A meta-analysis of selected studies on the effectiveness of bilingual education.' *Review of Educational Research* 55/3:269–317.

Willig, A. C. 1987. 'Examining bilingual education research through meta-analysis and narrative review: A response to Baker.' *Review of Educational Research* 57/3:363–376.

5 The components of research

Whatever phenomenon varies in any manner wherever another
phenomenon varies in some particular manner, is either a cause or
an effect of that phenomenon, or is connected with it through some
fact of causation.

(John Stuart Mill: *A System of Logic*)

The need for a plan

Designing research may be described as the process of planning and
organizing the elements or components that comprise the research
study. Research must be guided from the very beginning by a plan
of some kind. Without a coherent plan, it is not possible to give
concrete expression to hypotheses which have been developed from
general questions nor is it possible to pursue answers to general
questions.

In Chapter 1, we noted that scientific research is disciplined
inquiry characterized by terms such as 'structured', 'organized',
'methodical', and 'systematic'. The lack of a clear plan for the
conduct of research may stem from the lack of clarity in the focus of
the researcher or in the definition of the goals of the research and its
questions. (See Chapter 3.) The purpose of the discussions in
Chapters 5, 6, and 7 is to aid in the formation of clear plans for
research once the research questions have been precisely focused.

There is no one plan for researching a question but there are
many possible plans and different research formats. The nature of
the question or the hypothesis will determine which approaches
and objectives are preferable. Sometimes researchers appear to be
predisposed to a particular research format. For example, an
ethnographer might be convinced that the only valid way to
research a language question is by studying the language phenomena
within natural contexts. The experimentalist, on the other hand,
may believe that only after the particular phenomenon has been
totally isolated from other distorting factors can it be adequately
studied. Each of these approaches could be viewed as potentially
complementary to each other. Our approach here, as is evident
from Chapter 2 where we discussed the four *parameters* for second

language research, is that all of these approaches are valid but that each looks at different facets of the reality of second language acquisition.

The research plan and the type of research

In previous chapters, we have referred to different kinds of research formats or paradigms which one can use in second language research. As the quotation at the beginning of this chapter indicates, one way to view research is to see it as the search for explanations of cause-and-effect relationships. As Mill makes clear in his statement, wherever one factor regularly varies in the presence of another, we may be dealing with either a cause or an effect. It is important to note that we do not know what causes what; all we have is the *co-occurrence* of the phenomena. Another possibility is, of course, that co-occurring factors may not be related at all and their co-occurrence is purely coincidental. One of the functions of statistical tests in research, such as those to be discussed in Chapter 9, is to determine the degree to which the relationships found are significant or coincidental.

Aside from noting the co-occurrence of the phenomena, we might wish to concentrate on describing the phenomena without entering into the problem of whether phenomenon A causes phenomenon B or vice versa. In other words, rather than being concerned with trying to *predict* what will happen (A causes B), it may be sufficient to *describe* the phenomena or the patterns of their co-occurrence.

In Chapters 2 and 3, we noted that research might have either a *heuristic* or a *deductive* objective. In *heuristic* research, we claim that we do not know enough about the phenomenon or that perhaps a deductive approach is inappropriate because of the nature of the phenomenon being studied. (See Smith and Heshusius 1986, for interesting insights into the problem of matching the type of research to the characteristics of the phenomenon being studied.) We therefore attempt to describe it in order to *discover* possible underlying patterns or relationships from the description.

In heuristic research, which we will discuss in detail in Chapter 6, procedures are used to gather data which are then organized according to patterns or a structure which emerges with the research. Because of this, heuristic research is more *inductive* and more likely to arrive at new insights into the phenomena being studied. Planning heuristic research is concerned with deciding how to collect or gain access to data. In research describing the development of a sentence type in the interlanguage grammar of the second language learner, researchers do not attempt to decide in advance how the data will look. Rather they must first decide on the best methods of collecting such data and under what conditions, and then examine the data to see if instances of the target sentence type have been found.

On the other hand, in *deductive* research we make assumptions and try to predict cause-and-effect relationships or the co-occurrence of phenomena. We attempt to support our predictions by designing an investigation, collecting data, and statistically examining the results. However, because this kind of research attempts to demonstrate a clear relationship of cause and effect or co-occurrence, it becomes imperative that the research be so meticulously designed that other factors which may also be present in the research context cannot explain the relationship. It is because of this need to demonstrate a relationship *unambiguously* that deductive research is concerned with the problems of the control of these factors or variables, and internal and external validity.

Making predictions and controlling variables

Independent and dependent variables

In the simplest and most straightforward case, a single variable (or phenomenon in Mill's sense) which may be called the *predictor* will predict what will happen to a second single variable to which it is related in some way. The predictor variable is called the *independent variable*, while the variable about which predictions are made is called the *dependent variable*. In other words, variations in the independent variable predict corresponding changes in the dependent variable (the predicted). Another way to describe the relationship between the independent and the dependent variable is to state that the *independent variable* is that factor or phenomenon which the investigator manipulates in order to see what effect any changes will have. The *dependent variable* is the means by which any changes are *measured*.

Look at the following excerpt from the abstract of a piece of published research. The *independent* variable has been enclosed in brackets [. . .] and the *dependent* variable has been italicized:

The present research tested the hypothesis that predictions concerning second language (SL) achievement and use would be improved by considering [the motivational support the learner expects from the target language group]. . . The hypothesis was tested by asking adolescent English-speaking Canadian students why they were learning French as a second language and why French-speaking Canadians wanted them to learn English. Regression analyses were used to examine the relationships between the motivational predictors and *the respondents' SL proficiency and use.*

(Genesee *et al.* 1983)

As another example, let us assume that we suspect that a relationship exists between level of intelligence and success at language learning in a school environment. That is, our hypothesis is that intelligence (the *independent variable*) will predict success in second language learning as measured by some criterion such as a language test (the *dependent variable*). It must be remembered that whether a phenomenon is called *independent* or *dependent* depends on the role assigned to that phenomenon in the research. Intelligence could become a *dependent* variable if the research were concerned with the level of bilingualism predicting a child's performance on an intelligence test.

Other variables

Some types of research permit the researcher to investigate more than one variable at a time and it is possible to make multiple predictions concerning the interactions of the variables being studied. (See the discussion of multivariate research in Chapter 6 and factorial designs in Chapter 7.) However, one of the researcher's main problems is to account for all of the phenomena or variables which may affect the study. While the researcher may think that only one independent variable is being studied, there may be other, unrecognized variables which might also explain the results found. Because of this, much research design and methodology is concerned with controlling or explaining the effects of variables that may not be the focus of the research but which, nevertheless, can affect or interfere with the outcomes of the research.

Hypothesis: There is a correlation between level of intelligence and performance on a language achievement test.

Let us suppose it is decided to test this hypothesis among children learning a second language in a school setting. What other factors (variables) might affect the outcome of the investigation? We shall assume that the children in the study are of the same language and cultural background. In addition, in this culture, males and females are expected to play different sex-determined roles in educational settings. For example, it is expected that males will be more daring, outgoing, or extroverted while females are expected to be more introverted and more conformist.

It is decided that language ability will be measured with a language test which is very thorough but which takes two hours to administer. In addition, the research will be conducted over a period of approximately one school year. Finally, the children in the study are drawn from three different classes with three different teachers.

It should now be clear that the research is no longer simply a matter of comparing IQ scores with scores obtained on a language test at the end of the year. If it were indeed found that there was a relationship between IQ scores and achievement on the test, it would still be necessary to consider the other factors which may or may not affect the results of the comparison. The factors or variables that play a role in this study might be the following:

---

1 The first language of the subjects
2 Sex roles in the native culture and the distribution of males and females in the different classes being studied
3 The ages of the children
4 The teachers: personalities, teaching styles, etc.
5 Teaching methods used in different classes
6 Settings in which the tests are taken
7 How the tests are administered
8 Who administers the tests
9 The amount of time the test takes
10 The effect of the passage of time on the subjects
11 The problem of children moving to other classes or leaving the school before the study is completed

---

Table 5.1   Other variables which might affect the hypothesis that IQ predicts success in second language learning

The variables listed in Table 5.1 can be categorized into the following four general categories in Table 5.2.

1 The independent variable: IQ scores
2 The dependent variable: scores on a language test
3 Subject variables: sex roles, age, reaction to testing, distribution of
   males and females
4 Extraneous variables: teachers, method of language teaching, effect
   of time on subjects, attrition of subjects, and so on.

Table 5.2   Four categories for variables

For the researcher, the first two categories of variables, the
independent and the dependent, are the focus of the research. The
subject and *extraneous* variables are those whose effects must be
controlled so that they cannot be used as an explanation for the
interaction between the independent and the dependent variables.

In some descriptions of the role of variables in research,
categories 3 and 4 are collapsed together under the heading of
extraneous variables. However, in language research, because of
the central importance of human subjects and the role played by
subject characteristics, the subject variable should be maintained as
a separate category.

The allocation of any variable to one of the four categories is
dependent on the focus of the research. For example, a characteristic
associated with sex roles might become the independent variable in
a different study, while IQ might be transferred to the subject
variable category. In the next section, we shall discuss ways in
which the undesirable effects of variables in categories 3 and 4 can
be kept to an acceptable level.

Making the research more effective

There is much that can be done by the researcher before actually
beginning a study, in order to make certain that hypotheses will be
tested validly or, in the case of heuristic research, that data will be
authentic and collected reliably. These measures must be taken
before the start of the research and before data are collected.

In non-experimental research, case studies, and qualitative
research, the nature of the data may not be known until they are
actually collected. For example, in a case study of a child acquiring
a second language, there is no way to predict in advance what kind
of utterances the child will produce. However, in other cases, the
researcher may have some idea about the general characteristics of

the data which will be collected and the kinds of questions which have been addressed by previous researchers. In these latter situations, it is important to consider ways to strengthen the reliability of the data. Some of the ways in which this can be done will be discussed in the following sections.

Types of data and variables

Different categories of variables contribute different kinds of data to the study. In Chapter 2, we discussed the nature of data from the conceptual perspective of how to define 'data' in second language acquisition. In this chapter, we are concerned with operational definitions of data, because the way in which we categorize the data will decide how we will analyze it. For example, some kinds of data, such as test scores, can be manipulated mathematically, while other kinds, such as the sentences produced by learners or the country of origin of subjects, cannot.

Qualitatively, data may be grouped into three types – *nominal*, *ordinal*, and *metric* (or *interval*). It is important to consider the question of data type because all of the procedures (collection, analysis, and the drawing of conclusions) are a function of the kind of data in the study.

The term *nominal data* refers to *names* or categories of phenomena which cannot be treated numerically in terms of such operations as computing averages. The purpose of a nominal categorization is to group subjects or instances of data according to some attribute. The separate categories in themselves have no necessary relationship to each other and cannot be added together to form a single pool of data. For example, if a language class is made up of males and females, or students from Japan, Korea, France, and Switzerland, we cannot speak about the average sex of the class or the average nationality. These nominal categories can play a significant part if a subject group is biased in the direction of one language or nationality. In second language studies, other typical examples of nominal data are grammatical classifications such as *past tense, -ing forms, article*, etc., or subject characteristics such as attitude type (instrumental or integrative).

The fact that the category of nominal data does not lend itself to mathematical manipulation is important in decisions about which type of research approach (synthetic/holistic or analytic) and objective (heuristic or deductive) to employ. More will be said about this in the next chapter.

Ordinal data are data which can be *ordered* or *ranked* according to some hierarchical system such as test scores, degree of presence of some characteristic, or the relative number of occurrences of some sentence type among a group of subjects. In addition, while different rankings can be compared statistically in various ways, the ranks themselves have no numerical value. Ranks have an ordinal value only when they are relative to other ranks. On the other hand, dichotomized nominal data such as attitude type cannot be treated as ordinal data because two categories cannot be ordered in any meaningful way. In ordinal data, the top rank will always be *one* regardless of what that score is. The difference between the first rank and the second will always be exactly one rank regardless of how different the scores are.

Nominal data can be treated as ordinal data if we group different nominal categories of the same type such as *past*, *-ing*, *article*, *possessive*, and create a single class such as *grammatical morpheme*. Each of the different morphemes might then be treated ordinally by being ranked according to frequency of occurrence in the production of language learners. This is possible because there are enough different grammatical morphemes to allow for ranking.

An assumption that we must be able to make when a class of ordinal data is created is that the ranked categories belong together validly as a class. Some research in first and second language acquisition (Brown 1973, Dulay and Burt 1974, Bailey, Madden, and Krashen 1974) has been concerned with showing that the frequency of occurrence of members of the class referred to as grammatical morphemes is a reflection of a 'natural order' of language acquisition. However, we must keep in mind that the class itself is an artifact of the research and was created by grouping *nominal* data categories into a new class.

Metric or *interval data* are data which have numerical value and can be manipulated mathematically. If we are considering the actual scores of subjects on a test, or times on the performance of a task, these data can be averaged and manipulated arithmetically in order to find, for example, how far from the average scores range, what the median point of the scores is, and so on. While we cannot speak of the average attitude of a language class, it is possible to add up all of the test scores on a language test and divide the total by the number of tests to arrive at an average score.

If data are treated as metric, then actual numerical values are important. For example, if the scores of subjects in an experiment are treated as ordinal data and *ranked* from highest to lowest, differences in scores from one rank to the next will not be an important consideration. If, however, the scores are considered as numerical values and treated *metrically*, then the differences between the scores will become important to consider.

Internal and external validity

Any research can be affected by different kinds of factors which, while extraneous to the concerns of the research, can invalidate the findings. For example, in Chapter 3 we discussed the importance of translating research questions into conceptually consistent definitions and then operationalizing these concepts for the purposes of the research. If terms are not consistently defined and used in the research, the validity and the reliability of the results may be called into question.

Findings can be said to be *internally invalid* because they may have been affected by factors other than those thought to have caused them, or because the interpretation of the data by the researcher is not clearly supportable. They may be *externally invalid* because the findings cannot be extended or applied to contexts outside those in which the research took place.

Factors affecting internal validity

Sometimes the manner in which the research plan or experiment is conceived can affect the validity of the outcome. When the results of the research are deemed invalid because of the design or the manipulation of some of the internal components that make up the research, this is considered a problem of *internal validity*. We shall now discuss some of the major factors which can affect the internal validity of research. (See Table 5.3.)

---

1 Subject variability
2 Size of subject population
3 Time allotted for data collection or the experimental treatment
4 Comparability of subjects
5 History, attrition, and maturation
6 Instrument/task sensitivity

Table 5.3   Factors affecting internal validity

Subject variability

In order for research to be generalizable, that is, applicable outside the immediate research environment, it must be possible to assume that the population used in the research is representative of the general population to which the research would apply. Methods used to achieve this representativeness include *random sampling*, in which subjects for research are chosen at random from a much larger pool of potential subjects, as well as the *random assignment* of subjects from the subject pool to different groups. By using these procedures, we may claim that any *extraneous subject variables* are evenly divided by random chance, or that subjects chosen for study will have a random chance of being affected by these variables.

However, there may be situations in which randomization will still produce a result which will not be representative. This is especially true where small numbers of subjects are used. While there is no fixed number of subjects which a study must use, the smaller the number of subjects, the more the study is susceptible to biases created by an over-representation of some subject characteristic. When the number of subjects in a study is small, each subject exerts a greater influence on the performance of the group as a whole.

Example

In an experiment on second language teaching, two groups of learners have been randomly assigned. Each group contains ten subjects. After the experimental treatment using two different language teaching methods, a language test is given to both groups. The mean score (average) for group A is 9.3 while the average for Group B is 11.3.

The individual scores for each group are shown in Table 5.4.

The raw scores show that there are some subjects in group A who are far below the group average. One measure of a group's homogeneity or variability is the *standard deviation.* (See Chapter 9 for a more detailed discussion.) It tells us how close the members of the group are to the mean. The greater the standard or average deviation, the greater is the variability of the group. When standard deviations are computed for the two groups in the example, we see that while the means of A and B seem reasonably close, the standard deviations for the two groups are 4.15 and 1.56 respectively. The variability of group A is more than two and a half times that of group B. With this kind of difference between the

	Group A	Group B
	3	10
	10	12
	12	12
	2	9
	10	10
	6	11
	13	10
	14	13
	12	12
	11	14
Total	93	113
Mean	9.3	11.3
Standard deviation	4.15	1.56

Table 5.4   Scores obtained for group A and group B on language test

groups for the standard deviation, we would have to question whether test differences might not be due to some other, unidentified factor.

In this example, the scores seem to indicate that the two groups are drawn from different populations. One of the underlying assumptions in this kind of research, that the two groups are representative samples of the same general population, cannot be supported. The large difference in the standard deviation shows that a few very low scores can upset the assumption.

Two solutions to this type of problem are open to the researcher. One is to begin again by reassigning the groups but this time attempting to distribute those with weaker scores more evenly. This solution is not the most suitable for a number of reasons. Once subjects have been exposed to the treatment, they should not be used again. The homogeneity of the groups might have been improved if steps had been taken *before* the experiment to choose subjects who met some pre-established criterion, indicated, for example, by performance on a pre-test or grade averages.

How one increases the comparability of groups depends on the specifics of the study in question. However, such concerns should be kept in mind in order to avoid rejecting or confirming hypotheses for the wrong reasons. In the case above, the method used with group B would appear to be superior, but analysis of the standard deviation shows that this conclusion is unwarranted. The variability of group A is an indication that the two groups probably differ in other ways as well as in the treatment they received.

Analytic-deductive research will sometimes attempt to compare the performance of two different groups matched for identifiable extraneous variables, such as language proficiency. When the results are examined, we should be able to state that they are not affected by a trait that may have existed in group A but not in group B. Populations should be matched for subject variables as much as possible.

Two criteria commonly used for matching subjects are sex and IQ. In second language research, IQ is not a reliable criterion, since scores are not usually available for adult learners, and IQ tests for children have questionable validity because of cultural and linguistic biases. However, other criteria that can be used to match groups or subjects are first language, number of years of exposure to the second language, amount of formal instruction in the second language, and scores on language tests all of the subjects have taken.

Size of subject population

As we can see by the example above, small populations in a study tend to magnify the effects of individual variability, thus presenting a possible distortion. There can be no absolute rule regarding the optimum size of the subject population in an *analytic-deductive* study, but the problem can be controlled to a large extent by increasing the size of the sample population so that it is more representative of the population as a whole. The greater the size, the smaller the effect of individual variability or any other population-related variable on the outcome. Table 5.5 shows the effect of doubling the size of the group on the average and standard deviation of group A.

As can be seen, by doubling the size of group A, we have narrowed the range of variability. This example demonstrates the importance of the size of the sample in research concerned with group statistical measures such as averages or standard deviations. The effect of very low scores in this group is still noticeable and may affect the experimental results. These problems might have been alleviated by increasing the original sample size and employing other criteria in selecting members for the population

	Score	Number of subjects	Total
	2	1	2
	3	1	3
	6	1	6
	8	1	8
	9	1	9
	10	4	40
	11	3	33
	12	3	36
	13	3	39
	14	2	28
Totals	20		204
Average	10.2		
Standard deviation	3.3		

Table 5.5   Effect of doubling population size on group mean and standard deviation for group A

from which both A and B were drawn, in order to allow for a fair test of the original hypothesis.

Concern for the size of the subject population does not apply to research in which the objective of the research is heuristic and the focus is on individual variability, as in the description of the interlanguages of second language learners. The size of the subject population in a *synthetic-heuristic* study might be as small as one subject whose interlanguage grammar would be described in great detail. An *analytic-heuristic* study might focus on a specific linguistic aspect in the development of interlanguage grammars and follow this development for an individual or a group of subjects over a period of time. The size of the subject population in studies of language acquisition is not always a relevant factor and depends on the research design, the topic, and even the type of data which are the focus of the study.

Time allotted for data collection or the experimental treatment

All research is conducted in real time. Because second language acquisition also takes place over time, changes in language performance are often subtle. Whether we are conducting unstructured observations of language acquisition in the classroom or an experiment, time needs to be allotted for the collection of data or for the exposure of the subjects to an experimental treatment. One of the problems facing the researcher, therefore, is to know how much time will be needed to find the data sought or to show an effect for a treatment such as an experimental teaching method.

Johnson (1983) conducted a study of the effect of peer interaction in which second language learning children interacted in a day-camp context with children who were native speakers of English. At the end of five weeks, the second language learners were given language proficiency tests and the scores were related to levels of interaction with native speakers to see if interaction affected rates and levels of acquisition. No significant effect was found. Johnson examined several explanations for her findings, such as the possibility that the instruments may not have been sensitive enough to identify gains. (See below.) However, an additional factor might have been that the effects of interaction on proficiency take longer to reveal themselves than the five weeks in which the study was conducted.

Example

In a study on the effects of training on listening comprehension strategies, one group is given specific training in consciously developing ways of listening for information from taped or orally presented lectures. The second group is simply told to listen to the lectures. After two weeks of training, both groups are tested on the content of a lecture.

In this study, the researcher would have to decide how much time is sufficient for the effects of training to reach their full potential. If the groups are tested too soon, no difference might be found between the groups, or the untrained group might perform better on the post-test. The conclusion might be reached that training in listening comprehension strategies is of no value or that learners cannot be trained in these strategies.

Example

The goal of an analytic-heuristic study of language use in the classroom is to collect observational data on the frequency of different types of *request* forms in different instructional settings and with different types of teacher personalities.

The appearance or lack of appearance of a particular request form may be due to the sociolinguistic conditions necessary for its use or because, in the amount of time in which the subjects were observed, not enough opportunities presented themselves for using the target forms.

It should be obvious that there is no hard and fast rule for deciding when enough time has elapsed for collecting a valid sample of data or for a treatment to have an effect. This is relative to factors such as the *context* in which data are collected, the *amount of time* devoted to the treatment or the collection of data, the *sensitivity of the instruments* used to observe or elicit data, and the *criteria* used for deciding when a form has been used or should have been used.

History, attrition, and maturation

While time is necessary in order for a treatment to have an effect or for a valid sample of language performance in a naturalistic setting to be collected, the researcher needs to be aware of ways in which the research may be negatively affected because it takes place over time. *History* refers to the possible negative effects of the passage of time on the study. In a longitudinal study, one which is conducted over an extended period, subjects may be exposed to sources of language input other than those measured by the dependent variable. In a second language context, where the learner has access to sources of input other than the classroom, this is difficult to control. In a foreign language context, where there is little input outside the classroom, the effect of outside sources of input are more easily accounted for.

Another problem that can arise when studies are conducted over an extended period of time is *attrition*. By this we mean that the composition of the population studied may change the longer the study continues. Subjects may lose interest and drop out of the study or be ill on days when periodic data collection is conducted. For these reasons, it is sometimes preferable to begin with a larger than necessary number of subjects if the study is to go on for an extended period of time.

Maturation as an influencing factor will be more significant with younger subjects than with older subjects and should be considered an important variable to control. We know that children's language acquisition is affected by changes taking place in cognitive development, so that language development which is tracked over a longer period is bound to be affected by other factors, such as increased short-term memory capability (Berman 1987).

A child's performance on an experimental task such as sentence repetition may be different at time 1 and time 2 because of these non-linguistic factors, while adults may be less affected by these factors because they are cognitively mature. Comparing adult and child second language acquisition is especially difficult because of the *maturation* factor. Snow and Hoefnagel-Hohle (1978) studied the effects of the critical period on subjects in four age groups: adults, 12–15, 8–10, and 3–5. Tests lasting one-and-a-half hours were administered to all groups. Given the length of time for the test and the nature of a formal test setting itself, it is quite possible that the results were distorted by the maturational differences in the subject groups. In this case, older learners were probably more 'test-wise' than learners in the younger age groups.

Instrument/task sensitivity

We have mentioned the fact that a data gathering procedure may not be sensitive enough to identify subtle language acquisition changes. Here, we shall discuss the effect of the procedure or test on the subject. One of the possible experimental designs discussed in Chapter 7 employs a procedure in which subjects are given a test before the treatment or the experiment. The terms 'instrument' or 'task' will be used here to refer to any tool employed by the researcher to obtain information on the status of the subjects *before* the research commences. The purpose of such pre-testing is to establish a base line of information which can then be compared with the results on the dependent variable, often another test of the same type, or the very same instrument or task. In non-experimental research, such as case studies, tests or other instruments are also used to establish a base-line or norm.

There are several ways in which pre-testing can affect the internal validity of research and thus affect the generalizability of the final results:

1 Learners can become 'test-wise'. Being test-wise results from the experience of taking the test. The subject or learner is now familiar with its format. Being test-wise is different from being familiar with the content of the test. Being test-wise is not necessarily negative. In fact, there may be situations in which the researcher will want subjects to be test-wise in order to be sure that the strangeness of a test, instrument, or elicitation procedure will not become an extraneous variable affecting the final results.

2 The pre-test may create a 'practice effect'. This is considered by some to be the greatest danger in using pre-tests in research. Practice effect refers to the possibility that the act of taking a test will give the subject an opportunity to practice those things which will comprise the treatment in an experiment. Thus, the

results measured by the dependent variable may or may not be due to the treatment itself.

Example

A study is concerned with testing the hypothesis that a grammar rule presented before practice is more effective for long-term retention than either no grammar rule before practice or a grammar rule presented after practice. In order to be certain that subjects in all three treatments have no previous knowledge of the language material, a pre-test is administered to determine the level of their knowledge.

It may be argued that because all groups receive the same pre-test, they will also begin with the same effect from that test. While this is true, the real problem still remains that we do not know if any practice resulted indirectly from the pre-test, thereby contributing to the final results.

3 The pre-test instrument may affect the attitudes of subjects. One area of second language research is concerned with factors that are called 'affective'. These refer to feelings and attitudes which may affect the type and rate of second language acquisition, and include attitudes toward the second language speech community (Genesee *et al.* 1983), the second language itself, personality factors, the learning style of the language learner, and so on. Pre-test instruments which measure learner responses in the above areas may sensitize subjects to factors which they had not previously considered. If the research later requires subjects to respond in terms of these factors, their responses may no longer be considered 'naïve'. This, again, is a type of practice effect. However, the effect expresses itself primarily in increased awareness of or sensitivity to an attitude or learning behavior, rather than to a particular linguistic form in the second language.

One way to avoid a practice effect in pre-testing is to tap the desired area indirectly. There are also areas of language performance which are unlikely to benefit from a practice effect. For example, judgments of grammaticality depend on unconscious knowledge and cannot be directly taught but are the indirect result of becoming proficient in a language. Instruments which test cognitive or metalinguistic abilities are therefore less likely to benefit from a practice effect.

Internal validity in heuristic research

Validity in analytic-deductive research is concerned with being able to demonstrate an unambiguous relationship between treatment effects and results. Synthetic-heuristic and analytic-heuristic research is concerned with many of the factors affecting internal validity discussed above, as well as the ability to demonstrate unambiguously that phenomena have been observed and that the interpretation of these data is not dependent on the subjective judgement of an individual researcher.

Validity in this sense can be seen as relating to three areas: the *representativeness*, *retrievability*, and *confirmability* of the data.

Representativeness

The degree to which observed data represent the normal behavior of the second language learner is a factor which can affect the validity of descriptions of that behavior. The degree to which data are distorted by the research activity or the presence of the researcher may be seen as a measure of the invalidity of data. For this reason, research which is considered 'naturalistic' or 'qualitative' must be able to show that the act of research or the presence of an observer has not distorted the nature of the data collected.

Jacob (1987), who provides an extensive review of different qualitative research traditions, emphasizes the various measures that different kinds of heuristic methodologies adopt in order to ensure that the data collected are truly representative of the natural behavior of the group. For example, the observer may actually participate in the activity, or less noticeable or intrusive methods of collection may be found.

Retrievability

This aspect of validity refers to the researcher's access to the subjects' responses or to records or protocols of data, so that the same responses or behaviors may be inspected. Retrievability is important so that records, protocols, and other forms of data can be repeatedly reviewed for analysis. The retrievability of data can be increased by collecting it by some mechanical means, such as video or audio recording. Collected in this way, the original data are accessible for inspection by independent judges. However, measures taken to make data more representative may conflict with measures necessary to make data retrievable. For example, the presence of video cameras in a language classroom may alter the behavior, not only of the students, but also of the teacher.

Confirmability

This aspect of validation in heuristic research is related to representativeness and retrievability. Assuming that the data collected are representative of second language behavior and that they are retrievable for continued inspection, confirmability is concerned with the ability of the researcher to confirm findings, either by re-inspection or by demonstrating the same findings through different sources.

This latter process is referred to as 'triangulation' (Long 1983). While in theory, triangulation sounds feasible, it is not always possible to collect the same second language data using different sources. This is especially true in studies which use learner self-reports as data for studying strategies or metacognition. For example, asking a learner to self-report or 'introspect' about a language error immediately after the act and again some time later is not drawing on the same source. In this case we could not use one kind of self-report to support the other. However, data drawn from observation or manual transcription could be confirmed by data drawn from video or audio tapes made at the same time as the observation.

External validity

Internal validity is concerned with being able to state that the relationship between the independent and the dependent variables is unambiguous and not explainable by extraneous variables. A study may be said to have *external validity* if the findings can be applied or generalized to situations outside those in which the research was conducted.

Questions about the external validity of second language research relate to the categories of research identified in Chapter 1 as *basic*, *applied*, and *practical*. Often the questions arise when applying findings from one type to another, but they can also arise when the findings of two studies in the same category conflict.

1 Basic or applied to practical

This refers to the relationship between research and language teaching in general. Classroom practitioners expect language acquisition research to help them directly, that is, language acquisition research is viewed as applied science not as basic science.

2　*Basic to applied*

This involves the relevance of a specific theoretical development to a particular aspect of language learning. For example, recent developments in theoretical linguistics suggest aspects of a universal grammar may determine the order in which a first language is acquired. Recent research in second language has attempted to apply these theoretical findings to understanding the process of second language acquisition. In a sense, this research is testing the external validity of the theoretical claims. (For an example of this kind of 'application' of linguistics, see Flynn 1987.)

3　*Basic to basic or applied to applied*

This involves the comparability of research findings testing the same hypothesis but conducted under different conditions or using different research designs. For example, the critical period hypothesis applied to second language acquisition claims that adults beyond puberty will be unable to acquire the phonology of the second language to the point of having native speaker competence. One study may test this hypothesis by having native speakers judge taped interviews with non-native speakers (Oyama 1976). Another study may test this hypothesis by having non-native speakers produce phonetic segments under strictly controlled laboratory conditions (Olson and Samuels 1973).

The question of external validity arises with regard to the degree to which the two studies are testing the same hypothesis and to what degree their findings are comparable and generalizable. Given that one study used interviews in a free discourse context and the other recorded controlled responses in a laboratory, are they in fact testing the same hypothesis? Can the findings of one study be used to contradict or support the other? Table 5.6 summarizes factors which can affect external validity.

1　Population characteristics
2　Interaction of subject selection and research
3　The descriptive explicitness of the independent variable
4　The effect of the research environment
5　Researcher or experimenter effects
6　Data collection methodology
7　The effect of time

Table 5.6　Factors affecting external validity

1 *Population characteristics*

In the discussion of internal validity, we stated that sample populations used in research are thought to be representative of a larger group with the same characteristics. In the case of external validity, we are concerned with the degree to which the sample population in the study has the same characteristics as the population to which the research findings are to be applied. Is the population used in the research a specific subset of the larger population?

If the research is carried out with adults, can the findings apply equally well to children? In experimental research, the ability to perform a task may be dependent on the maturational or educational level of the subjects. Research which requires adult learners to respond in a manner dependent on adult cognitive abilities may not be generalizable to populations of child language learners. Research carried out with university students may not be valid when applied to foreign guest workers, even though both populations are adult.

2 *Interaction of subject selection and research*

One of the problems which all researchers experience is finding an adequate number of subjects. The problem is especially evident when subjects have to experience different treatments in an experiment or participate in a longitudinal study over an extended period. In most cases, experiments require subjects to take time from their normal schedules in order to participate. Because of this, subjects may be paid or asked to volunteer. In terms of external validity, to what degree do paid or volunteer subjects represent the general population to which the research will be generalized?

When the experimenter chooses the population for research, it may be claimed that the selection is random. In the case of volunteers, the question of *self-selection* arises. Perhaps there is something about the volunteers leading them to come forward when others would not. This is especially important to keep in mind in studies dealing with affective learner variables in second language, such as learning style, attitude and motivation, and metacognition.

3 *The descriptive explicitness of the independent variable*

As we have noted previously in this chapter and in Chapter 3, defining and operationalizing terms in a clear and consistent manner is important for both internal and external validity. In order for research findings to be either replicated or generalized to a broader population, the independent variable must be described as explicitly as possible. If the independent variable is a language teaching method, for example, not only must the components of the method be described, but also the conditions in which it was used, the characteristics of the teachers using it, and the size and nature of the classes.

The same is true if the independent variable is a language variable. If the study is concerned with the acquisition of relative clauses, what are the criteria for deciding whether the learner has produced a relative clause, a near-relative clause, or a sentence construction resembling a relative clause but intended to be something else? Unfortunately, if these details are not available, replication and application of research findings are at best difficult.

4 *The effect of the research environment*

The fact that learners are aware that they are participating in a study may affect them in ways that will make their behavior different from a population not participating in a study. Results in a study may be influenced by what is called the 'Hawthorne effect'. This effect is named after a manufacturing plant where it was found that workers in a study increased production whether working conditions improved or worsened. When workers were interviewed, they reported that they increased their production in order to remain in the study because it brought them added prestige in the eyes of their fellow workers.

Second language learners may become more motivated simply because they are told that they are participating in a study that will help the researchers understand the process of language learning.

Example
In a study of participation patterns in the language classroom, observers sat in the back of the class and, using a coded system, noted different types of turn-taking by the class members. The class members were not told of the purpose of the observation. One alert language learner noticed that the observer made marks on a paper whenever anyone seemed to speak. Not knowing what the marks were, he began to increase his turn-taking. When he saw that the observer noted his turn-taking, he increased it even more.

In the example above, the learner was reacting to the fact that some aspect of his behavior was being observed. It is possible that if the observers were present in the classroom over an extended period of time, their presence and their note-taking behavior would become less obvious and less distracting to the learners, and would, in time, be ignored. If there is a possibility that the research environment will distort the data in some way, longitudinal studies, conducted over a longer period of time, are preferable to cross-sectional studies, in which data are collected once and considered to be representative of data collected over a period of time.

5 Researcher or experimenter effects

This threat to the external validity of research stems from the possible effect of something which the researcher does either during the actual research or during the interpretation of subject behavior, while collecting or evaluating data.

For example, the researcher may unintentionally indicate to the subject the kind of response desired. In the examples on the effects of the research context, we stated that subjects may change their behavior when they become aware that they are participating in a study. The researcher may also inadvertently provide clues through changes in tone of voice, raising eyebrows, or other forms of body language.

6 Data collection methodology

In evaluating the external validity of a study, the method used to obtain the results must be considered. For example, data obtained through structured interviews may differ qualitatively from data gathered through a test, as in the examples of studies of the critical period hypothesis cited at the beginning of this section on external validity. In the Oyama (1976) study, the data consisted of taped anecdotes which the subjects related to the researcher, while in the Olson and Samuels (1973) study, data were collected through a pronunciation test.

It would be difficult to compare the findings of these studies since each approached the problem in a different way. The studies could be compared to show how different methods and different approaches to the same research question can produce different methodologies and different results. A comparison might also show how different approaches can be complementary to researching a question. But it would be difficult to claim that each was testing the same hypothesis.

The fact that findings obtained with different methods cannot be compared directly does not mean that one method is necessarily better than another. As we pointed out in Chapter 2, the diversity of second language research questions implies that different methods may be equally valid in investigating a question. What the researcher has to keep in mind is that each method of data collection has underlying theoretical assumptions about the nature of data.

7 *The effect of time*

The effect of time has already been discussed with reference to internal validity. We stressed that the effects of experimental treatments or the appearance of target data may not always occur within the time-frame defined by the research plan. There is, therefore, a possibility that the hypothesis may be rejected for the wrong reasons.

In applying this concept to external validity, we are concerned with the degree to which the time frame established by the research context can be extended to the real world to which the results of the research will be generalized. That is, will the results of the research be valid when they are applied to situations in which the conditions of time are not controlled and where, as in second language acquisition, the concern is with long-term change?

The question is especially important when a post-test is used as the dependent variable. The post-test may show that there is some significant difference between groups in an experiment. However, it may, in fact, be measuring short-term differences of recall after an experimental treatment. In real life, these seemingly significant differences between groups may disappear over the long term and may not be a measure of long-term retention. Therefore, when considering external validity, it is important to define the type of learning measured by the dependent variable.

The time allotted for the research can have important effects both on the replication of research (the same time constraints should be observed) and on the application of research findings to non-research environments such as the language classroom. Since second language acquisition is a long-term process and language teaching is concerned more with long-term effects, the time elapsing between treatment and testing will have important implications for evaluating the external validity of the research. That is, the success of applying research findings to non-research environments will be affected by the time constraints within which the research itself was conducted.

Summary

This chapter has been concerned with the stage of research which begins after the research question or hypothesis has been developed. (See Chapter 3.) Planning the research takes place after the researcher has identified the focus or objective of the research. In *synthetic* or *analytic-deductive* research, planning requires the careful development of a plan in which those factors to be controlled or manipulated – the independent, dependent, subject, and extraneous variables – are identified. Under the heading of *internal* or *external* validity, we discussed factors which might affect the findings or claims made for a study.

While research which focuses on variables is primarily of the *deductive* type, throughout this chapter we also discussed those aspects of planning which relate to *heuristic* research. Since heuristic research approaches the research context from a different perspective, using different methods, and does not attempt to control or manipulate variables, it necessarily measures validity differently. Validity in this type of research is more a question of the quality of the data collected, and is concerned with the representativeness, retrievability, and confirmability of the data.

Activities

1 Read the following abstract and identify the independent and the dependent variables.

   This article presents the results of an empirical concurrent validation study in which measures of musical ability (pitch, loudness, and rhythm), auditory discrimination, and memory were used to account for variance in attained ESL oral proficiency.

   (Brutten *et al.* 1985)

2 Select an article which is *synthetic* or *analytic-deductive* from a journal in the field. You may want to refer to the journals cited in Chapter 4. Read *only* the abstract and *do not read the article itself*. What problems of internal and external validity can you foresee for this research? How might some of these problems be limited or avoided? List the variables you have identified.

3 Now read the article. Has the researcher controlled the variables you have listed? How? What variables on your list were not controlled?

4 How did the research control for internal and external validity? How might the research have been made more sensitive?

5 Select an article which is *synthetic-heuristic* or *analytic-heuristic*. What are the problems of internal or external validity which this kind of study must control? How has the researcher done this?

References

Bailey, N. C., Madden, C., and Krashen, S. 1974. 'Is there a natural sequence in adult second language acquisition?' *Language Learning* 24/2:235–243.

Berman, R. 1987. 'Cognitive components of language development' in C. Pfaff (ed.): *First and Second Language Acquisition Processes.* Cambridge, Mass.: Newbury House.

Brown, R. 1973. *A First Language.* Cambridge, Mass.: Harvard University Press.

Brutten, S., Angelis, P. and Perkins, K. 1985. 'Music and memory: Predictors for attained ESL oral proficiency.' *Language Learning* 35/2:269–286.

Dulay, H. C. and Burt, M. K. 1974. 'Natural sequences in child second language acquisition.' *Language Learning* 24/1:37–53.

Flynn, S. 1987. *A Parameter Setting Model of L2 Acquisition.* Dordrecht: D. Reidel.

Genesee, F., Rogers, P., and Holobow, N. 1983. 'The social psychology of second language learning: Another point of view.' *Language Learning* 33/2:209–224.

Jacob, E. 1987. 'Qualitative research traditions: A review.' *Review of Educational Research* 57/1:1–50.

Johnson, D. M. 1983. 'Natural language learning by design: A classroom experiment in social interaction and second language acquisition.' *TESOL Quarterly* 17/1:55–68.

Long, M. H. 1983. 'Inside the black box: Methodological issues in classroom research on language learning' in H. W. Seliger and M. Long (eds.): *Classroom Oriented Research in Second Language Acquisition.* Rowley, Mass.: Newbury House.

Olson, L. and Samuels, S. J. 1973. 'The relationship between age and accuracy in foreign language pronunciation.' *Journal of Educational Research* 66:263–267.

Oyama, S. 1976. 'A sensitive period for the acquisition of non-native phonological system.' *Journal of Psycholinguistic Research* 5:261–285.

Smith, J. K. and Heshusius, L., 1986. 'Closing down the conversation: The end of the quantitative-qualitative debate among educational inquirers.' *Educational Researcher* 15/1:4–12.

Snow, C. and Hoefnagel-Hohle, M. 1978. 'The critical period for language acquisition: Evidence from second language learning.' *Child Development* 49:1114–1128.

6 Research design: qualitative and descriptive research

As you know, Bergson pointed out there is no such thing as disorder but rather two sorts of order, geometric and living. Mine is clearly living.

(Jean Piaget (in an interview, 1980))

Introduction

This and the following chapter will be devoted to a discussion of how the various components of a research study are assembled into a construction which is called the *research design* or *plan*. In this chapter, after a brief comparison of some of the major categories of design, we will examine those research approaches which attempt to describe second language phenomena as they occur *naturally*, such as *qualitative*, *descriptive*, and *correlational* and *multivariate* research. Chapter 7 will be devoted to experimental and quasi-experimental research designs which attempt to control or manipulate the research environment.

As we stated in Chapter 5, any research project needs a plan or design, even if that plan is minimal. We discussed the components of the design, the variables, and how various factors can affect the validity, internal and external, of the research.

While all approaches to second language research require some form of disciplined inquiry, some have developed quite explicit methodologies while others appear to have less explicitly developed methodological procedures. For example, one approach may be concerned with describing second language acquisition behavior in a natural context, with no manipulation or little intrusion from the researcher. Another approach may consider nature a difficult context in which to conduct an investigation because too many variables must be controlled.

The focus of this chapter will be on those research methodologies which, as a group, may be called *qualitative* or *descriptive*. In the research literature, they are referred to under a variety of names such as 'ethnography', 'participant' and 'non-participant observation', 'constitutive ethnography', 'interaction analysis' (Long 1983), 'holistic ethnography', 'cognitive anthropology', 'ethnography of communication', and 'symbolic interaction' (Jacob 1987). Given the limited scope of this chapter, we have grouped all of these under the generic headings of 'qualitative research' and 'descriptive research'. This is a simplification but it is sufficient for the purposes of an introduction to this area for the novice researcher.

Qualitative and quantitative research design

It is clear from our discussion thus far that designing a research plan is not simply a matter of deciding to carry out research but requires careful consideration of an appropriate approach (*synthetic* or *analytic*) and of the objectives or purpose of the research (*heuristic* or *deductive*) as we discussed in Chapter 3. A researcher can, of course, combine these approaches so that a hypothesis generated by synthetic-heuristic research might then be selected as the basis for investigation within an analytic-deductive design.

A question which must be considered is the degree to which research design can be *eclectic*, that is, freely combine elements from different kinds of research approaches. Is the difference between research which *quantifies* second language acquisition and that which examines the data *qualitatively* simply one of degree, or is there a substantive difference in the *philosophies* behind these approaches? Are the dichotomies expressed in Parameter 1, (the synthetic versus the analytic approach) or those of Parameter 2, (the heuristic or deductive objectives of research) differences of approach and purpose or also differences in underlying principle in the way second language phenomena are viewed?

As in all dichotomies, terminology such as *qualitative* or *quantitative* leads to oversimplification. For this reason, we have tried to present these differences along a continuum rather than as an either/or choice for the researcher. The question that arises is whether these different approaches represent simply another way to investigate questions or do they represent two different perspectives on the realities of second language acquisition? If the latter position is taken then:

> This conceptualization involves such basic questions as what is the nature of social and educational reality? What is the relationship of the investigator to what is investigated? And how is truth defined?
>
> (Smith and Heshusius 1986)

According to the above view, fundamental differences in the intrinsic nature of the subject matter, the role of the researcher in relation to the object of investigation, and whether truth is defined in terms of objective reality or in terms of subjective perception must be considered. For example, is the truth represented by the verbalized introspections of language learners about their language acquisition strategies (Cohen and Hosenfeld 1981) different from the truth represented in quantified group scores on metalinguistic judgment tests in controlled experimental research? (See White 1985.) In the first study the verbalized introspections of learners about their performance comprise the data, while in the latter the judgments of second language learners on metalinguistic tests of grammaticality are quantified as statistics and these become the data. In the first study, one must ask what quantification of learner verbalization would achieve and whether, as a result of quantification, valuable insights into learner processing at some level might not be lost. While *qualitative analysis* will allow us to study individual performance closely, it may or may not represent the behavior of other learners and is therefore of questionable value for generalization to language acquisition by others. On the other hand, when our interest is in the normative acquisition behavior of a population, quantification represents a reality for that group. Such a reality may be generalizable to other groups, assuming that sampling procedures are adequate (Shulman 1981).

The differences in these two approaches are significant and it is likely that the debate as to which approach is more valid will continue for some time to come. We have discussed this issue here because we feel that the novice researcher should be aware of it in considering possible ways of conducting second language research.

Research methodologies: similarities and differences

In Chapter 2, we discussed a research framework consisting of four parameters, each defining a different dimension of second language research. Here, we are concerned with the first three parameters, which apply to the conceptual and operational levels of research design and methodology. (Parameter 4 is concerned with data collection and analysis which will be discussed in Chapters 8 and 9.) Figure 6.1 shows where, on the continua represented by those parameters, we would place the kind of research designs or approaches to be discussed in this and the next chapter.

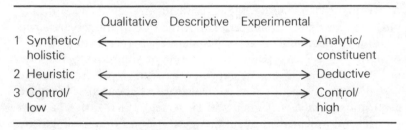

Figure 6.1   Types of designs and the research parameters

Earlier, we discussed the question of whether qualitative and quantitative approaches are *complementary* or whether they derive from different and incompatible philosophies about how to study second language acquisition. Figure 6.1 shows schematically where each type of research would fit into the framework of the parameters discussed in Chapter 2. It should not be interpreted to mean that various types of approaches to design should or should not be used eclectically.

Qualitative, descriptive, and experimental research: some differences

Qualitative and descriptive research

Both qualitative and descriptive research are concerned with providing descriptions of phenomena that occur naturally, without the intervention of an experiment or an artificially contrived treatment. While it is true that both types of research are concerned with description, they approach research from different perspectives.

Qualitative research is *heuristic* and not *deductive* since few, if any, decisions regarding research questions or data are made before the research begins. In addition, ethnographic methodologies such as cognitive anthropology, ethnography of communication (Jacob 1987), constitutive ethnography (Long 1983), and others (Green and Wallatt 1981) require that the research have a synthetic/holistic perspective of the research area or question in order to gather as much information as possible and to avoid any manipulation or interference in the research context. Some forms of qualitative research narrow the focus of the research scope as the research progresses, but this is viewed as an organic development dictated by the research *in progress* and not by a predetermined focus or hypothesis.

Descriptive research can be *heuristic* or *deductive*. While technically, qualitative research is also concerned with description, *descriptive research* as a type or category of research refers to investigation which utilizes already existing data or non-experimental research with a preconceived hypothesis. A descriptive study might describe an aspect of second language acquisition from a more *synthetic* perspective or might focus on the description of a specific *constituent* of the process, such as on the acquisition of a particular language structure or on one particular language learning behavior to the exclusion of others. That is, in a descriptive study the researchers begin with general questions in mind about the phenomenon they are studying or with more specific questions and with a specific focus. Because the questions are decided in advance, the research only focuses on certain aspects of the possible data available in the language learning context being described.

It has been claimed by some research methodologists (Kamil *et al.* 1985) that descriptive research may be distinguished from qualitative research by the kind of data analysis that is carried out. That is, descriptive research will be *quantitative* while qualitative research is not. This distinction is certainly not true for language acquisition qualitative research in which both qualitative and quantitative elements may be present. Quantification of data takes place in qualitative research only after data of a general nature have been collected and perhaps categorized. A classic example of a combination of approaches is found in Brown (1973) in which many procedures typically found in qualitative research, such as observation, tape recording, and manual transcription were used. The data were then analyzed first qualitatively and then quantitatively in terms of frequency orders and the mean length of utterances. Brown's study of three children later formed the basis for several studies on the acquisition of grammatical morphemes by adult and child second language learners. A descriptive case study might provide an in-depth linguistic analysis of the development of some aspect of grammatical ability with a second language learner, while an ethnographic study might provide quantitative analysis in the form of frequency of occurrence of an observed second language phenomenon.

Descriptive and experimental research

The essential difference between descriptive and experimental research is that *descriptive* research can be either synthetic or analytic in its approach to the second language phenomena being studied, while *experimental* research must be analytic. In addition, descriptive research may be conducted for heuristic reasons, for example, to find out more about a particular second language phenomenon, or to attempt to test an *a priori* hypothesis. Both types of research can be hypothesis-driven, in that the researcher starts out with a theory or a specific research question.

An equally important distinction between descriptive and experimental research is that in descriptive research no manipulation of naturally occurring phenomena occurs, while in experimental research, manipulation and control become important measures of both internal and external validity. (See Chapter 5 for a more complete discussion of these concepts.)

Correlational and *multivariate* analysis, while technically not research methodologies so much as different ways of manipulating data, allow us to 'research' different configurations or combinations of second language data and may be considered forms of descriptive research since they deal with already existing data. More will be said about these types of analysis in Chapter 9.

Qualitative research

Qualitative methods originally developed from the methodologies of field anthropologists and sociologists concerned with studying human behavior within the context in which that behavior would occur naturally and in which the role of the researcher would not affect the normal behavior of the subjects. These methods attempted to present the data from the perspective of the subjects or observed groups, so that the cultural and intellectual biases of the researcher did not distort the collection, interpretation, or presentation of the data (Jacob 1987). When ethnographic methods were developed, anthropologists and sociologists were concerned primarily with describing observable behaviors and activities within their natural context and describing these in their entirety from beginning to end. They avoided describing only certain selected aspects of behavior because the act of selection would be considered a distortion of nature. Unlike descriptive research, qualitative research avoids establishing research questions or hypotheses, or identifying, *a priori*, any variable which will become the focus of the research.

The procedures and methods associated with *qualitative* research have increasingly been incorporated into second language research in recent years. There are a number of reasons why investigators have selected these procedures:

– Much second language acquisition research is concerned with classroom learning, to which it is not easy to apply the controls necessary for experimental research. Initially, second language research was concerned with demonstrating the superiority of one method or approach to teaching second or foreign languages over others. For example, in the 1960s several studies tried to show the superiority of the audio-lingual method over the grammar-translation method. (See Scherer and Wertheimer 1964.) These studies, conducted within an experimental or quasi-experimental framework (see Chapter 7), were very ambitious and cumbersome and, in the final analysis, demonstrated very little about the relative efficacy of one method over another. Dissatisfaction with this kind of methods comparison research, and the realization that perhaps more was involved in the effects of instruction than merely teaching method, led researchers to seek more effective ways to investigate language acquisition in the classroom.

– There has been an increased use of qualitative or ethnographic research approaches in psychology, education, communication, and discourse analysis (Jacob 1987). A growing awareness of the necessity for careful data collection and analysis in this type of research has led to more sophisticated techniques. (See Ericsson and Simon 1984.) Although qualitative research methods do not control for variables, the development of rigorous methods for data collection and analysis have produced results that would not be possible through experimental designs.

– There has been a growing concern in second language research about the interactive or distorting effects of the research setting on the kind of language data collected (Tarone 1982). Experimental settings, being controlled and artificial, may elicit data different from those produced in natural settings.

In terms of the parameters discussed in Chapter 2 (see Figure 6.1), qualitative research is *synthetic* or *holistic* (Parameter 1), *heuristic* (Parameter 2), with *little* or *no manipulation* (Parameter 3) of the research environment, and uses data collection procedures with *low explicitness* (Parameter 4). Qualitative research thus avoids the pitfalls felt to exist when language research is carried out in experimental settings.

In Chapter 2, we distinguished between hypothesis-testing and hypothesis-generating research. Qualitative research is the primary example of *hypothesis-generating* research. Once all the data are collected, hypotheses may be derived from those data.

The ultimate goal of qualitative research is to discover phenomena such as patterns of second language behavior not previously described and to understand those phenomena from the perspective of participants in the activity. Researchers themselves may be *participant observers*, that is, participating in the very act that they are describing. A good example of participant observation would be the diaries kept by researchers, recording their experiences and observations while learning another language (Bailey 1983). The other kind of observation found in qualitative research is *non-participant observation*, in which the investigator observes and records or takes notes of the observed activity, but without the control or guidance of a questionnaire or other instrument (Long 1983). However, the purpose of non-participant observation should be to reconstruct what the subjects are experiencing as accurately as possible. In second language acquisition, this means trying to understand the phenomena of second language from the perspective of the second language learner and not from the perspective of the researcher.

The problems of non-participant observation in second language

Conducting qualitative research in second language acquisition presents unique problems to the investigator. The language itself may become a variable. Research of this type seeks to describe what is occurring and what it means to be a participant in an activity such as acquiring another language. However, conclusions about what participants are experiencing are not easy to reach. It is not simply a matter of asking language learners what they think, since the observer and the learner usually speak different languages. The language used by the learners to describe their experiences is also language which, at that point, is still incompletely learned. The researcher must therefore infer and extrapolate to a greater extent than in other kinds of qualitative research in order to arrive at as accurate a description as possible. This limitation makes it very difficult for the researcher to validate findings that have been observed. (See the discussion in Chapter 5 on validity in qualitative research.)

Because of these limitations, qualitative research in second language acquisition has been limited to describing observable second language acquisition behavior rather than attempting to describe actual language processing, which is by definition internal. Qualitative research appears to be more appropriate for describing the social context of second language, such as dyadic speech interactions (who says *what* to *whom* and *when*), frequencies and descriptions of speech acts in given language-use contexts such as the language classroom, and descriptions of teacher and learner language in the language classroom. (See Schinke-Llano 1983.)

Procedures for conducting qualitative research

What the reader may conclude from the foregoing discussion of qualitative research is that there is in this type of research no set of standard designs or procedures such as exist in experimental research. Jacob (1987) has described research design in this type of research as 'emergent'. The procedures have been likened to a funnel or an upside-down pyramid, meaning that the investigation progresses from the general to the specific. Another image to describe them is that of the spiral – while the researcher progresses from general to more specific data collection, there is also a repetition of the cycles of observation and analysis. As the research progresses, each successive stage of analysis may lead the researcher to focus on a different aspect of the phenomenon for observation, as the picture becomes more focused.

The procedures for conducting qualitative research are, therefore, much more open-ended than they are in either descriptive or experimental research, and are dictated by the context of the particular research study. For this reason, there are technically no prescribed procedures for this type of research, but only general guidelines. In Chapter 8 we will discuss the instruments for data collection in qualitative research. Table 6.1 (overleaf) summarizes the process of conducting qualitative research.

1 *Define the phenomenon to be described*

Since qualitative research is synthetic in its approach, this means that at some stage the focus of observation will have to be narrowed down. Sometimes, in the initial stages of research, the investigator will enter the research context without a focus and try to be open to anything that is happening. At later stages, some kind of narrowing of focus is usually necessary. However, all behavior

---

1 Define the phenomenon of second language to be described.
2 Use qualitative methods to gather data.
3 Look for patterns in the data.
4 Validate initial conclusions by returning to the data or collecting more data.
5 If necessary, return to step 1 and repeat the cycle, redefining the area of focus on the basis of the first cycle.

Table 6.1   Conducting qualitative research

consists of hierarchies of units and subsets of these units. For example, if the research is being conducted in a language class, the researcher will want to decide how to narrow the scope of the observations to be conducted or what possible subsets of the behavioral unit of the language class to focus on.

2 *Use qualitative methods to gather data*

Qualitative research utilizes a variety of means to collect data. Often, several different methods are used in the same study in order to compile a more complete picture of the activity or event being described. Because data are collected from different sources and with different means such as observations, tapes, questionnaires, interviews, case histories, field notes, and so on, qualitative research can provide insights not available through research methodologies dependent on a single approach such as an experiment or a test. The use of a variety of methods of data collection also facilitates validation and triangulation (See p. 105.)

3 *Look for patterns in the data*

Data which are gathered in qualitative research are raw data, in the sense that they have not been collected with any specific research question or hypothesis in mind nor have they undergone any initial sifting or selection. Once the data are collected, the researcher must sift through to find recurring patterns emerging from them.

For example, in a study of turn-taking in the language class, the first stage might consist of video taping lessons. The tapes would then be viewed to discover only what kinds of turn-taking patterns emerged. Are certain request forms more frequent than others? Does the teacher in the language class request information in ways different from those used outside? How do learners request information or clarification? On the basis of the patterns which emerge, the researcher begins to formulate hypotheses and even develop models to explain the findings.

4 *Validate initial conclusions by returning to the data or collecting more data*

Once patterns have been identified in the data, the qualitative researcher will want to validate the findings. The use of a variety of methods to collect data allows the researcher to validate findings through *triangulation*. In triangulation, the same pattern or example of behavior is sought in different sources. Use of the process increases the reliability of the conclusions reached. (See also the discussion in Chapter 5, p. 105.)

There are two sources of invalidity for this type of research:
- The research is not conducted in a natural environment or the data are not representative of what language learners normally do in non-research situations. That is, something in the data collection procedures causes the behavior being observed to be distorted in some way. This is also a problem with other forms of descriptive research. The solution is to replicate the study and observe what data are found the second time. Repetition of the study will show whether something happened during the first investigation to make the language learning behavior different from what it would be if it were not being observed.
- There is no control for the introduction of possible subjective factors in the interpretation of data in qualitative research. Subjectivity may, however, be controlled through *triangulation*. In Chapter 5, we pointed out that data should be *retrievable* and *confirmable*. That is, the protocols or corpus of the data should be in a form which allows them to be reviewed from an original source. In a study of turn-taking, the researchers should have access to the video tapes of the lesson, not just to the selective and subjective field notes taken during the lesson. In order to *confirm* findings, it is also good practice to have other judges to evaluate the tapes to see if they reach similar conclusions about the interpretation of the data. If the study utilizes live observers, it will be necessary to have more than one observer to control for the reliability of the observations.

5 *Recycle through the process or the data*

After the initial stage of data analysis, it may be necessary to redefine the area of research and to narrow the focus. This process has been described above as a 'funnel', in which the focus of the study becomes gradually narrowed. The researcher recycles through the data or through the data collection process as questions about the phenomenon being studied come into sharper focus.

For example, in the study on turn-taking, it may be discovered from the data that male language learners take more turns than females or that one group of learners is more dependent on teacher elicitation. If may then be decided either to re-examine the data or to collect additional data using similar but more focused methods.

The uses of qualitative research

Qualitative research is a useful approach wherever an investigator is concerned with *discovering* or *describing* second language acquisition in its natural state or context and where there are no assumptions about what that activity consists of or what its role is in acquisition.

Any conclusions reached in this kind of research are arrived at as a result of considering only the data and the possible patterns which can be inferred *inductively* from the data. Qualitative research may be said to be *hypothesis-generating* because questions are suggested by these recurring patterns which emerge from the data itself. We shall discuss the specific data gathering procedures for this type of research in Chapter 8 and the appropriate data analysis and statistical procedures used with qualitative research in Chapter 9.

Descriptive research

Descriptive research involves a collection of techniques used to specify, delineate, or describe naturally occurring phenomena without experimental manipulation. As we stated above in our comparisons of qualitative, descriptive, and experimental research, descriptive research shares characteristics with both qualitative and experimental research designs. This is shown in Figure 6.1. It is similar to qualitative research because it deals with naturally occurring phenomena, using data which may either be collected first hand or taken from already existing data sources such as data from other studies, student records, and so on. It differs from qualitative research in that it is often *deductive* rather than *heuristic*, and begins with preconceived hypotheses and a narrower scope of investigation. In this respect, it shares some of the qualities of experimental research. In addition, descriptive research is often quantitative.

Descriptive research is used to establish the existence of phenomena by explicitly describing them. For example, the research may attempt to establish the existence of a specific strategy used by learners in which hypothesis-testing is involved. Descriptive research may provide measures of *frequency*, for example, of the occurrence of a particular syntactic form in the speech of second language learners at some stage in development. It is important to emphasize that while this type of research may begin with a question or hypothesis, the phenomena it describes are not manipulated or artificially elicited in any way.

There are two ways in which descriptive research can be used to investigate second language acquisition:

Case studies

The case study approach is used where the investigator is interested in describing some aspect of the second language performance or development of one or more subjects as individuals, because it is believed that individual performance will be more revealing than studying large groups of subjects. If, for example, we are interested in tracing in detail the development of a particular subset of linguistic forms for a learner, the case study approach is more likely to provide an in-depth and detailed description of how these forms develop in individuals. Since we know that each individual may have their own idiosyncratic pathway to developing language competence, case studies are also able to show how the development of individual language acquirers may be different from that described for groups.

Group studies

Studies which utilize groups of subjects may be used in both descriptive and experimental research. The important difference is that in descriptive work, the groups are already formed or exist in natural contexts while in experimental research, these groups are carefully structured or selected so that they can be said to represent the general population of second language learners. (See also Chapter 7, p. 141.)

To take an example of the use of group studies in descriptive research, a researcher may be interested in describing the various types of motivation found in a second language learner group in order to see if it is related to achievement. Gathering the data for this study could be accomplished in a number of ways: surveys, questionnaires, interviews, and so on. Because the research begins with a particular focus or hypothesis, the scope of the data which are gathered is limited. On the other hand, in qualitative research, the kind of data gathered would be less focused because the goals of the research are less defined.

Data collection in descriptive research

Our discussion here will be limited to some major types of procedures which are related to the question of design in descriptive research. The methods used to collect data in this type of research can be categorized in terms of the relative degrees of explicitness which the data collection instruments require in the response of the subject. (See parameter 4 in Chapter 2.)

Tests

Language *tests* are used in descriptive research in a variety of ways. They may be formal language tests or test-like activities, such as a writing assignment or communicative activity, which are normally carried out in a language class and which later become a data source for the research. The activities might be specially constructed to elicit target data such as a learner's ability to negotiate directions in a dyadic setting. Already existing or archival test data could also be used.

Surveys and questionnaires

Surveys and questionnaires are useful for collecting data from large groups of subjects. The items on surveys and questionnaires may vary in the degree of explicitness with which they elicit data from subjects and the degree of specificity in which items are formulated. Items may consist of questions or other stimuli that either limit responses to a very narrow range of possibilities or allow more latitude in response. They may be administered directly by the researcher to a subject if the subject is unable to complete the questionnaire or if it is thought undesirable for the subject to do so. Surveys may be conducted in the presence of the researcher, or by mail, or telephone.

Self-reports and interviews

These instruments are used with increasing frequency in second language research, especially where the immediate goal of the research is to describe the state of the learner during particular language learning activities. Self-reports and interviews are also used in qualitative research. The difference in their use in descriptive research is that here there is a predetermined goal or objective and only specified kinds of information may be elicited or selected. In terms of Parameter 4 (Chapter 2), this kind of data collection would be considered relatively low on the scale of explicitness.

More structured methods are sometimes used in combination with less structured methods in the same study. For example, in a study of the use of the passive by Hebrew-English bilinguals, a specific task was followed by an interview in L1, in which subjects were asked to describe why they did not use the passive more for a particular topic in their L1 (Seliger 1988). The purpose of the question was to gather data on intuitions about differences in the use of the passive in English and Hebrew. It was not possible to predict what the responses would be; however, the response was limited to the area of focus of the research.

Observations

Descriptive data may be collected by observing the target language acquisition activity or behavior and noting only those aspects of the event which are of interest for the research. Depending on the observation instrument used, observations may record either very narrowly defined data such as a specific speech act or a particular language form, or more general kinds of language learning activity such as turn-taking in a language class (as opposed to a particular kind of turn-taking).

In descriptive research, observations usually focus more on the collection of data specified in advance before the research begins. In qualitative research such as ethnography, no decision is made about focus until after the observations have been conducted. In this sense, in the second, or focused stage, qualitative research resembles descriptive research. The primary difference is that descriptive research begins with a deductive premise about what to look for in the observation. For the purpose of the observation, much thought is given to the way the observations will be conducted, to the controls needed to ensure the reliability of the observations, and to the development of the observation instrument which will focus on the specific kind of data under investigation.

The use and development of data collection procedures in second language acquisition will be discussed in much greater detail in Chapter 8.

---

1 Decide on the question.
2 Select the population.
3 Determine methods for data collection.
4 Collect the data.
5 Organize and analyze the data.

Table 6.2   Procedures for carrying out a descriptive study

Table 6.2 summarizes some of the basic procedures involved in carrying out descriptive research.

1 *Decide on the question.* Descriptive research may be concerned with investigating a question or be motivated by a research hypothesis similar to that used in an experimental study. Whether the research is motivated by a research question or a research hypothesis depends on the nature of the study itself. (See Chapter 3 for a discussion of the distinction between the research question and the research hypothesis.) In many cases, the goal of descriptive research may be simply to describe a particular phenomenon in order to learn more about it.

2 *Select the population.* Descriptive research varies widely in the size of the populations involved. In a case study, for example, it may involve only one or two subjects. Some of the classic studies of first language acquisition have been conducted with only two or three subjects (Brown 1973).

3 *Determine method(s) for data collection.* At this point the researcher must decide on the *type* of data to be collected and the *means* of collection. Making a decision about the type of data to be collected is a theoretical decision as well as a practical one. Since descriptive research is derived from a theoretical position held by the researcher, the type of data to be collected will also be a function of the theory.

Example
A study wishes to describe the role of transfer in second language acquisition. It is decided that the research will focus on performance errors made in the speech of second language learning adults in interview situations. The interviews will be with native speakers of the second language and will be tape-recorded and transcribed. At the time of transcription, it is found that the language learners produce many errors in speech which they themselves correct or change. These changes do not

necessarily result in the correct form. Does the researcher transcribe the errors *before* the speaker changes them, as well as *after* the speaker's correction or note only the final product after all the changes and corrections have been made?

In this example, deciding what to define as data will have very real consequences for what will be described as errors in the research. For this reason, the decision on the type of data collection is often a theoretical decision as well as a practical one.

4 *Collect the data.* Depending on the type of procedure used, this is usually the simplest part of descriptive research. Assuming that the procedures and instruments have been well thought out and field-tested, this step in a descriptive study follows naturally from the preceding three stages.

5 *Organize and analyze the data.* Once descriptive data have been collected, they must be organized into manageable units which can be analyzed and from which meaningful conclusions can be drawn. In descriptive research, this phase is facilitated by the fact that data are not collected randomly or without focus, as they are in qualitative or ethnographic research. In studies which describe linguistic aspects of language development, specific examples representative of categories may be extracted from the data, and a more detailed linguistic analysis performed on these selected sentence types. If the data are collected from groups of subjects, they may be organized into categories, after which frequencies or percentages may be computed. Other statistical procedures may be carried out, such as correlating the frequencies and percentages with other categories of data. In Chapter 9, we will discuss the analysis of these kinds of data in detail.

Summary: The uses of descriptive research

Descriptive research in second language acquisition provides descriptions of naturally occurring phenomena connected with language development and processing. It does this by collecting data through non-intrusive and non-manipulative procedures. It is motivated by specific questions or hypotheses derived from theories of second language acquisition or related fields.

Descriptive research is useful for providing a picture of factors connected with second language development. These descriptions can form the baseline for data for more controlled research or can be used as the basis for inferences about second language, without further controlled research. For example, a descriptive case study of two learners acquiring a second language may provide a basis for making important universal inferences about second language acquisition for a wider population from the same language background, age, or educational level.

Multivariate and correlational research

Technically speaking, multivariate and correlational research are not research methodologies or designs in the same sense that *qualitative, descriptive,* and *experimental* research are. They are discussed here because they may be regarded as a form of descriptive research. However, they are more properly regarded as methods for analyzing data than as methods for research. In fact, multivariate and correlational research can use data from all of the other research methods.

Because multivariate and correlational research are not concerned with the conditions in which the data are gathered, they are used in both descriptive and experimental contexts. These two methods of research are concerned primarily with discovering relationships between categories of data. The statistical procedures for demonstrating these relationships will be described in Chapter 9, where correlational and multivariate research will be discussed as *data analysis* procedures rather than as research designs *per se.*

In multivariate and correlational research, the investigator may be interested in studying possible relationships between or among sets of variables. As with descriptive research, data may be collected as part of the study or the researcher may use existing data from an archive, a data bank, or from previously completed studies. For example, Purcell and Suter (1980) investigated which of twelve factors correlated most highly as predictors of *pronunciation accuracy*, by using correlational and multivariate methodologies.

In experimental research, we may investigate no more than a few variables at a time, and these variables are manipulated by the experimental conditions. The same limit on variables applies to descriptive research. The difference is that here variables are not experimentally manipulated. Correlational research looks at the interrelationship of two variables at the same time, while multivariate research can investigate the interrelationships of a large number of variables at the same time. This is facilitated today by the use of statistical computer software.

Multivariate research has become increasingly popular in second language studies because it takes into consideration the unique and complex characteristics of this field. As we shall see in the next chapter, while experimental research is very valuable when we are studying the interaction between a limited number of independent variables and one or more dependent variables, multivariate research allows the researcher to consider a much wider spectrum of manipulable and non-manipulable variables at the same time.

Experimental research

Dependent variable: Pronunciation ability

$\updownarrow$

Independent variable: Type of lab practice

Multivariate research

Figure 6.2   Multivariate and experimental research compared

Example
A study is set up to examine the relationship between ability to pronounce a second language with near-native accuracy and variables such as IQ, attitude toward the second language, type of motivation, sex, socio-economic status, job, educational aspirations, degree of ethnocentrism, schooling, other second language experience, number of years of residence in the second language environment, type of method used in teaching the language, type of instruction in pronunciation, marital status, language used at home, language used on the job, number and type of social contacts which use the second language, amount of TV watched in the second language, performance on a test of hearing acuity, and so on. The study wishes to investigate the contribution of all these independent variables to the dependent variable of second language pronunciation.

If we wished to examine the relationship of each of the variables mentioned here separately with the variable of pronunciation, it would involve a long and tedious procedure. The above list is not exhaustive; many other variables could be added that might logically have some effect on the acquisition of second language phonology. Note also that the data from each of these categories is of the three different types discussed in Chapter 5 (nominal, ordinal, and metric). Multivariate research allows us to mix these data types and compare them. (See Figure 6.2.) Purcell and Suter (1980) cite a study in which a battery of twenty variables were correlated with pronunciation accuracy.

Another advantage of multivariate analysis is that it allows us to statistically manipulate the variables and group them together to see if any particular cluster of variables affects the dependent variable more than any other. This type of analysis is referred to as *multiple regression*. Basically, this means that we are looking at several correlations at the same time. That is, this type of research allows us to reduce the size of the variable set by combining sets of variables together to see whether, in combination, they seem to correlate more highly than other combinations. For instance, in the example given above, we might decide to cluster attitude toward the second language, number and type of social contacts in the second language, and measures of ethnocentrism within one category. It may be that these combine to form a category that demonstrates a better correlation with ability to pronounce the second language.

It should be remembered, however, that this still does not demonstrate a causality relationship between these factors and pronunciation, but rather that where one is present, the other is also likely to be present. How these relationships are statistically demonstrated will be discussed in Chapter 9.

Summary: multivariate and correlational research

This type of research (unlike experimental and descriptive research) while not technically a research methodology, is nonetheless useful for investigating, simultaneously, the relationship between many variables. Multivariate research may be used with data collected from many different sources, such as previous descriptive or experimental research, or data collected specifically for the current study using tests, questionnaires, observations, and so on. The data are then statistically analyzed in terms of their relationship and contribution to the dependent variables. Independent variables can also be grouped or clustered together into subsets to form stronger correlations with the dependent variable(s). This form of analysis is sometimes referred to as multiple regression analysis.

Summary

This chapter has discussed one of the major groups of research designs, all concerned with various forms of description. Qualitative research is carried out without preconceived notions about what to look for. This type of research would be characterized as *synthetic* or *holistic* in its approach to second language phenomena, and *heuristic* in its research objective.

Descriptive research can be *synthetic* or *analytic* in its approach and *heuristic* or *deductive* in its research objectives. Descriptive research begins with a preconceived focus or research question; it may also test a hypothesis, and utilize already existing data from other studies.

What these methods have in common is the fact that they *describe* what is, and do not attempt to control or manipulate any of the factors in the research environment. Descriptive research may test hypotheses on the basis of pre-existing data or focus on selected aspects of data occurring naturally in second language acquisition. *Correlational* and *multivariate* research approaches, unlike qualitative and descriptive research, are not concerned with methods for conducting the research but rather with ways of looking at the relationships between variables and their possible multiple contribution to the dependent variable.

Activities

1 Select from second language research journals such as *Language Learning, TESOL Quarterly, Second Language Research* or others, one example each of *qualitative, descriptive, multivariate* and *correlational* research. Why do you think each researcher chose that particular research format and not another?

2 Select a research question in your field of interest and discuss how the research would be carried out, using each of the three research types discussed in this chapter.

3 Discuss the relative advantages and disadvantages of conducting qualitative and descriptive research with children acquiring a second language. Give examples of the kinds of information on child second language acquisition you can obtain using each of these approaches.

4 What are some of the validity problems that can result from using qualitative research such as diary studies? How might these problems be overcome or minimized?

References

Bailey, K. M. 1981. 'Competitiveness and anxiety in adult second language learning: Looking at and through the diary studies' in H. W. Seliger, and M. H. Long (eds.): *Classroom Oriented Research in Second Language Acquisition*. Rowley, Mass.: Newbury House.

Brown, R. 1973. *A First Language*. Cambridge, Mass.: MIT Press.

Cohen, A. and Hosenfeld, C., 1981. 'Some uses of mentalistic data in second language research.' *Language Learning* 31/2:285–314.

Ericsson, K. A. and Simon, H. A. 1984. *Protocol Analysis: Verbal Reports as Data*. Cambridge, Mass.: MIT Press.

Green, J. L. and Wallatt C. (eds.) 1981. *Ethnography and Language in Educational Settings*. Norwood, N.J.: Ablex.

Jacob, E. 1987. 'Qualitative research traditions: A review.' *Review of Educational Research* 57/1:1–50.

Kamil, M. L., Langer, J. A., and Shanahan, T. 1985. *Understanding Reading and Writing Research*. Boston: Allyn and Bacon.

Long, M. H. 1983. 'Inside the "black box": Methodological issues in classroom research on language learning' in H. W. Seliger and M. Long (eds.) *Classroom Oriented Research in Second Language Acquisition*. Rowley, Mass.: Newbury House.

Purcell, E. T. and Suter, R.W. 1980. 'Predictors of pronunciation accuracy: A reexamination.' *Language Learning* 30/2: 271–287.

Scherer, A. C. and Wertheimer, M. 1964. *A Psycholinguistic Experiment in Foreign Language Teaching*. New York: McGraw-Hill.

Schinke-Llano, L. A. 1983. 'Foreigner talk in content classrooms' in H. W. Seliger and M. Long: *op. cit.*

Seliger, H. W. 1989. 'Semantic transfer constraints on the production of English passive by Hebrew-English bilinguals' in H. Dechert and M. Raupach (eds.): *Transfer in Language Production*. Norwood, N.J.: Ablex.

Shulman, L. S. 1981. 'Disciplines of inquiry in education: an overview.' *Educational Researcher* June/July: 5–12.

Smith, J. K. and Heshusius, L. 1986. 'Closing down the conversation: The end of the quantitative-qualitative debate among educational inquirers.' *Educational Researcher* 15/1: 4–12.

Tarone, E. 1982. 'Systematicity and attention in interlanguage.' *Language Learning* 32: 69–84.

White, L. 1985. 'The acquisition of parameterized grammars: subjacency in second language acquisition.' *Second Language Research* 1/1:1–17.

7 Research design: experimental research

> Science, after all, is fundamentally about process; learning why and how things happen is the soul of our discipline. You can't abandon the search for cause in favor of a dry documentation of pattern. You must take risks of uncertainty in order to probe the deeper questions, rather than stopping with sterile security.
>
> (Stephen Jay Gould: 'Darwinism defined: The difference between fact and theory.' *Discover*. January 1987.)

Introduction

In Chapter 6 we discussed qualitative and descriptive research procedures in second language acquisition. In this chapter, we will discuss experimental research. This order reflects the current interest among second language researchers in descriptive investigation, and also reflects what may be considered a 'natural order' or developmental sequence. That is, qualitative and descriptive research, being hypothesis-generating, often culminate in testing those hypotheses experimentally. The idea of a conceptual, developmental sequence in the research process was implied in our discussions in Chapters 2 and 3.

As we noted in Chapter 3, research questions and hypotheses may emerge from different sources, such as observation. A theory, which is a set of interrelated hypotheses, can then be drawn upon for research which tests these hypotheses in a controlled context such as an experiment.

In this chapter, we are concerned with how the basic elements of an experiment can be arranged in order to give results which are both internally and externally valid. The various aspects of validity were discussed extensively in Chapter 5. In this chapter, we will discuss only those designs that relate to *experimental* research. In Chapter 6, we discussed non-experimental approaches to research (qualitative and descriptive research) and compared these approaches to experimental research in relation to the research parameters introduced in Chapter 2.

Experimental research is carefully constructed so that variables can be controlled and manipulated. In terms of the research parameters discussed in Chapter 2, experimental research is *analytic* and *deductive*. Figure 7.1 shows where experimental research would be placed relative to the research parameters.

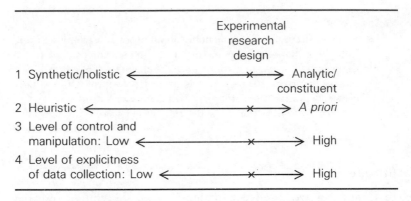

Figure 7.1   Experimental research and the research parameters

The major components of experimental research

All experimental approaches involve the control or manipulation of the three basic components of the experiment: *the population, the treatment,* and *the measurement of the treatment.* This chapter will only be concerned with those aspects of these components relating to the design of the research, and not to questions of statistical analysis. The latter are dealt with in Chapter 9.

1 The type and number of groups

Experimental research is concerned with studying the effects of specified and controlled treatments given to subjects usually formed into groups. Groups can be formed especially for the purposes of the experiment or they can be 'natural' in the sense that they already exist prior to the research. Natural groups often correspond to 'nominal' data categories such as those discussed in Chapter 5, for example, males, Spanish speakers, subjects who have learned a language for at least five years, or the class in room 405. The researcher has to decide whether to use pre-existing groups, as they occur in nature, or to construct them for the experiment. This difference between natural groups and those formed specifically for an experiment is one of the features that distinguishes true experimental designs from quasi-experimental designs.

2 The treatment

This refers to anything done to groups in order to measure its effect. The treatment is not a random experience which the groups might have, but a *controlled* and *intentional* experience, such as exposure to a language teaching method specially constructed for the experiment, or materials presented under controlled circumstances, say, in a language laboratory. Treatments are the *independent variable* in the research.

3 Measurement or observation

Measurement or observation refers to how the effects of the treatment will be evaluated or observed. The effects of a treatment might be evaluated by means of a language test, a judgment, or a communicative task; or physical measurements such as response time can be measured electronically or spectrograms can be taken.

Following conventions established by Campbell and Stanley (1963), the components of experimental research designs will be symbolized as follows:

X = an experimental treatment such as a teaching method, or exposure to specially constructed materials, and so on.
O = observation or measurement of the effects of the treatment.
R = randomization, or the random assignment of subjects to groups in order to control for extraneous variables.

Experimental research design consists primarily of various ways of organizing a treatment (X) and an observation or measurement (O). We will examine a representative sample of possible research designs and discuss their advantages and disadvantages.

Experimental research designs may be grouped into several categories, all of which have a number of variations, depending on the conditions under which the research is being conducted. The discussion here will be limited to *single group designs*, in which research might be conducted with only one group; *control group* designs, in which one group receives a treatment while the other, representing the same population as the experimental subjects, does not receive a treatment; *factorial designs*, which allow for the investigation of a number of independent variables at the same time; and *quasi-experimental* designs, in which experimental research is conducted in situations which cannot be completely controlled or manipulated.

All of the designs discussed in this chapter have numerous variations that depend on the specific conditions under which the research is conducted. It is important, therefore, for the reader to understand the *general principles* of experimental design in order to be able to construct satisfactory variations of these designs dictated by different conditions, research questions, and so on.

Single group designs

1 One-shot design: X O (Pilot study design)

This is experimental research design at its most basic. In this design, a single treatment is given to a single group or individual. The group or individual is then observed, tested, or measured.

This design might also be referred to as the 'pilot study' design because it does not control for any of the extraneous variables discussed in Chapter 5. The design is problematic and, for many researchers, it is never seriously considered as a viable design for experimental research. The main problem with this design is that there is no way of knowing the characteristics of the group or individual before the treatment or experience. However, the design is useful as a means of pinpointing what to avoid in experimental research. It can also be used for preliminary testing of instruments or 'run throughs' of experimental procedures.

Example

A second language teacher employs a new method for teaching the communicative use of the target language. After three weeks of using this new method, a test is administered to the class. The class performs well on the test.

It is clear that there are serious problems with this design, and that claims made for findings using it must be made with great caution. The discussion on extraneous variables in Chapter 5 indicates that this design does not control for many factors.

There are instances in which the 'one-shot design' is all that is available to the researcher because it is not possible to set up experimental conditions and control for extraneous variables. It might be that there are not enough subjects for randomization into groups, or it may be impossible to find out what the pre-treatment conditions were. An example of such a situation would be the study of language acquisition by transient populations whose past educational history is unobtainable. In such cases, the researcher is limited to this type of design.

Because of its limitations, it is important to qualify the findings of 'one-shot' research in terms of the factors which affect internal and external validity. This research design is more appropriate to pilot studies in which the researcher wishes to try out instruments or treatments before running a full-scale experiment.

2 One group pre-test + post-test: O1 X O2

This design attempts to use the subjects as their own controls and to eliminate the need for a control group design. This design is sometimes referred to as a 'repeated measures' design because subjects are observed or measured twice on the dependent variable.

The design is efficient because it controls a number of extraneous variables which can affect the homogeneity of subjects when more than one group is involved. To some degree, the design also controls for attrition or loss of subjects. Since the same group is used for both pre-test and post-test, it does not need to be matched to another group.

Unfortunately, there are a number of disadvantages to this design that the researcher must be aware of. One of the primary problems is that there is no certainty that the possible differences that appear in O2 are the result of treatment X; they might simply be changes that would have taken place anyway. (See the discussion of history, attrition, and maturation in Chapter 5.) For example, in classroom research where the independent variable might be a set of materials or a language teaching method, there is no way of knowing whether changes between the before and after treatment measures (O1 and O2) were the result of incidental exposure to language material or to some other experience that the subjects may have had. In the case of second language learners, incidental exposure to the second language outside the classroom may affect performance. In foreign language contexts, this may be a less important factor because incidental exposure can more easily be controlled.

Another possible disadvantage of this design is that the pre-test, O1, may sensitize the subjects to specific aspects of the treatment, X, and thus confound what is measured by the post-test, O2.

Example
In a study on the effects of second language instruction, the researcher wishes to establish that the group has no knowledge of a grammatical structure which will be taught in the lesson (X). In order to establish this, two tests are constructed which specifically test for the target structure in a discrete point test. One test will be used as the pre-test and the other will become the post-test.

In this case, the pre-test may highlight or draw attention to the target structure. Because the group has been sensitized to this structure by the pre-test, it may learn differently from a group which has not been sensitized in this way. The pre-test here acts not only to establish a baseline norm for knowledge of the language being measured, but also acts as a pre-instruction phase for the treatment X. This problem may be mitigated to some extent by using more indirect measures to establish baseline norms of knowledge before the treatment. For example, a pre-treatment speaking or writing sample might reveal levels of knowledge, without drawing attention to the language forms which will be taught during the treatment stage.

3 Time-sampling designs: O1, O2, O3, On . . . X, On + 1, On + 2. . .

These are also referred to as 'time-series' designs because a number of samples or observations are taken over a period of time. They can be distinguished from non-experimental longitudinal research because they have a controlled treatment, X, inserted after a number of observations or measurements. The use of this type of design is another way of overcoming the problems inherent in the previous design.

The procedure of taking a number of measurements or observations of the subject population before and after the treatment allows us to ascribe any changes in the subjects' performance to the treatment with greater assurance. It allows the researcher to develop a norm for the population over time and thus discount *history* as a possible factor. After a series of observations, a regular pattern of change should emerge, thus revealing the amount of change that would be expected as a result of time, incidental exposure to other language sources, and maturation. A sudden or noticeable difference between the observation (On) immediately preceding the treatment and the observation following treatment (On + 1) can then be said with more confidence to result from X. Other variants of this design include a time-series in which several treatments are paired with several observations over time.

In this type of design, the researcher does not have access to a control group, and must be content with results obtained from one group. Since this design also operates under real-life conditions and not necessarily with groups specially constituted for the research, it may also be considered one of the 'quasi-experimental' designs discussed below.

As we have noted a number of times, *history* is one of the greatest threats to internal validity. In the case of second language acquisition, it is possible that certain changes in language ability could be the result of natural developmental processes unrelated to a specific treatment.

Example

A study wishes to investigate the effectiveness of teaching students the use of relative clauses in English. For the purposes of the research, a 'treatment' is constructed consisting of a lesson which gives the formal features of relative clause formation in English along with practice in using relative clauses in speech and writing. The treatment is preceded by several in-class writing assignments (O1, O2, O3) spaced over several weeks. For each writing assignment, the number of relative clauses in learners' writing is tallied and categorized. After the treatment, several similar writing assignments are given (On + 1, On + 2, On + 3) and the number of relative clauses are counted and categorized.

In summary, collecting data over an extended period before and after the treatment allows us to establish a normal pattern of performance for the language or acquisition behavior under investigation. This allows the researcher to exclude the possible interaction of incidental exposure to language material outside the classroom, or any natural developmental change which may take place regardless of instruction.

Designs using control groups

Conducting an experiment means that at least one independent variable is manipulated and its effect measured by some dependent variable while other factors are controlled in various ways. In the single group designs, the experimental group acts as its own control; the comparison is between its performance without treatment and its performance with treatment. In the designs discussed below, the comparison will be for the treatment effect between two or more groups. Implicit in the use of control groups is the important assumption that the control group represents the same population as the experimental group: it is as if we are comparing the same individuals with and without treatment. For this reason, the multi-group designs are concerned with measures to standardize the groups being compared, so that claims for difference in the performance on the dependent variable (O) have both internal and external validity.

1 Static group or 'pre-experimental' design

$$\frac{\text{X O1}}{\text{O1}}$$

This would seem to be an 'economical' design because it allows us to utilize groups which already exist, such as classes found in a school. In this design, a treatment is administered to one group and its performance is compared with another, seemingly equivalent group which has received no treatment. The problem with this design is that there is no way of knowing whether the groups are, in fact, equivalent before 'X'. That is, differences in performance on the dependent variable (O) may be due to intrinsic group differences such as the first language background, sex, exposure to the second language, the time of day during which instruction takes place, the level of motivation of the groups, and the effects of different teachers on group response.

This design may also be considered 'quasi-experimental' (see below) and is most appealing for second language experiments conducted in school environments because it requires the least amount of disruption of school routines. It does not require the reassignment of subjects to groups different from those in which they are already found and it requires no rearrangements of schedules or reassignment of teachers. These apparent advantages, however, can also be sources of invalidity if variables are not controlled. For example, if the same instructor teaches both groups, teacher variables may be better controlled; or if the groups compared receive their instruction at about the same time of day, fatigue may be discounted as having a variable effect.

One way to avoid some of these problems when using a *static* design is for the experimenter to match subjects in the two groups for various characteristics such as placement test scores, sex, first language, and teacher rankings to make the groups more comparable. Matching is a way of increasing the comparability of the groups when subjects cannot be randomly assigned. Thus, the variation on the *static* design will look like the pre-test designs discussed below, but without randomization. This will not solve all of the problems discussed above but it will give some indication of the comparability of the static groups.

Group A: matching $\dfrac{\text{X O1}}{}$
Group B: matching $\dfrac{}{-\ \text{O1}}$

A variation on the control group matching design

A variation on the control group matching design can be found in the study conducted by Lightbown and Libben (1984), in which the use of cognates by francophone ESL learners was compared with a control group of native speakers. In this study, the treatment consisted of both control and experimental subjects viewing a film and then taking a modified cloze test in which target concepts were left blank. The test was then followed by an acceptability task in which the same text was presented with the blanks filled in, some with acceptable cognates and others with unacceptable cognates. The acceptability performance of the ESL learners was compared with that of the native anglophones (NS). In this case, the cloze acted as a form of pre-test to establish that the ESL learners did have the concepts with which to judge acceptability later. The design, therefore might be described as follows:

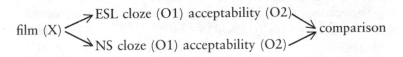

film (X) ⟨ ESL cloze (O1) acceptability (O2) ⟩ comparison
         NS cloze (O1) acceptability (O2)

2 Pre-test/post-test with randomization of groups

Group A → R ⟨ Group A': O1 X O2
               Group A": O1 — O2

Randomization is a procedure with which to reduce the amount of systematic error that might result from biases in the assignment of subjects to groups. It also provides better control of variables that could affect internal validity. By randomizing, we are claiming that any effects of extraneous variables occur by chance and that chance is equally distributed between both groups.

An important advantage of randomization is that it provides the option of not using a pre-test as a method of making groups more comparable. If subjects are assigned to groups randomly, it is safe to assume that the effect of many subject variables is spread evenly throughout the two groups. This is more likely to be the case when the size of the groups in the experiment is large. The larger the number of subjects in each group, the more likely it is that subject variables will negate each other through the randomization process. (See also 'Size of subject population' in Chapter 5.)

The following example demonstrates another possible threat to internal validity which can be solved by randomized assignment of subjects.

Example

Volunteers are solicited for a study on the effects of computer-assisted instruction on second language achievement. From the population of volunteers, subjects are assigned to the computer-assisted group first and to the control group receiving no computer-assisted instruction second. (Reversing the order of assigning volunteers will not change the effect.)

Even though the assigning of subjects to the treatment or the control group would seem to be random, it is likely that those volunteering first are different from those who may have been cajoled into participating in the study. The order of assignment may be a reflection of motivation at some level and is also likely to affect the results of the study.

Sometimes the problem of how to assign volunteers cannot be overcome. In a study reported by Eubank (1987) on the acquisition of negation in German as a foreign language, only six subjects volunteered from a total of approximately three hundred students registered for a beginning German course, even though all of the potential subjects had been offered money for participation. Given such small numbers and the likelihood that these six stalwarts were highly motivated, the results of such a study must be viewed with caution.

With a sufficient number of subjects, the problem of biases in levels of motivation or other factors can be controlled, and internal validity heightened, by assigning subjects to groups by using a randomization (R) procedure. This can be done through the use of a table of random numbers found in the back of statistics books, by drawing names out of a hat, or by any other means which will guarantee that subjects are not assigned on the basis of some conscious or unknown bias.

In the pre-test/post-test with randomization design, it is assumed that all subjects are members of some group A, which is in turn a representative sample of the greater population of second language learners. That is, Group A, from which the experimental and control groups will be drawn, is itself representative. The population of Group A is fed through a randomization process (R), and members are randomly assigned to either Group A' or Group A". Once the two groups are formed, the pre-test, O1, is administered to both.

There are variations on Design 2. For example:

$$R \begin{cases} \nearrow X \ O1 \\ \searrow — \ O1 \end{cases}$$

shows that randomization can eliminate the problem of pre-testing. This design, without pre-testing, is useful when assumptions can be made about the baseline knowledge of the population from which the groups are formed.

For example, if we wish to test the effect of laboratory training on the ability to pronounce second language sounds, we may wish to start with a population defined as beginners and assign them randomly to experimental or control groups. In this way we can avoid giving them a pre-test of phonological ability, which might sensitize them to the treatment itself.

Factorial designs

Factorial designs are similar to the true experimental designs discussed above and include all of the elements found in those designs, such as grouping by randomization, pre- and post-testing, and treatments. The difference is that the effects of several independent variables may be tested at the same time.

In simple experimental designs, the additional variables are referred to as extraneous variables. (See Chapter 5.) These variables must be controlled if an effect is to be attributed to a specific independent variable. However, in factorial designs, more than one variable may be treated as an independent variable.

Example
In a study to test for the effect of language laboratory training on pronunciation, it is also decided to measure for the effect of such training on learners of different proficiency levels, as well as the effect of different kinds of language laboratory practice.

In this example, we are hypothesizing that the effect of practice versus no practice in the language laboratory could be a function of both the proficiency level of the learner and the type of practice administered in the laboratory.

It may be that only learners of a more advanced proficiency level are able to utilize the focus on pronunciation because they are aware of the problems they are having with pronunciation, while beginning-level learners are not able to become aware of pronunciation differences because they are concentrating on more global aspects of the language learning task.

We might further hypothesize that the *type* of practice will also be a factor in the efficacy of pronunciation practice in the language laboratory. Here we are referring primarily to differences between *contextualized* laboratory drills, in which pronunciation is practiced in a communicative setting, and *decontextualized* practice such as minimal pair drills requiring little or no communicative use of the sounds. If we include all of these variables in a factorial design, we arrive at the following:

$$
R \left\{
\begin{array}{l}
Gb1 \rightarrow O1 \rightarrow Xd \rightarrow O2 \\
Gb2 \rightarrow O1 \rightarrow Xc \rightarrow O2 \\
Gb3 \rightarrow O1 \rightarrow\!\!- \rightarrow O2
\end{array}
\right.
$$

$$
R \left\{
\begin{array}{l}
Ga1 \rightarrow O1 \rightarrow Xd \rightarrow O2 \\
Ga2 \rightarrow O1 \rightarrow Xc \rightarrow O2 \\
Ga3 \rightarrow O1 \rightarrow\!\!- \rightarrow O2
\end{array}
\right.
$$

In this design, beginning (b) and advanced (a) proficiency subjects are randomized (R) separately, since level of proficiency is defined here as one of the independent variables. It is assumed that some other criterion measure has been used to categorize students as either advanced or beginning before the randomization. Both beginning (Gb) and advanced (Ga) groups are assigned randomly to one of three groups:

1 those receiving decontextualized pronunciation practice in the laboratory (Xd)
2 those receiving contextualized laboratory practice (Xc)
3 those receiving no laboratory practice at all.

All groups are given the same pre-test and post-tests before and after treatment.

There are, of course, other variables which might be considered, such as the amount of time practiced, the students' motivation to improve pronunciation, and so on. In the above design, each additional variable would require a treatment group and, if necessary, a corresponding control group. If no additional proficiency levels were added to this design, the already existing control groups would suffice.

Variations on factorial designs in second language research

The factorial design is often used in second language research with a minor variation on the classical factorial design described above. In many second language studies there is no formal stage which can be regarded as a 'treatment' (O) in which something specific is done to the subjects. Typically, instead of a formal treatment stage in the experiment, a task is devised and administered to the subjects. However, this task serves the double purpose of the 'treatment' and the post-test stage in the design. Often, this is a linguistic task in which the subjects, divided into groups, are asked to judge or imitate a set of stimuli. The performance of the subjects on the set of stimuli (sentences, sounds, and so on) are then used as the data with which to test the experimental hypothesis.

A variation of the factorial design can be found in Flynn (1984) in a study of the ability of Japanese and Spanish speakers to correctly imitate sentences with right or left branching adverbial phrases. Her hypothesis was that the 'primary branching direction' of the first language would affect the ability of the learner to imitate such sentences in the target language, English.

In this study, subjects were not randomized as would be the case in true experimental designs. Learners were given a pre-test to establish proficiency level and were then divided into three levels: beginning, intermediate, and advanced. They were further grouped according to first language. There was no experimental treatment, but an experimental task was administered, in which learners were asked to imitate a set of stimulus sentences.

A similar design is found in Kilborn *et al.* (1987). In this study, Dutch-English bilinguals were tested on sets of sentences in which they had to identify the subject or agent in various stimulus sentences. Subjects were grouped according to proficiency before the task and the treatment stage consisted of the stimulus sentence task as in the Flynn study above.

In these kinds of studies, it may be argued that the 'treatment' took place *before* the experiment and consisted of the subjects' exposure to the second language. The purpose of the pre-tests in these studies is basically to establish levels of ability before the task is administered. In addition, there is no randomization in assigning subjects to groups, because .the experimental groups consist of 'natural' first language groups (Dutch, Japanese, and Spanish). Randomization may be used in another way in these types of studies: In the Kilborn *et al.* study, the tasks consisted of different lists of sentences randomly assigned to subjects for the processing task. These designs combine elements from the factorial designs and from the quasi-experimental design principles discussed below.

Quasi-experimental designs

Quasi-experimental designs (Campbell and Stanley 1963) are constructed from situations which already exist in the real world, and are probably more representative of the conditions found in educational contexts. Some of the designs described above have also been termed 'quasi-experimental' because the research is conducted under conditions in which it is difficult to control many of the variables and in which subjects cannot be assigned to special groups for the purposes of the research.

Typical of experimental research which is carried out under normal school conditions is the study by Cziko (1980) on the reading strategies of learners of French as a second language in Canada. In this study, the author compared the contextually based versus graphically based oral reading strategies of second language learners at the intermediate and advanced levels, using native speakers of French as controls. All three groups consisted of already existing classes in a Canadian high school.

In the real world in which schools and classes exist, serious limitations are placed on the freedom of researchers to manipulate and control the conditions under which they conduct research. Language program administrators are generally unwilling to disturb their ongoing programs and allow reorganization of classes in order to randomize the assignment of subjects to different experimental groups. Teachers are under pressure to advance the abilities of their students and are jealous of time taken from class, unless they feel that there will be some immediate beneficial effect, such as learning improvement or more effective teaching.

Students, especially adult learners, are often reluctant to participate in experiments or research because they may perceive it as interfering with their learning or work routines. This may explain the small number of subjects who volunteered for the Eubank (1987) study discussed earlier. Many second language programs are aimed at immigrant or guest-worker populations, which are transient and unstable because of changing work or family demands.

One of the alternatives discussed above under *one-group* designs, the *equivalent time-series* design, is an attempt to overcome the limitations of conducting research in the real world. Even though this design uses only one group and is not considered truly experimental because it cannot assign subjects through randomization, other measures are employed to ensure control of extraneous variables that may affect internal validity.

Quasi-experimental research is more likely to have external validity because it is conducted under conditions closer to those normally found in educational contexts. For this reason, research conducted under a quasi-experimental design format is often less likely to meet resistance from the 'consumers' of research, such as language teachers. Furthermore, since these designs are less intrusive and disruptive than others, it is easier to gain access to subject populations and thus easier to conduct such research. For these reasons, quasi-experimental designs are also ideal for teacher-conducted research and for pilot studies, in which the exploration of a research idea is the primary goal. In short, the researcher must consider the relative merits of using true experimental designs and quasi-experimental designs. It should be noted again that the greatest problem is controlling for sources of internal invalidity.

Separate sample designs

Separate sample pre-test/post-test design

This design is useful for those situations in which the researcher has access to only one group of subjects at a time.

Example
As in the previous example, the aim of the study is to measure the effects of language laboratory training on the pronunciation of advanced level learners. However, the program has only one advanced level class entering every three weeks.

In order to gather enough subjects for a study, it will be necessary to pool the results of at least three classes. This can be accomplished by repeating the one-group pre-test/post-test design discussed above, but treating the separate groups as one group in a time-series design. In a sense, we are replicating the same experiment each time with a different class, the population characteristics of which are assumed to be the same.

Group 1: (Week 1) O1 X O2
Group 2:   (Week 3) O3 X O4
Group 3:   (Week 6) O5 X O6

There are several advantages to this design. It allows for a larger population to be treated, and overcomes the problem of lack of access to large enough groups of subjects at any one time. This design could be continued further to include several groups and would be useful for investigating variables over long periods of time. It also allows us to control for changes due to history and in that sense, becomes like a time-series study with one group. In the one group design, if the results of O2 are greater than O1, it might be possible to claim that some other event outside of the experiment caused the result. If, however, we conduct inter-group comparisons and find that for successive semesters, scores on post-tests (O2, O4, and O6) are greater for all groups, it is unlikely that the same event could have occurred in all three semesters at the same time.

Another way to control for history using this design, is to conduct inter-group comparisons between post-tests and pre-tests. It might be argued that changes in pronunciation were not due to the practice in the language laboratory but rather to exposure to language over time. An additional comparison *across groups* can control for this variable. By comparing O2 to O3, and O4 to O5, and finding differences in favor of post-tests, it may be claimed that at the onset of each experiment all groups were at the same level and that any changes are due to practice in the language laboratory.

Another possible source of internal invalidity is the sensitizing effect of the pre-tests. The experimenters need to use pre-tests which will enable them to claim that the groups are similar at the outset of the research and yet not sensitize the groups to the language material in the treatment.

Summary

The designs presented in this chapter are not meant to be used as recipes for experimental research. Rather they should be used as examples of possible experimental and quasi-experimental designs for second language research. Keeping in mind the basic components of experimental research (subjects, treatment, and measurement of the effects of the treatment) as well as the factors which affect the validity of experimental research, the researcher may create variations on the basic design types discussed in this chapter.

We have looked at various ways of manipulating or managing the variables under investigation. Single group, control group, factorial, and quasi-experimental designs were discussed. However, many possible variations on these designs have not been discussed. Descriptions of such variations can be found in the research literature, and in the references listed at the end of this chapter.

Activities

1 Select articles describing experimental research from second language journals. Describe the design used. What are the advantages and disadvantages of that design for the research question? What other designs might be used to investigate the hypotheses of the research?

2 Some texts on educational research describe a set of procedures called 'ex post facto' experimental designs. Why is this term used? In terms of Parameters 1 and 2, why might these designs be better grouped under the research designs discussed in Chapter 6?

3 The critical period hypothesis for second language acquisition claims that some aspects of a second language cannot be acquired after puberty. Read Neufeld (1987) who tested this hypothesis experimentally. Use a different design from that used by Neufeld to test this hypothesis. Describe what aspect(s) of language you will investigate, the characteristics of the population you will use, the problems of internal and external validity that may affect your research, and how you will control for them.

References

Campbell, D. J. and **Stanley, J. C.** 1963. 'Experimental and quasi-experimental designs for research on teaching' in N. L. Gage (ed.): *Handbook of Research on Teaching*. Chicago: Rand McNally.

Cziko, G. A. 1980. 'Language competence and reading strategies: A comparison of first and second language reading errors.' *Language Learning* 30/1:101–116.

Eubank, L. 1987. 'The acquisition of German negation by formal language learners' in B. Van Patten, T. R. Dvorak, and J. F. Lee (eds.): *Foreign Language Learning: A Research Perspective*. Cambridge, Mass.: Newbury House.

Ferguson, G. A. 1971. *Statistical Analysis in Psychology and Education* (third edition). New York: McGraw-Hill.

Flynn, S. 1984. 'A universal in L2 acquisition based on a PBD typology' in F. R. Eckman, L. H. Bell, and D. Nelson (eds.): *Universals of Second Language Acquisition*. Rowley, Mass.: Newbury House.

Hatch, E. and Farhady, H. 1982. *Research Design and Statistics for Applied Linguistics*. Rowley, Mass.: Newbury House.

Kamil, M. L., Langer, J. A., and Shanahan, T. 1985. *Understanding Research in Reading and Writing*. Boston: Allyn and Bacon.

Kilborn, K. and Cooreman, A. 1987. 'Sentence interpretation strategies in adult Dutch-English bilinguals.' *Applied Psycholinguistics* 8/4:415–431.

Lightbown, P. and Libben, G. 1984. 'The recognition and use of cognates by L2 learners' in R. Andersen (ed.): *Second Languages: A Cross-Linguistic Perspective*. Rowley, Mass.: Newbury House.

Neufeld, G. 1987. 'On the acquisition of prosodic and articulatory features in adult language learning' in G. Ioup and S. H. Weinberger (eds.): *Interlanguage Phonology: The Acquisition of a Second Language Sound System*. Cambridge, Mass.: Newbury House.

Sax, G. 1979. *Foundations of Educational Research*. Englewood Cliffs, N.J.: Prentice-Hall.

Siegel, S. 1956. *Nonparametric Statistics for the Behavioral Sciences*. New York: McGraw-Hill.

8 Data and data collection procedures

I've made me a moon-catchin' net
And I'm goin' huntin' tonight,
I'll run along swingin' it over my head
And grab for that big ball of light

So tomorrow just look at the sky,
And if there's no moon, you can bet
I've found what I sought and I finally caught
The moon in my moon-catchin' Net'.
(S. Silverstein: 'Moon-Catchin' Net' in A Light in the Attic, 1981)

Introduction

Once the researcher has selected a specific design for the study consistent with the objectives of the research, as described in the previous chapters, it is time to collect the research data. In collecting the data it is important to use procedures which elicit high quality data, since the quality of any research study depends largely on the quality of the data collected, and the quality is directly related to the data collection procedures. Thus, well thought-out data collection procedures will generally elicit high quality data leading to valid research findings and conclusions, while unsuitable procedures may often lead to invalid conclusions.

In Chapter 2 we presented the second language research paradigm and its four parameters, of which the fourth focused on data and data collection. As we discussed, the data collection parameter consists of two components: the need to determine what constitute data in a given second language acquisition study, and the procedure(s) used for collecting the data.

Determining what constitute data

In terms of the first component of the parameter – determining what constitute data – we noted in Chapter 2 that second language acquisition data can be drawn from any of the behaviors involved in a second language acquisition event. They may cover a wide variety of phenomena such as learner utterances, conversations, strategies used for producing and solving language problems, attitudes toward learning a language and toward its speakers, language used by teachers and students in classroom lessons, performances of learners on metalinguistic tasks such as judgments, translations, imitations, and so on.

However, determining what constitute data in a specific piece of second language acquisition research depends primarily on the focus of the study and on the specific variables to be identified. Thus the first step in the process is to arrive at a clear, precise, and exact definition of the variables of the study. Since most variables are abstract, the researcher needs to *operationalize* them, that is, identify specific behaviors which could provide acceptable evidence for describing them. These behaviors are those recognized by current theories in the field of applied linguistics and other related disciplines as realizing the abstract variables, and this justifies accepting them as the data of the study.

Let us consider the hypothetical example of a research project in which the variable 'language proficiency' needs to be investigated. The researcher will first need to *operationalize* this abstract variable as defined above, in order to determine what will constitute relevant data. The behaviors identified for this purpose will then serve as appropriate pieces of evidence for the existence, or lack of, language proficiency. Such behaviors may include ability to pronounce words correctly, and to speak the language with a certain degree of fluency, possession of certain vocabulary, use of the appropriate register in a conversation with native speakers of a given status, mastery of specific grammatical structures, or any other behavior considered to be compatible with the current theories on language proficiency. Any of these behaviors, when elicited by means of a variety of data collection procedures, will be considered as the data of the study, since each provides an indication of language proficiency. Clearly, the behaviors considered appropriate evidence of language proficiency nowadays will be different from those considered appropriate twenty years ago, when there were different theories about language proficiency.

Let us consider another hypothetical example of a research study where the abstract variable 'teacher effectiveness' needs to be studied. Here, too, the first stage is to operationalize the variable by identifying specific behaviors which exemplify the variable, based on current theories of what an effective teacher is. These may suggest that an effective teacher is one who has knowledge of the subject matter, is familiar with the latest teaching methods and pedagogy, and has a good relationship with students. These behaviors will be considered the data of the study. The assumptions at this point are that an effective teacher is one who possesses those behaviors, while an ineffective teacher is one who lacks them. The behaviors can be investigated by means of a variety of data collection procedures such as questionnaires, tests, and observations which will be described in the next section of this chapter.

The two examples just given show that determining what constitute data involves a number of steps. The first is to arrive at a precise and clear definition of the variables which need to be investigated in a given research study. This is done through operationalizing the variables by identifying a set of behaviors associated with them according to current theory. The data collected through the assessment of those behaviors occur in a variety of forms, such as test scores, descriptions, conversations, answers to questionnaires, interviews, verbal descriptions, or observations of language behaviors in a classroom.

Procedures for collecting the data

Once the researcher has decided *what* data to collect, the next step is to decide *how* to collect them. At this point the researcher will select the appropriate data collection procedure(s) from a large pool of available procedures. Certain types of procedures are more suitable for certain types of data, but similar types of data can often lend themselves to a variety of procedures.

Thus, if the behavior selected by the researcher as indicative of language proficiency is 'ability to pronounce words accurately', then the researcher needs to search for appropriate procedures to study that ability. If specific phonemes have been defined, the researcher may collect data through a *test* where the subject is required to pronounce these while being recorded in a language laboratory. Alternatively, if the researcher wants to collect data in the form of the subject's pronunciation in a natural conversation, the subject's speech in that natural setting may be *observed* and recorded. In addition to the two procedures just mentioned, other data collection procedures, such as *questionnaires* (where learners are asked to assess their own proficiency), or *interviews* (where learners are asked to assess the proficiency of their peers), can be applied as well. Similarly in the case of teacher effectiveness, data about the relationship between teachers and students can be collected through interviews (with teachers and students), questionnaires (administered to both), or observations (of actual behaviors of students and teachers during class time). Data about the teacher's knowledge of the subject matter and of current teaching methods can be collected by means of a test and/or observations (of actual lessons). It is also possible, at times, to use *multiple* procedures in one study and thus to obtain data from a variety of sources simultaneously.

We will now consider the criteria for the selection of data collection procedures. These criteria are based on the different types of research designs described in earlier chapters.

Criteria for selection

In discussing the criteria for selecting particular data collection procedures, we will refer back to Chapter 2 and to parameter 4, 'Data and data collection'. We stated there that this parameter can be viewed as a manifestation of the relationship between the conceptual and operational levels of the research. Thus, the approach, objective, and design of the research can be expressed both in *what* will be regarded as data and *how* the data will be collected and analyzed. Accordingly, the procedures used to collect the data will often depend on whether the research is synthetic or heuristic, analytic or deductive, since the type of data is usually related to the design of the research and the nature of the research problem.

The data collection parameter

The main feature of parameter 4 is the *degree of explicitness* of the data collection procedure. This can be viewed on a continuum. At one end of the continuum we often find data collection procedures which are broad and general and do not focus on particular types of data, while at the other end we tend to find procedures which are more explicit and structured and usually determined in advance. The broad and general procedures can be considered to be of a *low* degree of explicitness, while the structured procedures can be considered of a high degree of explicitness. Figure 8.1 illustrates the continuum of the data collection parameter according to the degree of explicitness.

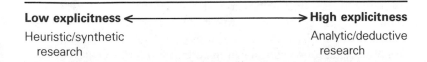

Figure 8.1   Parameter 4: A continuum representing the degrees of explicitness of the data collection procedures

Collecting data by procedures of a *low* degree of explicitness is often done by means of open and informal procedures which tend to be used simultaneously. Typical of such data collection procedures are field notes, records, diaries, observations, and open, informal interviews or conversations with the subjects. These types of data collection procedures are to be found mostly in heuristic/synthetic type of research (described in Chapter 6), which focuses on understanding a phenomenon within the interactive framework of the environment where it occurs, without isolating variables from the general context and without making precise pre-data-collection decisions.

Collecting data by means of procedures of a *high* degree of explicitness involves the use of 'formal' and structured types of data collection procedures which determine in advance the specific focus of the data that will be sought. Examples of such procedures are structured questionnaires, discrete point tests, formal interviews, and metalinguistic judgment tests. In all of these procedures, the subject is constrained to respond to specific questions or stimuli determined in advance, often with little or no elaboration. These types of procedures are typically used in studies of the analytic or deductive type (described in Chapter 7), where the researcher usually has a specific hypothesis or research question, and where the data to be elicited can be determined in advance.

Thus, the use of procedures of high or low degrees of explicitness will usually, though not always, depend on the design of the study. A point worth noting is that the same type of data collection procedure may vary in its degrees of explicitness; sometimes it may be of a high degree of explicitness and at other times it may be of a low degree of explicitness. For example, an interview can sometimes be open (of a low degree of explicitness), when the researcher uses general and broad questions and does not determine in advance the exact and specific questions of the interview. An interview in a different type of research may be more structured (of a higher degree of explicitness), when used in an experimental study, for example. In that type of research the interview will consist of pre-determined and specific questions and the subjects will be required to answer in a specific way.

Similarly, an observation can in certain types of research designs be of a low level of explicitness; the researcher observes and records everything that is taking place in a research setting without deciding in advance what to focus on. On the other hand there can be structured observations which observers make with the aid of instruments such as checklists, which guide the observer to the exact behaviors which are to be observed and recorded. It is also possible, at times, to use a number of different data collection procedures in a given study and thus to obtain data from a variety of sources (Denzin 1978 and Mathison 1988).

The reader should be aware here of the current debate, described in detail in Chapter 6, and discussed at length by Firestone (1987) and others, on the relationship between the data collection procedures and the research paradigm. A distinction is made between, on the one hand, researchers who are viewed as 'purists', in that they claim that qualitative and quantitative methods are incompatible because they are based on paradigms that make different assumptions about the world and about what constitute data, and on the other hand those who are viewed as 'pragmatists', for whom methods are just a collection of techniques, and have no such paradigm implications. 'Pragmatists' would claim that in principle all data collection procedures are legitimate for almost all research designs (qualitative, correlational, experimental, and so on), but that some data collection procedures are more *typical* of one design than of another.

We will now proceed to describe a number of commonly used procedures for collecting second language acquisition data. The next section will discuss specific criteria for assuring the quality of the procedures, followed by guidelines for developing, adapting, and using such procedures.

Description of data collection procedures

In this section we will describe a variety of procedures which the second language acquisition researcher can use to collect the research data. The procedures will be described according to the framework of the data collection parameter just discussed. In Figure 8.2 we list the procedures which will be discussed in this section. They are shown on a continuum: on the left hand, we list those of a low degree of explicitness (more typical of the heuristic/synthetic type of research) while those of a higher degree of explicitness (more typical of the analytic/deductive type of research) are shown on the right hand side of the continuum. Some procedures are placed in between the two points, since they share features of both types of research.

We will begin by describing procedures of low explicitness and proceed along the continuum toward procedures of high explicitness.

Low explicitness		High explicitness
←		→
Heuristic		Deductive
Diaries		Metalinguistic tests
Record reviews	Structured interviews	
Journals		
Letters	Semi-structured questionnaires	
		Grammatical judgments
Unstructured interviews		Structured
Conversations		questionnaires
Open observations		Structured observations
		Discrete point tests

Figure 8.2   Examples of data collection procedures typical of research types

Procedures for collecting data in qualitative research

In qualitative types of research (heuristic/synthetic, described in Chapter 6), where a phenomenon is studied within a natural context, data are often collected by means of a number of procedures used simultaneously, with one piece of data leading to the next.

Example

A researcher is interested in finding out how a number of immigrants acquire the language of the country where they reside. She *interviews* a number of learners and asks them to *report* on their experiences and to reflect on the processes that help them learn the language. She also *observes* the immigrants using the language as they interact with colleagues at work and with spouses and children at home. In addition, she *reviews records* which are believed to provide further insights about their language learning processes. These records include letters they write in the target language, notes and reports they write at work, as well as their grades and papers in the language classes in which they are enrolled during the time they are acquiring the language. She also *reviews* a diary of one of the learners which describes the process and problems of learning the language and some experiences he had as an immigrant in the first few months of arriving in the new country.

In the example above, the researcher uses a variety of data collection procedures for collecting data about the process of second language learning by immigrants. All these procedures may be considered of a low degree of explicitness since the aspects and data to be collected by the procedures are not specified beforehand. The researcher does not determine in advance the exact data that will be sought, and may even have only a rough idea of the procedures that will be used, since it is not known whether those data even exist. By using a variety of procedures and by obtaining data from a variety of sources the researcher often obtains rich and comprehensive data. Such data usually provide an expanded and global picture of the phenomenon, as each source provides additional data.

Smith (1987) states that in this approach, data are often collected inventively by data collection procedures tailored to the situation and played off against each other. So there is no real catalogue of 'certified' methods; a variety of procedures are recognized as legitimate.

Some of the typical devices and procedures used for collecting data in this type of research are interviewing informants, compiling biodata about them, administering open questionnaires, eliciting ratings and rankings, and using various unobtrusive measures such as studying students' notebooks, handouts given by the teachers, and official documents.

Short descriptions of some examples of such data collection methods now follow. Most of these procedures are described more extensively in later sections of this chapter.

Interviews. A variety of interview types are used in second language acquisition research. However, in qualitative research the most typical interviews are those which are open, informal, and unstructured. These interviews can take many directions, according to the information being sought by the interviewers and the responses provided by the subjects. The responses often include extensive elaboration and expansion; such an interview may resemble a conversation rather than an interview. So as not to make the subjects conscious of the fact that they are taking part in a research study, they may not always be made aware that any information is being obtained from them or that they are being asked to respond to certain questions. (See the section on open interviews later in the chapter.)

Open observations. Observations are very common in qualitative research, in which the researcher usually observes a number of behaviors taking place simultaneously, often without determining in advance the particular aspects that will be observed. The observation is performed either by a participant observer, who becomes an integral part of the observed situation as one of the subjects without the other participants being aware of the fact, or by a non-participant observer who records in detail as an outsider, all the behaviors which take place. (See also the discussion of participant and non-participant observation in Chapter 6, and the section on unstructured/open observations later in the chapter.)

Record reviews. This, another commonly used procedure in qualitative research, involves collecting data from documents and other materials, the content of which is reviewed and analyzed by a process known as content analysis. Examples of such records and documents are records of meetings, report cards, letters, notebooks, historical records, documents, correspondence, tests, papers, and teachers' comments.

Diaries. The subjects or the researcher record in writing, different aspects of a process or a phenomenon. Diaries have been used in a number of second language acquisition studies, especially to collect data on subjects' experiences as students or as teachers of a second language (Bailey 1983, Schumann and Schumann 1977).

The type of data obtained from the above procedures can take a variety of forms: verbal descriptions when the data is based on notes taken by the researcher, tapes (audio or visual), or even simply 'impressions' or 'anecdotes', which the researcher carries away and may record later. Often data of this type need to be transformed so that they become more manageable. For example, audio or visual tapes are often transcribed or described in a summary form. When the researcher transcribes the data, everything that is being said is written down verbatim. Transcriptions may, however, exclude information such as the speaker's accent, intonation, stress, or other non-verbal elements which may be relevant to the understanding of the phenomenon under study. Ways of analyzing such data are discussed in Chapter 9.

We turn now to other procedures for collecting second language acquisition data, moving along the explicitness continuum.

Observations

We have already briefly mentioned observations in the previous section as one of a family of procedures used to collect data in qualitative research. In this section, we will describe a variety of observation types ranging from low to high degrees of explicitness.

Observations have always been considered a major data collection tool in qualitative research. Recently, however, the more structured types of observations have also been used for collecting data in quantitative studies. In second language acquisition research, observations are most often used to collect data on how learners use language in a variety of settings, to study language learning and teaching processes in the classroom, and to study teachers' and students' behaviors.

The main use of observations is for examining a phenomenon or a behavior while it is going on. Observations can be made in many situations. A researcher who collects observational data on code switching, for example, may observe how learners use language at home, at work, at school, or in the classroom.

The main advantages of using observations for collecting data are that they allow the study of a phenomenon at close range with many of the contextual variables present, a feature which is very important in studying language behaviors. However, this advantage may become a disadvantage when the closeness introduces biases which may affect the researcher's objectivity; in addition, the presence of the observer in the research situation may alter the behavior of the subjects observed, as discussed in Chapter 6.

Observations can be made by insiders who are part of the group observed, by participant observers, or by outsiders. They can focus on a single subject, on a number of subjects, or on a whole group (a whole class, for example). They can last one session, a number of sessions, or be made at intervals, such as every three seconds, for example.

Observations can also vary in their degree of explicitness. Those of a high degree of explicitness are 'structured' observations, in which the researcher has determined in advance what to look for in the observed context. Those of a low degree of explicitness are 'unstructured' or 'open' observations, in which the data being recorded are broad and more general. In structured observations, the researcher will utilize tools which specify in exact terms what the observer should focus on, and the specific data that should be gathered. *Interaction analysis* is an example of observation made with a high degree of explicitness. The researcher observes what takes place in the classroom with the aid of an instrument which standardizes *both* the observer's data collection procedure *and* the focus of the observation. This instrument defines *a priori* the focus of the observation. A large number of such instruments have been developed over the years by different researchers for a variety of aspects of classroom research (Flanders 1970, Fanselow 1977, Bialystok 1979, Allwright 1983). These instruments consist of lists of behaviors for trained observers to look for and record, often in the form of tallies or numbers. The records are compiled either while observing the lesson, or by working from video, audio recordings, or written transcriptions. *Checklists* of the kind illustrated below require the observer to check whether a specific behavior is present or absent. *Numerical scales* and *rating scales* are additional examples of other types of tools which help the observer to rate and quantify the observed behaviors or phenomena.

Examples

A Checklists

Observed behavior: Student's activities in the language classroom.

Task: Check whether or not the student performed the following:

	yes	no
1 Asked for translation of unknown words	____	___
2 Used L1 in conversation with teacher	____	___
3 Used L2 in conversation with teacher	____	___
4 Used L2 in conversation with peers	____	___
5 Referred to textbook/dictionary for unknown words	____	___
6 Asked for grammatical explanations	____	___

B Numerical scale

Observed behavior: Students' use of L2 in asking questions

Task: How often does each student ask a question in L2?

Always_____; Usually_____; Sometimes_____; Never_____

C Rating scale

Observed behavior: Students' involvement in a specific classroom task.

Task: Please mark how involved students are:

Very involved   1   2   3   4   5   Not very involved

In the other group of observations (those of a low level of explicitness), observations are more open, and data gathered may vary during the course of the observation as a reflection of the observer's developing understanding of what is being observed. These types of observations will require the observer to describe the observed scene in more general terms and in an impressionistic manner as in examples D, E, and F that follow.

D Open observations (1)

Observed behavior: Students' involvement in the language class.

Task: Describe the level of involvement of three students in the language class activities.

_____

_____

_____

E Open observations (2)

Observed behavior: Teacher's and students' use of L1 in an L2 class.

Task: Describe the type and amount of language used by the teacher and by the students during a groupwork activity.

_____

_____

_____

_____

F Follow two students during class time and during the intermission (while they play in the school yard) and describe the type of language they use.

_____

_____

_____

_____

Data obtained from more structured observations will be in the form of checks, tallies, frequencies, and ratings, while data obtained from the open observations will be in the form of impressions, field notes, tapes, or transcripts. Impressions often have no records, and this may create a problem if it is necessary to return to the data.

Notes provide records, but depend on the opportunity and ability of the observer to record accurately what is observed. In addition, the presence of the observer may alter the subjects' behavior. Audio tapes can not only be intrusive; they are limited to capturing the vocal aspect of verbal interaction, and may vary in recording quality. Video tapes provide more elaborate data, although they are also dependent on the capability of the camera and what it focuses on; they may also be even more intrusive than audio tapes. Transcriptions, which are a way of converting oral data into a written form, usually screen out significant contextual elements which are an integral part of oral interaction in the observed scene. The researcher therefore needs to determine the best method for recording the observed data, and that will depend to a large extent on the purpose, goal, and design of the research. However, for all types of observations it is recommended that observers be trained in observational techniques such as note-taking and recording. Training can significantly increase the accuracy and validity of the data collected.

The use of observation as a data collection procedure has been gaining increased attention with the recent emphasis on classroom research. The reader is advised to refer to the article 'Inside the black box' (Long 1980), for an extensive review of a classification of observational procedures used in classroom research. In that article Long classifies observational procedures according to features such as the recording procedures used, the types and categories of items observed, the coding options, the level of cognitive activity, and the unit of analysis. He contends that the most problematic feature of the structured type of observation instruments is their validity, that is, the strength of the theoretical claims upon which they are based.

It is suggested that a variety of observational procedures for different aspects of classroom research could be employed simultaneously, some being of the more structured type, such as interactional analysis, and others of a more open nature. Each observational procedure addresses different aspects in the classroom, so each complements the other. Thus together they provide a more comprehensive picture of what takes place in the language learning classroom or in other research settings under observation. (See Allwright (1988) for an extensive and detailed description of the use of observations as research tools in the language classroom.)

Example

A researcher (Bejarano 1987) compared the effect of three teaching methods on achievement in EFL. In order to examine whether the teachers of each of the methods actually implemented them correctly, observations were conducted by three observers. They were first trained in methods of observation with videotapes and in classrooms, until close agreement was obtained among the different observers. The real observations were conducted by three observers visiting every class twice during the experimental period using a 20-item observation schedule. Ratings were recorded every 15 seconds for a 7-minute period at the beginning, middle, and end of a classroom session. In addition, the observers were asked to write an impressionistic report of whatever they could detect in the classes concerning students' behaviors while they were carrying out the various activities.

In the above example the researcher was using observations in order to verify that the methods of teaching were being implemented correctly. While these observations were conducted with structured observational instruments which specified exactly what to look for in the observed situation, they were also supplemented by unstructured, open observations, in which the observers reported on everything that took place in the classroom.

Interviews

The purpose of the interview is to obtain information by actually talking to the subject. The interviewer asks questions and the subject responds either in a face-to-face situation or by telephone. Interviews are personalized and therefore permit a level of in-depth information-gathering, free response, and flexibility that cannot be obtained by other procedures. The interviewer can probe for information and obtain data that often have not been foreseen. Much of the information obtained during an open/unstructured interview is incidental and comes out as the interview proceeds. There are disadvantages, however. Interviews can be costly, time-consuming, and often difficult to administer. They depend on good interviewing skills that might require extensive training. They may introduce elements of subjectivity and personal bias, and rapport may cause the interviewee to respond in a certain way to please the interviewer.

In second language acquisition research, interviews are used to collect data on covert variables such as attitudes (toward the target language, or the ethnic group whose language is being learned) and motivation for learning the second language. They can be used as tests for obtaining information about learners' language proficiency. They have also been used recently for obtaining information about strategies which language learners use in the process of producing and acquiring language in a variety of contexts. In these types of studies the language learner is asked to report verbally on the cognitive strategies and processes used in producing different features of language. A detailed description of these procedures, known as *verbal reports*, is provided in the next section.

Interviews can be differentiated by their degree of explicitness and structure, ranging from very open interviews to very structured ones. 'Open' interviews provide the interviewee with broad freedom of expression and elaboration and often resemble informal talks. They allow greater depth, and one question leads to another without a pre-planned agenda of what will be asked. There is usually a topic for the interview but, by allowing the respondent maximum freedom of expression, ample and often unexpected information emerges. This kind of information probably could not be obtained if the interview was more structured. This type of interview is therefore used mostly in qualitative and descriptive studies.

In 'semi-open' interviews there are specific core questions determined in advance from which the interviewer branches off to explore in-depth information, probing according to the way the interview proceeds, and allowing elaboration, within limits. The 'semi-structured' interview consists of specific and defined questions determined beforehand, but at the same time it allows some elaboration in the questions and answers. The 'structured' interview consists of questions defined from the start and presented to the interviewee. No elaboration is allowed in either the questions or the answers. This type of interview is usually employed when uniform and specific information is needed and when it is necessary to interview a large number of subjects.

In administering semi-structured and structured interviews, the interviewer will use an *interview schedule* which lists the questions to be asked or the topics to be discussed, and provides space to record the information produced during the interview. For more open interviews, the interviewer may at times supplement the interview with audio or video taping, or may take notes of the main points.

Below are a number of examples of questions used in interviews of different degrees of explicitness.

Examples

a) Which of the following best describes your level of proficiency in the second language?

1 a new immigrant_____
2 native_____
3 residence of 10 years or more_____
4 residence of less than 10 years_____

b) While reading a second language text and encountering an unknown word, do you:

1 turn to a dictionary? yes/no
2 ask the teacher for its meaning? yes/no
3 not worry about it and just go on? yes/no

c) What do you think of the people whose language you are now learning?

(This open question can be followed by probes as to the reasons the subject feels that way: Where do these feelings originate? How are they expressed in the classroom situation? Do these feelings transfer to the learning of the language?)

d) What do you do when you encounter a word you do not know?

(This can be followed by questions such as: Why? Where? How come? It can also be followed by tasks such as: Let's read a text together, and show me how you do these things. Do you do it with all types of texts? How often does it occur?)

e) Please describe orally what you do when you are presented with this text and need to comprehend its content.

(This can also be done in a more structured way when the researcher provides the learners with a number of strategies that students usually use in a similar situation, and asks the interviewees whether they use them, as in the example below.)

f) When answering this test question, what did you do? 1) Did you refer back to the text? 2) Did you guess the answer? 3) Did you answer it based on your previous knowledge about the subject?

The nature of the interview will determine the type of data obtained. Specifically, more structured interviews will elicit brief and concise data in the form of checks, marks, and short responses, while open interviews will elicit generally more elaborated data in the form of impressions, descriptions, and narratives obtained from interviews.

The procedures for analyzing the data will depend on 'the type of data obtained, so that descriptive and narrative data will be analyzed by looking for patterns and categories within the data, while data obtained from structured interviews will be analyzed with the aid of statistics. Both types of analysis will be discussed in Chapter 9.

Interviews are becoming very useful in second language acquisition research. An important element in obtaining data in interviews is the training of interviewers in effective interviewing strategies and techniques. Such training can increase the probability of obtaining significant data from an interview. Other ways of assuring the quality of interviews are discussed later in the chapter.

Verbal reporting

The use of the interview as a data collection procedure in second language acquisition research has increased recently with the growing emphasis on collecting data about linguistic and cognitive aspects involved in processing language. *Verbal reporting* refers to a set of data collection procedures in which research subjects report orally to the researcher on the processes they are engaged in while performing a cognitive or linguistic task (Cohen and Hosenfeld 1981, Mann 1983). The assumption underlying the procedure is that learners can provide insightful information on how they learn and function in the second language.

Verbal reporting has been used in a number of second language acquisition studies. Brown (1983) collected verbal reports on how experts formulate written summaries of reading texts. Mann (1983) elicited subjects' self-reports in order to identify problems in reading in L1, and readers' attempts to solve them. Olshavsky (1977) investigated reading strategies by obtaining verbal reports from readers. A recent edited collection (Faerch and Kasper 1987) contains a number of research studies which utilize a variety of verbal reporting procedures for various types of second language learning problems.

There are three main techniques for eliciting verbal reports:

Thinking aloud involves externalizing the content of the mind while engaged in a particular task without inferring mental processes. In that method subjects are told to say aloud everything they think and everything that occurs to them while performing the task, no matter how trivial it may seem (Hayes and Flower 1980).

Introspection requires the subjects to observe the workings of their minds when involved in a particular task, and report on them as they occur.

Retrospection probes the subjects for information after completion of the task. This requires the subjects to infer their own mental processes or strategies from their memory of the particular mental event under observation. (For a more detailed description of these techniques, see Ericsson and Simon 1980, Cohen and Hosenfeld 1981, Garner 1987, Faerch and Kasper 1987.)

The 'think aloud' procedure is believed to yield rich data, since it elicits information which is kept in short term memory and is thereby directly accessible for further processing and verbalization. The other methods cannot always be relied on to produce data stemming directly from subject's actual experience or thought processes.

It is important that researchers become aware of some of the problems associated with the different types of verbal reporting. For example, the subjects may infer a process, not as a direct reflection of the activity recently engaged in, but rather from prior knowledge or experience of a similar activity on a previous occasion. There are also social or psychological factors which result from the interaction between the experimenter and the subject, the subject's willingness to cooperate, and the experimental setting itself. Again, there may be subjects who are not accustomed to carrying out 'think aloud' tasks and who may find it difficult to perform two tasks simultaneously, and thus fail to verbalize important information. Another problem is that in an effort to please the experimenter the subjects may over-compensate and provide information they feel the researcher is hoping to obtain but which does not really reflect their true mental states. The researcher's hope of obtaining certain data may also indirectly bias the subjects' behavior. There are doubts, therefore, about the reliability and validity of the data obtained from verbal reporting procedures. (The concepts of reliability and validity are discussed later in this chapter.) Garner (1987) points to situations where insufficient data are obtained and it is not possible to know whether this is a result of limited cognition, limited language skill, or some combination of these factors. The method may also be difficult to use with young children. Finally, there is the possible effect of the task of verbalization itself: the need for additional verbal processing may interfere with the processing that is being commented on.

In order to counteract some of these problems, researchers collect secondary data through questionnaires, or written responses to questions to corroborate the primary data and to obtain some indication of either intra- or inter-rater reliability. Some of the problems can also be minimized by training the research subjects to use the procedures.

We will conclude this section by providing a number of suggestions on how to collect 'think aloud' data:

– A preparatory meeting should be held with each of the subjects to prepare them for the session, to acquaint the researcher with the subjects, to explain the purpose of the study, and to illustrate the task they are about to engage in, and thus allow practice.

– Subjects go through the task and are asked to verbalize their thoughts while doing so. They are encouraged to point out any difficulties they encounter in comprehending the text or questions and to express verbally any confusion or uncertainty they experience when reading. Subjects who feel they cannot verbalize the processes are not forced to do so.

– Each of the subjects is interviewed individually, usually in the L1, and the interviews are recorded. Subjects are not given a time limit in which to complete the task and there is as little intervention on the part of the researcher as possible. When a long pause in verbalization occurs, the researcher probes to elicit information with a question such as 'What are you thinking about now?' or 'What are you deliberating about?'

– During the session the researcher occasionally notes down the subject's overt behavior (referring back to the text, underlining words).

– The tapes are later transcribed and analyzed using the 'protocol analysis' procedure, which is described in Chapter 9.

In conclusion, while verbal reporting procedures may be valuable for retrieving and eliciting certain types of data, they may also raise doubts as to whether the data elicited are a true reflection of the actual processes which occur in the mind of the learner. In spite of their recent popularity in second language research, verbal reports should be interpreted with caution or, as Meichenbaum (1980) noted, used mainly to provide clues to the underlying processes.

Questionnaires

Questionnaires are *printed* forms for data collection, which include questions or statements to which the subject is expected to respond, often anonymously. They do not differ greatly from interviews in that both require subjects to provide information in response to a stimulus provided by the researcher and they are, in fact, often used in combination. In questionnaires the answers are usually expressed in a written form, whereas in interviews they are oral. In second language acquisition research, questionnaires are used mostly to collect data on phenomena which are not easily observed, such as attitudes, motivation, and self-concepts. They are also used to collect data on the processes involved in using language and to obtain background information about the research subjects, such as age, previous background in language learning, number of languages spoken, and years of studying the language.

Questionnaires have a number of advantages: a) They are self-administered and can be given to large groups of subjects at the same time. They are therefore less expensive to administer than other procedures such as interviews. b) When anonymity is assured, subjects tend to share information of a sensitive nature more easily. c) Since the same questionnaire is given to all subjects, the data are more uniform and standard. d) Since they are usually given to all subjects of the research at exactly the same time, the data are more accurate.

However, one of the main problems with questionnaires is the relatively low response rate (especially with mailed questionnaires), which poses questions about the reasons why certain subjects respond and others do not. A low return rate may therefore influence the validity of the findings. Another problem with questionnaires is that they are not appropriate for subjects who cannot read and write. This is especially relevant to research in second language, as subjects very often have problems reading and providing answers in L2. Thus there is no assurance that the questions used in a questionnaire have been properly understood by the subjects and answered correctly.

As with observations and interviews, questionnaires can also vary in their degree of explicitness. Unstructured questionnaires, those with a low degree of explicitness, will include open questions to which the subject will be expected to respond in a descriptive manner. Those of a high degree of explicitness, the structured questionnaires, may require the subject to mark responses, to check agreements or disagreements, or to select among a number of alternatives. Structured questionnaires are considered to be more efficient than open ones, and can also be scored by machine. It is possible to use different types of questions, open and closed, in the same questionnaire.

The type of data obtained from questionnaires will vary according to the degree of structure of the procedures used; open questionnaires will elicit data of a more descriptive and open nature, such as essays or narratives. Structured questionnaires will elicit data in the form of checks, numbers, or rankings.

In developing questionnaires, especially those of a low level of explicitness, there is a need to include a *number* of questions, since a single question is meaningless. Moreover, questionnaires will often include a number of *scales*. Each scale is capable of eliciting data on a certain aspect of the behavior which needs to be measured, and each scale includes a number of questions. For example, in developing a questionnaire to collect data about 'attitudes toward learning the language', the researcher is likely to have a number of scales, such as 'attitudes toward learning the language in school', 'toward the people speaking the language', 'toward the teacher', 'toward the learning material and content', and so on. Each scale will consist of a number of questions. The score of 'attitude toward learning the language' will be based on all the scales combined.

It is important to stress that before using any questionnaire it is necessary to try it out and examine whether all the questions on the scales and all the scales provide an actual indication of the variable. Trying out or field-testing the questionnaire *before* using it in the real study is also important in order to obtain information about the relevancy and clarity of the questions, the format, and the amount of time required to answer the questions, so that the questionnaire can be revised if necessary. This process will significantly improve the quality of the data obtained.

A number of techniques are used to collect data through questionnaires. The *Likert scale* (Likert 1932) asks individuals to respond to a series of statements by indicating whether they 'strongly agree' (SA), 'agree' (A), 'are undecided' (U), 'disagree' (D), and 'strongly disagree' (SD) with each statement. 'Strongly agree' may be assigned a weight of 5 points, while 'strongly disagree' may get a score of 1. Thus, in an attitude questionnaire, for example, favorable attitudes are reflected in higher scores, as is shown in example A below.

Another procedure, the *semantic differential* (Osgood, Suci, and Tannenbaum 1975), requires the subjects to give a rating to the subject of the attitude scale on a number of bipolar adjectives such as good/bad; high/low; active/passive; positive/negative. The respondents indicate the point on the continuum between the extremes that represent their attitude. Based on their research, the developers of this approach reported that most adjective pairs represent one of three dimensions which they labeled 'evaluative' (good/bad), 'potency' (strong/weak), and 'activity' (active/passive). Each position on a continuum has an associated score value; by totalling score values for all items, it can be determined whether the respondents' attitudes are positive or negative. Semantic differential scales usually have 5 to 7 intervals with a neutral attitude being assigned a score of 0 as in example B below.

Below are examples of different types of items or questions on questionnaires. Examples A, B, and G are of structured questions; examples C, D, E, and F are of open types of questions and example H is of questions used for obtaining background information about the subjects.

Examples

A Data collected about attitude toward the study of a second language.

Instructions: Mark with 'X' the extent to which you agree with each of the statements:

1 In using the foreign language in conversation, I feel:*

	1 Strongly disagree	2 disagree	3 agree	4 strongly agree
Hesitant				
Comfortable				
Confident				
Talkative				
Cooperative				

2 Learning the grammar structures is:

Difficult				
Challenging				
Boring				
Important				

3 When meeting speakers of the language I:

	Always	Sometimes	Rarely	Never
Try to avoid conversations	_____	_____	____	__
Tend to switch to my native language	_____	_____	____	__
Ask questions for clarification	_____	_____	____	__

B Semantic differentials (measuring attitudes toward the language class).
Instructions: Mark an 'X' at the place that best reflects your attitude:

Learning French is:

Good	_____	Bad
Worthless	_____	Valuable
Strong	_____	Weak
Unpleasant	_____	Pleasant
Relaxed	_____	Tensed

(-3) (-2) (-1) (0) $(+1)$ $(+2)$ $(+3)$

* Note that in this example there is an even number of choices (4). This forces the subject to make a choice regarding the direction of the attitude. It is also possible to give an odd number of choices (3, 5, 7).

C Comment in a sentence or two on your feelings about studying the language.

_____

_____

_____

D What is the best thing about your language class? (attitude toward the language)

_____

_____

_____

E What is the thing you like best about this language?

_____

_____

_____

F Describe your feeling when using the foreign language in conversation with native speakers.

_____

_____

_____

G Describe the steps you take when reading a text during a test. What are the steps you use when you read the same text in your own time?

_____

_____

_____

H Background information

1 Where do you live?_____

2 Where were you born?_____

3 What languages do you speak at home?_____

4 When?_____ With whom?_____ For how long?_____

5 Do you wish you spoke more languages?

6 What do you do after school in order to improve your language? (check 'yes' or 'no')
— read newspapers? YES/NO
— talk on the phone to native speakers? YES/NO
— watch TV? YES/NO
— read books in the language? YES/NO

Tests

A test is a procedure used to collect data on subjects' ability or knowledge of certain disciplines. In second language acquisition research, tests are generally used to collect data about the subject's ability in and knowledge of the second language in areas such as vocabulary, grammar, reading, metalinguistic awareness, and general proficiency. We will therefore focus in this section on testing procedures which can be used to investigate knowledge of the second language. Collecting valid language data is a complex and controversial issue since it relates to the problem of: 'What does it mean to know a language?' We will discuss some of these issues in the next section.

As with the other data collection procedures discussed in this chapter, tests also vary in their degree of explicitness. Tests with a high level of explicitness employ a variety of structured techniques to *elicit* language data while tests of low explicitness collect/record/gather language which is produced *spontaneously*, often without the subjects being aware that their language is being assessed.

For high explicitness tests, the researcher will use elicitation techniques in which subjects are required to answer predetermined questions, to select among a number of alternatives based on a given text, or to fill in blanks, for example. The low explicitness tests will assess spontaneous language by the researcher observing the research subjects interacting with native speakers in social situations or by reviewing notes or letters which the subjects have written.

The type of language data which will be collected by these different tests will also vary. Tests of high explicitness will often yield more isolated and discrete types of language, such as short sentences, structures, or lexical items, while tests of low explicitness will yield more holistic, descriptive, and integrative language data in the form of continuous discourse, protocols, essays, speeches, and conversations.

Between these two types of tests, there are tests of varying degrees of explicitness. For example, at the low explicitness end of the scale, there are tests in which the researcher creates an elicitation task with the intention of eliciting certain aspects or factors of language, but the subject is not aware of *what* aspects are being elicited. Or the researcher can set up situations where specific language elements will be elicited within a spontaneous and more natural context, referred to as an *obligatory context*. For example, a researcher who is interested in eliciting the use of specific structures in the past tense can create a task in which the subjects will talk about their past experiences and thus will have to use the past tense forms in a pseudo-spontaneous context. There can also be tests of high explicitness and low explicitness which elicit more elaborate and integrative language, such as when the task, determined *a priori*, is to produce a writing sample, give a talk, or respond to a true/false question in a reading comprehension test which relates to the text as a whole and not to isolated language elements.

Below, we will describe a number of examples of testing techniques used for collecting language data. We will begin with those of high explicitness, and move along the continuum toward those of low explicitness.

Judgment test. This is an elicitation technique where the test-taker is presented with correct and incorrect language items and is expected to decide whether they are acceptable or not. This procedure is widely used to test the metalinguistic ability of learners. This ability is believed to indicate competence in the language. Judgment tests can also be used with full discourse.

Multiple choice. This technique requires the test-taker to *select* a correct answer from a number of alternatives, usually based on a text or other stimulus that precedes it. It is used to test reading, listening, grammar, vocabulary, and writing.

True/false. This procedure requires the test-taker to determine whether a statement is correct or incorrect. It is often based on a text or an oral stimulus and is usually used for testing grammar, vocabulary, reading, listening, or metalinguistics, as in the judgment tests mentioned above.

Elicited imitation. The test-taker is presented with an oral or reading stimulus and is expected to repeat it, or read it aloud. It is used for testing pronunciation and comprehension.

Cloze. The subject is presented with a written (or oral) text from which a number of words (or letters, clauses, or sentences) have been deleted. The subject is expected to fill in the missing parts. It is used for testing reading, writing, and overall language proficiency.

Completions. The subject is presented with partial oral or written questions, and is expected to complete them orally or in writing. This procedure is used to test aspects such as reading strategies, writing, vocabulary, grammar, and so on.

Translation. In this technique the subject is presented with an oral or written stimulus and is expected to translate it verbatim into L1. It is used to assess aspects such as comprehension, written production, lexicon, grammar, transfer from L1 to L2, and so on.

Recall. After reading or listening to a stimulus the subjects are asked to write down or to report orally all that they can recall from the text, in L1 or in L2. It is a widely used tool for researching the process of reading and listening.

In addition to the above, other data collection procedures, which do not really look like 'tests', are often used to collect similar types of language data. In using these techniques, all of a low level of explicitness, the subjects are less aware of the fact that their language is being assessed and therefore concentrate more on the meaning than on the form. The *oral interview* is a technique used to collect data on the oral language of the subjects. In this procedure oral language is assessed in an interview in which the subject talks to the interviewer on a variety of topics. Information about the subject's pronunciation, fluency, use of language functions, and various other features of oral language use can all be assessed through the procedure. Similarly, the techniques of *role play* and simulation, in which the subject and the tester act out given roles, or imitate real life situations are effective procedures for collecting more natural language. Role play and other types of simulations are considered to be very effective procedures for collecting oral and written language data in research. Most subjects are able to participate effectively in role plays or simulations and thus produce more natural language samples. These can then be used for the assessment of oral features such as the use of speech acts, vocabulary, and pronunciation. *Observational* procedures also collect data about the subjects' use of language in a variety of real life situations without the subjects realizing that they are being assessed. *Reviewing documents* is yet another procedure by which the written language ability of the subjects is collected from various types of written documents, without an official test. The researcher may deduce facts about the subjects' writing ability from letters, notes to peers, homework, and so on.

The procedures which the researcher uses for analyzing the language obtained from the different techniques will depend on the type of data. Language obtained from tests which provide highly explicit data will generally be analyzed by totalling the correct or incorrect responses, and computing means and standard deviations. The language data obtained from the less explicit procedures can be analyzed impressionistically and holistically, often with the aid of *rating scales* which define different levels of language knowledge on scales such as from 1 to 5, 1 being equivalent to 'no proficiency' and 5 equivalent to 'native-like' proficiency. A rating scale can be used for holistic analysis as well as for a more analytic scrutiny of the language sample, focusing on specific aspects such as grammar, lexicon, cohesion, discourse, and fluency.

As with other data collection procedures, it is important to try out the tests before using them in the real study and to revise or omit items or questions which do not provide meaningful information. These issues are also discussed in the next section.

Standardized tests. Researchers often use ready-made tests developed by different agencies. These are referred to as *standardized tests.* They are developed by experts and are therefore considered to be well constructed. Individual test items are analyzed and revised until they meet given standards of quality. In such tests, directions for administering, scoring, and interpreting the scores are carefully specified. One characteristic of a standardized test is its objectivity. This means that the score a subject obtains does not differ with different scorers. Another major characteristic is the existence of reliability and validity information. As will be explained in the next section, reliability and validity are important features for determining the quality of the data collection procedure. Standardized tests also have certain conditions for administration and this ensures that the test is always administered in the same way and always provides the same kind of data. Standardized tests generally include directions for scoring and guidelines for interpretation of scores, that is, the acceptable criteria for correctness, number of points to be assigned to various responses, and ways of computing the total scores. In addition, performance on the test can be compared to the performance of a group called a normative group. Information about the normative group is contained in the manual accompanying the test. Often, standardized tests will be administered by testing agencies, as is the case with the TOEFL test (Test of English as a Foreign Language), which is administered and scored by the Educational Testing Service.

The best source for obtaining information about available tests is the *Buros Mental Measurements Yearbook* (Buros 1978). This yearbook has. been published in several editions and contains descriptions of more than one thousand commercially available tests. Each entry contains information such as a description of the test, the age and group for which it is intended, the number and area of subtests, details concerning answer sheets, scoring, and related costs, the time estimated for completing the test, the names of the test authors, and how it can be obtained. The book covers tests on a variety of subjects as well as batteries on achievement, personality, intelligence, and aptitude.

Considerations on the use of self-developed tests, standardized tests, or adapted tests are given later in the chapter. The reader is advised to refer to the bibliography in the Appendix for references on the development and use of tests. Some references are related to general testing, but others focus specifically on the construction and use of language tests.

In this part of the chapter we have discussed different procedures for collecting data in second language research. We began by describing specific procedures used in qualitative type of research, and continued through descriptions of observations, interviews, questionnaires, and different types of tests. It is important to note here that in an actual research study a researcher will often use a number of data collection procedures and will not rely on one procedure. This approach usually yields extensive, rich, and more valid type of data based on a variety of sources. (See a discussion on this issue in Denzin 1978, Jicks 1983, and Mathison 1988.) We shall now look at the relationship between data collection procedures and the *quality* of the language data obtained by these procedures.

Issues and problems in collecting language data

Tests are used to collect data about features of language. A number of problems arise, however, in the process of defining what are considered to be appropriate 'language' data, since language is known to be affected by a variety of contextual variables which may affect the reliability and validity of the data.

As was mentioned at the beginning of this chapter, in order to determine what are considered data, it is necessary first to define the variable or the feature that needs to be measured and then to select behaviors which will be indicative of the variable. Such definitions, it was noted, depend on current theories of language. Defining linguistic variables is clearly a complex and controversial issue which has direct implications for what will be considered valid language data.

In defining language data, the theory concerning the difference between *competence* (what the learner knows) and *performance* (what the learner is able to do) must be considered. Is all language performance by a second language learner indicative of underlying grammatical knowledge? In other words, is the distinction between competence and performance valid for second language acquisition? If it is valid, how will this be reflected in the manner in which data are collected? What can be considered valid language data in terms of this distinction? How will the procedures used to collect those language data affect the data obtained?

Tarone (1981) claims that interlanguage data consist of systematic and non-systematic elements, that language users and language learners do not process their knowledge of the language in the same way under all conditions, and that their performance varies as a product of the stylistic norm they are drawing on, which again depends on whether they are participating in planned or unplanned discourse. In second language acquisition research this variability is manifested in the type of task which the learner performs in supplying the researcher with data. Tarone claims that L2 learners can be observed to make different use of their interlanguage systems in different tasks. Thus, performance in one set of circumstances does not guarantee an identical or even similar performance in a different situation. There is considerable evidence in second language acquisition research to show that the nature of the task and situational factors such as where, when, and how language is assessed influence the kind of language that is obtained (Fillmore 1976, Schmidt 1977, Beebe 1980, and Dickerson 1975).

If the type of task and other contextual variables affect the language produced then how can second language acquisition language data be considered to be valid?

Tarone (1983) proposed a continuum which represents the effect of situational contexts on the interlanguage styles. At one end of the continuum is the vernacular style, which is summoned up when the learner is not paying particular attention to speech. This is the style that is both most natural and most systematic. At the other end of the continuum is the careful style, most clearly evident in tasks that require the learner to attend closely to speech, when making grammatical judgments, for example. Thus, this continuum is the product of the differing degrees of attention reflected in a variety of performance tasks, since the variability is a result of both the contextual aspects and the strategies learners develop for dealing with tasks. The continuum is illustrated below in Figure 8.3.

Vernacular style	Style 2	Style 3 . . .	Careful style
Spontaneous speech	Various elicitation tasks	Grammatical judgments	

Figure 8.3   The interlanguage continuum (Tarone 1983: p. 152)

According to this claim, the vernacular is the most stable type of data, while tasks which require more attention to speech may result in data which could not represent the real language of the speaker. This claim led Ellis (1985) to suggest that in all other styles, the normal pattern of language is disturbed, since the subjects produce certain strategies which will not occur in natural conversations. These may lead to erratic performance in data collection situations in which the subjects pay attention to the task. As a result, the language produced will be different from their real, natural language. Thus, there are grounds to believe that the vernacular is more basic than the other interlanguage styles (see Ellis 1986, p. 67 for an extensive discussion of this issue).

However, Ellis claims that the best data are the type of data representative of the specific interlanguage style which the researcher wishes to examine. Thus:

> . . . if the researcher is interested in the vernacular style, he will need data from spontaneous speech, but if he is interested in a careful style, he will need elicited data that reflect monitored performance. If he is interested in interlanguage as a variable system, then he will need data from a range of tasks (p. 89)'..

A number of suggestions are made in the light of the above discussion: one is that false claims about the data used should be avoided. First, a researcher should not make statements about natural language on data that have been collected by means of elicitation instruments, since language data obtained from elicited speech cannot provide an indication of naturally occurring speech.

Second, mixing data from different sources makes it impossible to distinguish one interlanguage style from another. (Findings from a number of second language acquisition studies may have resulted from varying tasks such as speaking, listening, reading, writing, or elicited imitation. Much of the heterogeneity of language learner language reported may have derived from pooling data which reflect differing degrees of attention on the part of the language users.)

Models must be developed which do not ignore this inherent variability but still give explicit recognition to it. In addition, a plea is made by Richards (1980) for language testers to devise appropriate procedures which will enable researchers to obtain valid language data by concentrating on the development of testing instruments for research purposes where the monitoring is minimized, where attention is on the meaning of the utterances rather than on grammatical forms, and where the task constrains speakers to produce the language which the researcher is interested in obtaining.

In the meantime it seems that in relatively unmonitored situations, most procedures available cannot replicate the language system in a sufficiently 'natural' way to produce the type of responses which the researcher is interested in describing. So far there has been little attempt to overcome what Labov (1970) termed the 'observer's paradox', which makes the following claim: The vernacular provides the most systematic data since minimum attention is given to monitoring it. It is best collected through systematic observation. However, systematic observation prevents access to the speaker's vernacular style and it is therefore not possible to investigate the vernacular of the user through systematic observation in research situations.

Assuring the quality of the data and the data collection procedures

In the previous sections we described a variety of procedures for collecting data. We also noticed that any data collection procedure, by the very fact of its use, is already creating some effect on the data, and that there are no foolproof procedures that do not affect the data. All data collection procedures, to different degrees, have some effect on the type of data that are elicited. The important point, however, is that the researcher will be aware of these effects in explaining the results obtained. Many factors affect the quality of the data and most of these factors have already been mentioned in the discussion of the specific data collection procedures; others were discussed in Chapter 5.

Over the years, researchers have developed a number of techniques to assure the quality of the research and the quality of data collection procedures used in the research. Techniques appropriate to the research as a whole were discussed in Chapter 5 in the section on internal and external validity. Here we will discuss techniques used specifically to assure the quality of the data collection procedures.

Reliability and *validity* are the two most important criteria for assuring the quality of the data collection procedures. Reliability provides information on the extent to which the data collection procedure elicits accurate data, and validity provides information on the extent to which the procedure really measures what it is supposed to measure.

It is important to examine the quality of the procedure *before* it is administered in the actual research, so that it is still possible to insert changes and revisions if necessary. It is recommended that data collection procedures be tried out in the *pilot* phase of the study. In this phase, the researcher examines the different data collection procedures in order to avoid problems during the administration of the actual research. Results of the pilot can therefore be used to revise the data collection procedures and the research as a whole. In situations when it is not possible to try out the procedures before the administration of the real study, the researcher is taking the risk that if the procedure is found to be unsatisfactory, there will be no valid data to use for arriving at conclusions and results.

Trying out the instrument before the administration of the real study is as important with the use of adapted and revised procedures as it is with ready-made procedures. In using ready-made procedures there can never be a guarantee that they have been tried out with exactly the same type of subjects as the researcher is using in the research. It is therefore always advisable to try out the procedure beforehand, regardless of the type of procedure used.

We will now elaborate on the different types of reliability and validity. We will focus only on *what* each of the procedures for establishing reliability and validity does, and *when* it should be used. We refer the reader to the references listed at the end of the chapter and in the Appendix to obtain information on *how* to use the procedures to compute reliability and validity.

It is important to note that the decision regarding the specific type of reliability and validity which the researcher should measure for assuring the quality of the procedure will depend on the data collection tool used in a given piece of research. Different types of procedure call for *different* ways of examining their quality.

Reliability

The criterion of reliability provides information on whether the data collection procedure is consistent and accurate. Inaccuracies and inconsistencies may arise for a number of different reasons. For example, researchers using observations to assess the type of language used in the classroom may suspect that inaccuracies will occur when no formal observational tools such as check lists are used. The reason to suspect this is that the observers may unintentionally impose their own biases and impressions on the observed situation. However, when the same observation is made with the aid of a formal tool, such as a check list, which specifies what the observer should focus on, there is less reason to suspect inaccuracies.

Different types of reliability need to be computed, depending on where the researcher suspects that inaccuracies in the data collection procedure could occur.

In using data collection procedures of low explicitness, it is important to estimate *inter-rater reliability*. This examines the extent to which different raters (in this case, observers) agree on the data collected from the observation. In the above example, it is possible to estimate the amount of inaccuracy by having another observer judge the type of language used in that classroom. Thus there should be at least one more observer who will also be independently observing the language output in that classroom. If the two observers agree on what they see, then the data collection procedures can be considered reliable. Inter-rater reliability is therefore crucial when there is a need to estimate the extent to which judgments based on the evaluation of one rater will also be arrived at and agreed upon by another rater examining the same data. Because of their subjective nature most of the open data collection procedures (those of a low degree of explicitness, such as open interviews, or open observations) would need to be examined for their inter-rater reliability.

Test-retest reliability is used when the researcher needs to examine whether the data collection procedure is stable from one administration to another. For example, when researchers use a test to measure reading comprehension, they assume that performance on that test does not change from one time to another (providing, of course, that no 'learning' has occurred in between the two occasions). In order to examine how stable the data collection procedure is from one administration to another, the researchers will use test-retest reliability, which will indicate the extent to which the procedure is stable over time.

Regrounding is another type of test-retest reliability, used with procedures of low explicitness. Here, the researcher goes back to the data a second time and compares the patterns obtained with the results obtained the first time. This procedure is also described in Chapter 6.

When the researcher is using two versions of the same data collection procedure and wants to ensure that the two versions are really equal, and gather the same type of data, *parallel form* reliability will be used. This examines the extent to which two versions of the same data collection procedure (say, two versions of an attitude questionnaire) are really collecting the same data and are in fact parallel, by comparing the results of the two versions. This is especially important in experimental research using pre-tests and post-tests.

When the researcher is using a data collection procedure which consists of a number of independent items, such as questions in tests or questionnaires, the researcher needs to find out whether all the items elicit the same information. For example, a researcher using a test intended to measure reading comprehension in the second language needs to find out whether all the items measure the same thing. For that purpose the researcher will employ the procedure of *internal consistency* reliability to provide that information. If it is found that some of the items do not measure reading comprehension, those items are then revised or removed from the test.

In the above discussion on reliability, we saw that for different types of data collection procedures different types of reliability will be relevant. The choice of the specific type of reliability which a researcher will use for a specific data collection procedure will be determined by the type of data collection used, and where the researcher suspects inaccuracies occur.

Reliability is expressed as a coefficient ranging from 0.00 to 1.00. The higher the coefficient, the more reliable the procedure is. Determining whether the reliability is acceptable depends on what the commonly acceptable reliability for a procedure is. In general one would expect reliability to be at least .70 or .80. It is important that the researcher obtains high reliability and does not compromise when this is not so.

The main advantage of assessing the quality of the data collection procedures *before* the real data are collected, that is, in the pilot or the try-out phase, is that it is still possible at that stage to change, revise, and modify the procedure on the basis of new information. There are a number of ways by which a researcher can improve the reliability of the procedure.

One way by which reliability can be increased is·through lengthening the data collection instrument by adding more items and questions. Another way is to remove the items that cause the problem or revise them by rephrasing or changing them. Yet another way to increase reliability is through extensive training. This procedure is especially relevant for interviewers, observers, and for researchers who analyze open data obtained from procedures of a low level of explicitness. Training can be directed toward aspects such as recording the data, asking questions, using rating scales, and taking notes efficiently.

An example for computing the reliability of procedures of a low explicitness is given in Chapter 9, in the section 'Analyzing qualitative research data'.

Validity

Validity refers to the extent to which the data collection procedure measures what it intends to measure. For example, a procedure which is supposed to measure speaking proficiency in the second language will be considered valid only when it really measures second language speaking proficiency.

Just as there are different types of reliability, there are also different types of validity, all providing 'evidence' for validity. Validity cannot really be *proven* but it is necessary to obtain *evidence* of validity.

Evidence on *content validity* will need to be accumulated in order to find out if the data collection procedure is a good representation of the content which needs to be measured. For example, a researcher is constructing a language test to find out whether the research subjects have learned the material they were supposed to learn during a school year. The content validity of that test will be examined by comparing the test content with the content of the material which the students were supposed to learn during that year. Showing that it is a good representation of that material will provide evidence for its content.

Criterion *validity* provides an indication as to whether the instrument can be measured against some other criterion. When researchers are developing a test for obtaining information to distinguish between people who are field dependent and field independent, they will need to compare the instrument with another procedure which is acceptable as a valid measure of these variables. If the two procedures correlate with one another, that will provide evidence of the validity of the instrument. This type of validity is also referred to as *concurrent validity*. *Predictive validity* is another type of criterion validity which provides information on whether the procedure is capable of predicting certain behavior. For example, if an entrance test is used to place students in different levels of language classes, its predictive validity will be determined by whether those placed by it actually function well in those classes.

Construct validity is used when the researcher needs to examine whether the data collection procedure is a good representation of and is consistent with current theories underlying the variable being measured. In the example of a researcher using a procedure to collect data on the language proficiency of the subjects, the construct validity of such a procedure will depend on whether that procedure is consistent with current theories on language proficiency.

This type of validity is the most important and also the most difficult type of validity to obtain evidence for.

A procedure used to examine the quality of items or questions on an instrument is *item analysis*. By using this procedure the researcher can obtain information on whether the items are too easy or too difficult, and whether the items are well phrased and easily understood by the respondents. Items or questions found not to be of a high quality can be either revised or removed from the instrument. It is important that any instrument should provide varied information, and differentiate and discriminate among the research subjects, thus providing meaningful information. Through the process of item analysis it is possible to ensure that the questions provide such information.

Other factors, such as the time it takes for administration, the efficiency of scoring, fairness, and so on, also affect the quality of the procedure. Table 8.1 (overleaf) is a summary list of the techniques needed for determining the quality of the data collection procedures, and shows the type of information they provide.

It is recommended that the researcher examines all these aspects in the pilot phase of the research, when it is still possible to insert changes in the procedure. When this is not possible, it is important that the data collected and used in the research should be based only on those parts of the data collection procedure found to be reliable and valid.

The above applies mostly to procedures of high explicitness. There have been discussions as to the appropriate procedures for low explicitness, that is, whether the same procedures should be used as for high explicitness, or whether entirely different types of techniques should be used.

Using, adapting, and developing data collection procedures

In using data collection procedures, the researcher has three choices: a) to use ready-made procedures developed and tried out by other researchers; b) to adapt and revise existing procedures; or c) to develop new data collection procedures.

Using ready-made procedures

In most research studies, a researcher should first begin by searching for available data collection procedures. Using a ready-made instrument which has been developed by experts and for

Technique	The information it provides
Reliability	whether the scores are accurate
Test-retest	whether the scores are stable over time
Inter-rater	whether there is agreement among judges about the score assigned
Intra-rater	whether a rater will assign the same score after some time has elapsed
Parallel form	whether two similar instruments supposed to measure the same thing actually do
Internal consistency	whether the test items are related to one another and measure the same thing
Validity	whether it measures what it is supposed to measure
Content	whether the procedure represents accurately the content it is supposed to measure
Concurrent	whether it correlates well with a different type of instrument which is supposed to measure the same thing
Predictive	whether the measure can predict accurately a certain future behavior
Construct	whether it represents accurately the theory of the variable which it measures
Item analysis	whether the items and questions which appear on the instrument are difficult or easy, and whether they discriminate among the subjects of the research.

Table 8.1   Information needed for determining the quality of data collection procedures

which information regarding reliability and validity is available is more advantageous than developing a new procedure, providing that it is appropriate for the given research.

Finding out about available ready-made data collection procedures calls for steps similar to those described in Chapter 4 for locating information for contextualizing the research problem. A review of the literature and the general indices (those which specifically list instruments as well as personal communication) will provide information on the availability of ready-made data collection instruments. The Appendix lists different sources for locating these.

Once the researcher locates a ready-made instrument, other information is needed before it is put to use.

Table 8.2 lists examples of the type of information researchers need to obtain before deciding whether to use the procedure as it is, to adapt it, or to develop their own.

Title
Developer
Author
Year of publication
Description
Requirements for administering the procedure
Time needed for administration
Availability of a manual
Scoring procedures
Procedures for analyzing the results
Reliability (different types)
Validity
Norming group
Availability of parallel forms
Other studies where the procedure was used
Cost

Table 8.2   Information researchers need for using ready-made procedures

Adapting data collection instruments

A common research problem is that a researcher cannot find instruments which exactly suit the research goal. However, with some revisions and adaptations, most instruments can be made to match the specific research context. For example, a researcher may locate a questionnaire on using strategies in second language acquisition designed for children, while the subjects of the research are adults. Since adapting an instrument is still a preferable alternative to developing a totally new one, the researcher may decide to use the ready-made instrument even though it does not exactly match the research needs. This can be done by shortening it, lengthening it, validating it on another population similar to the one used in the specific research study, deleting or adding questions or new categories, translating it into another language, or rephrasing the questions.

Once the changes are inserted, a new procedure has been created. This 'new' procedure needs to be tested for quality according to the criteria described in the previous section. Specifically, information must be obtained about the reliability and validity of the procedure, since the adapted and revised version is in fact a new procedure and no longer has the reliability and validity of the original. In fact, a common error made by researchers is to insert changes in a ready-made instrument but to overlook the need to reexamine the quality of the 'new' instrument. The most important point to consider in adapting instruments is that changes made should not change the theory, that is, the assumptions upon which the instrument was constructed. For example, a language test based on a lexical and grammatical view of language cannot be revised or adapted to become a language test for communicative language, because the underlying assumptions and theory on which the two tests are based are different. Once the theory and assumptions change, the researcher is in fact developing a completely new instrument. This is the borderline between *adapting* a procedure and *developing* a totally new one.

Developing data collection procedures

Although the researcher may find a ready-made instrument or adapt an existing instrument for the purpose of the research, there will often be a need to develop a new data collection instrument tailored to collect the specific data that the researcher is interested in.

Developing new instruments is a complex process, since most variables the researcher wants to measure are complex ones. That is, variables such as 'aptitude', 'motivation', 'language proficiency', and 'grammatical ability' are complex in the sense that there are no agreed definitions and interpretations of what they are and what they mean. Thus, measuring variables requires first translating them into measurable terms. The next step in the process of developing instruments is to select the appropriate data collection procedures to measure the variable. This is followed by assigning values to the behavior, for example, what is 'high' and what is 'low' aptitude. Once this decision has been made, the instrument is put together. At this stage, the researcher has an instrument that needs to be piloted and tried out with real subjects. The results of this pilot phase will provide the researcher with information on revisions and changes that may need to be made so that the instrument can be used with confidence in the research, and provide reliable and valid data. Table 8.3 lists the steps researchers can follow in developing data collection procedures. In the next section we will discuss each of the steps.

---

1 Converting complex, abstract variables into measurable ones (operationalizing)
2 Converting the behaviors into interpretable information
3 Selecting procedures for investigating the behaviors
4 Putting the instrument together
5 Piloting the instrument and obtaining information about its quality
6 Revising the instrument and using it

Table 8.3   Stages in developing data collection instruments

1 *Converting complex, abstract variables into measurable ones (operationalizing)*

This is the phase in which the researcher needs to find agreed definitions to allow the transformation of complex abstract variables into more concrete measurable ones. Operationalizing requires the selection of concrete *behaviors* which are believed to represent the complex variables or constructs. Once these behaviors are selected, the researcher looks for ways to measure them. In the first step, then, the researcher selects behaviors believed to serve as indicators of the variables.

As was discussed at the beginning of this chapter, in order to measure the variable 'language proficiency', it is necessary to identify specific behaviors which are an acceptable basis for describing it. That is, in accordance with current theories about language proficiency or language knowledge, what does a proficient language learner know? It will probably be agreed that behaviors which can be identified as the basis for making inferences about language proficiency are: ability to communicate in the language, use of appropriate registers and appropriate speech acts, and knowing conversation strategies in appropriate contexts, for example. (In the 1960s such behaviors may have included aspects such as the use of accurate structures and vocabulary, and native-like pronunciation, aspects which are likely to get less attention nowadays.)

2 *Converting the behaviors into interpretable information*

Once the behaviors which describe the variable are identified, it is necessary to determine the criteria of what good and bad, high and low mean in accordance with current theories in the field. In the example above, such criteria may be that a person who uses specific functions frequently and also has mastered conversation rules in a number of situations is of higher proficiency than one who has not mastered them. In this phase, then, the researcher quantifies the construct in terms of high and low, good or bad, appropriate and inappropriate use of register, and so on, so that the data to be collected will become interpretable.

3 Selecting procedures for investigating behaviors

Once the behaviors for describing the abstract variable have been selected (step 1), the researcher must determine which specific data collection procedures are most appropriate for assessing these behaviors. At the beginning of this chapter we discussed these procedures and emphasized that certain procedures are appropriate for certain designs, purposes, and contexts. In the example of measuring language proficiency mentioned above, one such procedure may be a test which will investigate these behaviors. In order to be congruent with these identified behaviors, the test will require subjects to use appropriate registers, show different language functions, and apply appropriate conversation rules in specific communicative situations. In addition to a test, the researcher may decide to use a questionnaire which asks the subjects to assess their own level of proficiency in accordance with the identified behaviors, or to use an interview in which the subjects' teacher will provide an opinion about their proficiency in accordance with the selected behaviors. Observation may be yet another procedure by which data about the proficiency of the subjects will be assessed; the researcher may observe the subjects using the language in a variety of interactive situations.

To sum up, different types of data collection procedures are available for the researcher to use to collect data on the behaviors which have been identified and quantified. Different types of behavior will lend themselves to different types of data collection procedures.

4 Putting the instrument together

At this stage, the researcher plans and writes the items and tasks in the selected data collection procedure, and puts it together so it can be administered to the subjects of the study, and the data collected. The content of the procedure(s) will depend on the behaviors selected and quantified and the type of procedure(s) selected to collect the information.

5 Piloting and trying out the instrument

However, before an instrument can be administered to the research subjects, it needs to be tried out. The aim of the try-out (or pilot) is to assess its quality while it can still be revised and improved and *before* it is used with the actual subjects in the research. The researcher collects information about the instrument, its items, and the criteria for scoring and rating its items, and this provides the basis for improving the instrument.

The type of information collected in the pilot phase is of two types. One relates to practical aspects of administering the data collection tool, such as the time required to administer the instrument, and the clarity of the instructions. The other relates to the reliability and validity of the instrument, as described in the section 'Assuring the quality of the data collection procedures'. When it is not possible to administer a pilot, the researcher should compute reliability and validity *after* the instrument has been used in the real study and make the necessary adjustments, such as deleting certain items, before the data of the whole study is analyzed. This will help ensure that the data analysis is based only on reliable and valid data.

6 Revising the instrument and using it

The information obtained from the pilot is then used to revise the data collection procedure, that is, to remove or modify items, to extend or shorten the administration time, or to clarify some of the tasks. It may sometimes be necessary to pilot the procedure again, but in most situations the researcher can now administer the procedure and collect the research data.

Ethical considerations in collecting research data

Most of the research in second language acquisition uses human subjects, who may be involved in experiments in which a certain 'treatment' is administered to them. In most studies it is the human subjects from whom the data are collected. Often school or other records are used as sources of data, and these records contain important information about the subjects.

In recent years much attention has been given to the ethical and legal considerations involved in conducting research and collecting data from human participants. The National Research Act of 1974 deals with these matters. This act requires that universities and agencies engaging in research with human participants have an institutional review board for proposals. The board must approve the proposal and certify that the project and the data collection will be conducted in accordance with the law. Universities have committees through which such proposals must be channeled, while school systems often have defined procedures of approval for any proposed research or data collection. Any researcher carrying out research with human participants at a university or in a school system must follow the institution's rules and procedures.

A number of points are made:
- The researcher must protect the dignity and welfare of the participants.
- The individual's freedom to decline participation must be respected.
- Confidentiality of research data must be maintained.
- The researcher must guard against violation or invasion of privacy.
- The responsibility for maintaining ethical standards remains with the individual researcher, and the principal investigator is also responsible for the actions of co-workers or assistants.
- Individuals should not be specifically identified with their data unless it is necessary, and then only after the individual has given consent.
- The researcher should take every precaution and make every effort to minimize potential risk to subjects.

Even if there is no risk to subjects, they should be completely informed concerning the nature of the study. Frequently, for control purposes, subjects are not aware of their participation in a study, or if aware, do not know the exact nature of the experiments. Such subjects should be given that information as soon as the study is completed. If school children are involved, it is also a good idea to inform their parents, before the study is conducted, about the purpose and procedures of the study. When tests are conducted, it is recommended that sample items from the test be shown to the parents. This may be done in writing or through a meeting with the parents' organization. The subject's right to privacy is also an important consideration. Collecting information on subjects or observing them without their knowledge or without appropriate permission is not ethical. Moreover, any information or data which are collected, either from or about a subject, should not be made public. It is usually sufficient to present data in terms of group statistics. If individual scores, or raw data need to be presented, they should be coded and should not be associated with subjects' names or other identifying information. This is especially important with regard to language data, which are often recorded on video or audio tapes. Access to such data should be limited to persons directly involved in conducting the research and tapes should not be made public without the written consent of the individuals.

After describing the different procedures for collecting data and the ethical considerations which the researcher should follow, in the next chapter we will discuss ways of analyzing the data collected, using the various data collection procedures described in this chapter.

Summary

In this chapter we first differentiated between data collection procedures of high and low degrees of explicitness. We then described different procedures used to collect data in second language research. We began by describing procedures used for qualitative research and then discussed observations, interviews, questionnaires, and tests. Each procedure was described according to its purposes and uses. This section was followed by a discussion of the problems associated with collecting valid language data and then by a description of ways to assure the quality of the data collection procedures, focusing specifically on reliability and validity. The chapter proceeded to describe criteria for using ready-made procedures, for adapting available procedures for specific needs, and for developing new ones. We ended the chapter with a discussion on ethical considerations which should concern researchers in collecting data and conducting research.

Activities

1 Refer to two articles in journals of applied linguistics which present research, and do the following:
   a) List the data collection procedures used.
   b) Describe them and assess their degree of explicitness.
   c) What are the criteria used by the researcher to assure their quality? (If they are not reported, think of how the researcher might have done it.)

d) Specify the behaviors on which the instrument is based.
2 Select two data collection procedures such as an interview or a questionnaire used with adult second language learners.
   a) Modify these procedures so they can be used with child second language learners.
   b) What procedures should the researcher use to assure the quality of the newly adapted instrument?
3 Select a variable on which you would like to collect data. Obtain definitions of the variable. Select behaviors which will be indicative of it, and suggest data collection procedures that could be used to collect the relevant data.
4 Look for three instruments used for observing interactions in the classroom. Compare and contrast them. What type of data could have been collected had the researchers used observation tools of a low level of explicitness?
5 Give examples of actual data that can be collected using verbal reports. What would you do to validate those data?

References

Allwright, R. 1983. 'Classroom-centred research on language teaching and learning: A brief historical review'. *TESOL Quarterly* 17:191–204.
Allwright, R. 1988. *Observation in the Language Classroom*. New York: Longman.
Bailey, K. 1983. 'Competitiveness and anxiety in adult second language learning: Looking *at* and *through* the diary studies' in H. W. Seliger and M. Long (eds.): *Classroom Oriented Research in Second Language Acquisition*, Rowley, Mass.: Newbury House.
Bejarano, Y. 1987. 'A cooperative small-group methodology in the language classroom.' *TESOL Quarterly* 21/3:483–504.
Beebe, L. 1980. 'Sociolinguistic variation and style shifting in second language acquisition.' *Language Learning* 30/1:433–447.
Bialystok, E. 1979. 'An analytic view of second language competence: A model and some evidence.' *The Modern Language Journal* LXIII, 257–262.
Brown, A. L. 1981. 'Metacognition and reading and writing: The development and facilitation of selective attention strategies for learning from texts.' Center for the Study of Reading, University of Illinois.
Buros, O. K. (ed.) 1978. *The Eighth Mental Measurement Yearbook*. Highland Park, N.J.: Gryphon Press.
Cohen, A. and Hosenfeld C. 1981. 'Some uses of mentalistic data in second language research.' *Language Learning* 31/2:285–313.

Denzin, N. K. 1978. *The Research Act: A Theoretical Introduction to Sociological Methods.* New York: McGraw-Hill.

Dickerson, L. 1975. 'Interlanguage as a system of variable rules.' *TESOL Quarterly* 9:401–407.

Ellis, R. 1985. *Understanding Second Language Acquisition,* Oxford: Oxford University Press.

Ericsson, K. and Simon, H. A. 1980. 'Verbal reports as data.' *Psychological Review* 87:215–251.

Fanselow, J. F. 1977. 'Beyond Rashomon – conceptualizing and describing the teaching act.' *TESOL Quarterly* 11:17–39.

Faerch, C. and Kasper, G. 1987 *Introspection in Second Language Research.* Clevedon, Avon: Multilingual Matters.

Fillmore, C. J. 1982. 'Ideal reader and real reader' in D. Tannen (eds.): *Analyzing Discourse: Text and Talk.* Washington, D.C.: Georgetown University Press.

Firestone, W. 1987. 'Meaning in method: The rhetoric of quantitative and qualitative research.' *Educational Researcher* 16/7:16–21.

Flanders, N. A. 1970. *Analyzing Teaching Behavior.* Reading, Mass.: Addison-Wesley.

Garner, R. 1987. *Meta Cognition and Reading Comprehension.* Norwood, N.J.: Ablex.

Jick, T. D. 1983. 'Mixing qualitative and quantitative methods: Triangulation in action' in J. Van Maanen (ed.): *Qualitative Methods.* Beverly Hills, CA.: Sage.

Labov, W. 1970. 'The study of language in its social context.' *Studium Generale* 23:30–87.

LeCompte, M. D. and Goetz, J. P. 1982. 'Problems of reliability and validity in ethnographic research.' *Review of Educational Research* 52:31–60.

Likert, R. A. 1932. 'A technique for the measurement of attitudes.' *Archives of Psychology* No. 40.

Long, M. 1980. 'Inside the "black box": Methodological issues in classroom research on language learning.' *Language Learning* 30/1: 1–42.

Mann, S. 1983. 'Verbal reports as data: A focus on retrospection' in S. Dingwall, S. Mann, and F. Katamba (eds.): *Problems, Methods and Theory in Applied Linguistics.* Lancaster: Lancaster University.

Mathison, S. 1988. 'Why triangulate?' *Educational Researcher* 17/2:13–17.

Meichenbaum, D. 1980. 'A cognitive-behavioral perspective on intelligence.' *Intelligence* 4:271–283.

Olshavsky, J. 1977. 'Reading as problem solving.' *Reading Research Quarterly* 12/4:654–74.

Osgood, C. E., Suci, G. J., and Tannenbaum, P. H. 1957. *The Measurement of Meaning.* Urbana: University of Illinois Press.

Richards, D. R. 1980. 'Problems in eliciting unmonitored speech in second language.' *Interlanguage Studies Bulletin* 5/2:2.

Schmidt, R. 1977. 'Sociolinguistic variation and language transfer in phonology.' *Working Papers on Bilingualism* 12:79–95.

Schumann, F. and **Schumann, J.** 1977. 'Diary of a language learner: An introspective study of second language learning' in H. D. Brown *et al.* (eds.): *On TESOL '77*, Washington, D.C.: TESOL.

Tarone, E. 1981. 'Some thoughts on the notion of communicative strategy.' *TESOL Quarterly* 15:285–295.

Tarone, E. 1983. 'On the variability of interlanguage systems.' *Applied Linguistics* 4/2:143–63.

9 Analyzing the data

A foolish man always thinks only of the results, and is impatient, without the effort that is necessary to get good results. No good can be attained without proper effort, just as there can be no third story (on a house) without the foundation and the first and second stories.

(The teaching of the Buddha)

Data analysis and the design of the study

Once the research data have been collected with the aid of different types of data collection procedures as described in Chapter 8, the next phase of the research is to analyze those data. *Data analysis* refers to sifting, organizing, summarizing, and synthesizing the data so as to arrive at the results and conclusions of the research. Thus, data analysis becomes the product of all the considerations involved in the design and planning of the research.

A variety of techniques are available for analyzing data; here too, as with the data collection procedures, the selection of a specific data analysis technique will depend mainly on the nature of the research problem, the design chosen to investigate it, and the type of data collected. Thus, in the data analysis phase, the researcher does not have much choice as to the specific data analysis technique to use, certain types of data lending themselves to certain types of analysis techniques. Figure 9.1 illustrates this dependence. Data analysis is therefore valuable to the extent that there is a valid relationship between it and the other components of the research.

As a result of this dependence, certain data analysis techniques will be more appropriate for quantitative research, while others will be more appropriate for qualitative research. In quantitative research the data is in numerical form, or some form which can be converted into numbers, and the analysis almost always utilizes statistics. Qualitative data analysis techniques deal with non-numerical data, usually linguistic units in oral or written form. While quantitative data analysis techniques have been well defined and differentiated, and there are specific approaches for analyzing data obtained from descriptive, correlational, multivariate, and experimental research

---

The research problem

↑

The research design

↑

The data collected

↑

| The data analysis technique |

Figure 9.1   Dependence of the data analysis technique on the other components of the research

(see pp. 211, 218, 222), it is only recently that attention has been devoted to defining and describing approaches for analyzing qualitative data.

Figure 9.2 gives examples of *typical* data analysis techniques used with the different research designs discussed in the previous chapters. On the left hand side of the figure there are examples of techniques for analyzing data obtained from qualitative research, such as drawing patterns and categories from the data, with a minimal amount of computation. This type of analysis is subjective rather than objective. At the other end of the table there are examples of techniques for analyzing data quantitatively, utilizing different types of statistics for descriptions, predictions, generalizations, and inferences.

A common misconception of the novice researcher is that *not* using statistics makes the research 'easier' to conduct. In fact, analyzing data *with* the aid of statistics usually makes the research more manageable and more efficient, as there are acceptable procedures for doing it. Using qualitative procedures, on the other hand, often puts a heavier burden on the researcher, who then needs to develop good insights, intuitions, and understanding concerning the data, and that is a complex and lengthy task. Statistics is the discipline which has developed a variety of techniques for analyzing numerical data in an efficient and accurate way. Too often, however, researchers develop an anxiety about statistics and as a result fail to appreciate its value as a means for analyzing research data.

In this chapter we will discuss both qualitative and quantitative data analysis techniques. We will not discuss in great detail *how* to

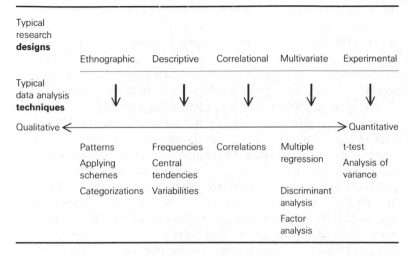

Figure 9.2   Typical data analysis techniques for various research designs

use the specific techniques, but rather emphasize *what* they are, *when* they should be used, and the type of answers they provide: in other words, what type of problem needs what type of analysis. This will be illustrated by discussing specific examples in second language acquisition research which utilize the different analysis techniques. Thus, the researcher will be able to select the techniques most appropriate for his or her own type of research. Detailed guidance and description of *how* to use the different statistical procedures can be found in the Appendix and at the end of this chapter.

Since all the statistical techniques discussed in this chapter can be carried out with the aid of a computer by using a variety of available statistical packages, the last section of the chapter will be devoted to the use of such packages for analyzing research data.

It is important to note that different statistical procedures have certain requirements for their use since certain techniques will only work with certain types of data. *Parametric* statistics, although having a number of set assumptions, are far more powerful than *non-parametric* statistics. Non-parametric statistics, used for nominal and ordinal data, have, in general, weaker assumptions, but they are also less powerful in the sense that it is not possible to utilize them for rejecting the null hypothesis at a given level of significance. One of the assumptions of parametric statistics is that the variable measured is normally distributed in the population. Since most variables studied in this field are normally distributed, this assumption is usually met. A second assumption is that the data represent an interval or a ratio scale of measurement. Measures used in second language acquisition often represent interval data, so this assumption is also usually met. A third assumption is that the subjects are selected independently for the study, so that the selection of one subject does not affect the selection of the others. This is usually the case whenever the sample is randomly selected. Thus when randomization is involved in subject selection, this assumption is met as well. A further assumption is that the variances of the population of the comparison groups are equal or at least known. (Variation, which indicates the spread of scores, is discussed later in the chapter.) With the exception of independence, some violation of one or more of these assumptions is not usually crucial. However, if any of the assumptions are violated, a non-parametric test should be used, since these do not make assumptions about the shape of the distribution and they are usually used when the data represent an ordinal or nominal scale. With one exception, the Chi square, all the statistics discussed here are parametric statistics. Readers who need to use non-parametric statistics are advised to refer to the statistical references listed in the Appendix. (See specifically Siegal 1956 and Hollander and Wolfe 1973.)

It is important, therefore, to become aware of the requirements of certain types of data *before* analyzing the data.

We will now proceed to describe the different techniques for analyzing data; these will be presented in the same order as the types of research are presented in Chapters 6 and 7: beginning with types of qualitative techniques, and going through quantitative techniques appropriate for descriptive, correlational, multivariate, and experimental research.

Analyzing qualitative research data

In qualitative (heuristic/synthetic) research (see Chapter 6), where qualitative data have been collected by procedures such as unstructured observations, open interviews, examining records, diaries, and other documents, the data are usually in the form of words in oral or written modes. These units, though, come in different forms: some are words within a specific context, or text segments, such as 'meaning units'; others are structural segments of texts, such as individual phonemes, morphemes, parts of words, lexical and grammatical elements, sentences, phrases, or paragraphs; others again are holistic and represent longer texts such as narratives. Each of these units calls for a different type of analysis.

While the analysis of qualitative data is a complex task, especially since there is only limited literature in which the principles of such analysis are described in sufficient detail, some typical features of the analysis can be identified.

Typical of all qualitative analyses is that at different stages of the analysis the researchers identify, delimit, and sort the relevant segments of the text according to an organizing scheme. They look for commonalities, regularities, or patterns across the various data texts (although it is also possible for researchers to look specifically for *differences* and *variations* in the data). Sometimes categories emerge from the data themselves rather than a specific analysis being imposed on the data; at other times, the researchers approach the data with predetermined categories (usually obtained from other sources) in mind. In both cases the data are summarized and collapsed in a systematic way. They then need to be validated and verified either by independent reviewers, who will obtain their own categories from the data, or by the researchers themselves when they return to the data in order to examine whether the same patterns and categories emerge again.

Thus, two main types of techniques can be identified in analyzing qualitative data: (a) deriving a set of categories for dealing with text segments from the text itself. This is an inductive procedure. Once the categories have been established they are applied to the remainder of the data; this leads to refinement of the categories and the discovery of new commonalities or patterns. Thus they serve as an ordering system for the data content. This type of research study is usually descriptive and exploratory in nature. (b) An ordering system of categories already exists at the beginning of the process and the researcher applies this system to the data. The system is derived either from a conceptual framework or from the specific research questions. These studies are more confirmatory and aim at some kind of explanation. The segments are selected and sorted according to the existing system. Then, in a second phase, the categories are investigated, for instance by cross-referencing, to see whether there are relationships that will assist in the understanding of the phenomenon under study (Tesch 1987).

We will now consider an example of a qualitative study in which the two different analysis procedures were used.

Example
A researcher collected observational data on immigrant children acquiring
a second language while interacting with native speakers. The researcher
was interested in observing the morphological and syntactic errors of the
learners and the reactions of the native speakers to these errors in a
conversational context. The material collected was in the form of audio
tapes of the verbal interactions of the immigrant children with the native
speakers in the classroom, working in small groups.

In this research study two sets of data were collected, and each
was analyzed separately. One set consisted of the morphological
and syntactic errors of the learners and the other, the reactions of
the native speakers to these errors. Both sets of data were analyzed
qualitatively by the researcher identifying, sorting, extracting, and
reorganizing the verbal interactions and then grouping them
according to topic. However, each set of data was analyzed using a
different type of qualitative analysis. The first set, the errors, was
analyzed with the aid of an organizing scheme. The second set,
reactions of the native speakers, was analyzed by deriving
categories from part of the data and then confirming them with the
rest of the data.

Below is a description of the steps the researcher followed in the
process of analyzing the syntactic and morphological errors with the
organizing scheme (technique (b)).

1 The researcher transcribed the tape data, so that he could focus
   directly on the morphological and syntactic errors of the
   learners.
2 Since research on the types of morphological and syntactic errors
   made by immigrant children in their first year of residence in a
   new country already existed, the researcher took an ordering
   system which he found in the literature on error analysis and
   applied it to his own data. He then counted the frequencies of
   errors for each of the categories in the organizing scheme.
3 The analysis of the data led to the results of the study, which
   were the frequencies of errors in each of the categories listed
   in the organizing scheme. The researcher then provided some
   explanations and suggested hypotheses as to why these particular
   types of error patterns occurred in this group of learners and why
   these categories were different from those found in the literature.
4 As part of this process, the researcher applied measures of
   reliability in order to verify and confirm that the scheme had
   been applied accurately to the data without being influenced by

possible biases of his own. He asked an independent researcher to repeat the task and apply the scheme to some portion of the transcribed data. Only those categories on which close agreement between the researcher and the independent rater were obtained were reported as the results of the study.

In order to analyze the reactions of the native speakers to the errors, the researcher used a qualitative data analysis in which categories of reaction were derived directly from part of the data without an organizing scheme. Once categories had been identified, they were applied to the remainder of the data for refinement and also to see if commonalities or patterns emerged. In this phase the researcher decided not to transcribe the tapes but rather to study the original recordings. He believed that by doing so he would be able to use the full information from the original data and would not lose aspects that might be relevant and important for valid interpretation of the data, such as the accent, intonation, and stress of the speakers.

Below are the steps which the researcher followed in analyzing the data of the native speakers' reactions to the errors made by the learners (technique (a)).

1 A portion of the tapes was carefully reviewed and notes were made about the types of reactions of the native speakers.
2 A list of the different types of reactions derived from the data was compiled.
3 The list was analyzed in an attempt to collapse and combine certain categories of types of reactions.
4 A finite group of patterns and sub-patterns was formulated.
5 The categories and patterns identified were applied to the remainder of the data for further refinement.
6 A definitive group of patterns and categories of reactions was formulated.
7 To examine the reliability of the data, the tapes were given to other researchers who went through the same steps and obtained their own categories of types of reactions. These categories were then compared with those of the first researcher. The patterns on which two researchers agreed were considered valid in this context.

It should be noted that different types of data analysis could have been applied to each set of data. For example, had there been no theory or previous research that had already classified the types of morphological and syntactic errors which learners make, then these classifications of errors would have had to be derived from the data themselves. In the same manner, if categories of types of reactions of native speakers to errors made by learners had been previously identified in some other research, then these categories could have been applied by the researcher to his data.

In summary, in the example above we have followed two different techniques for analyzing qualitative data. In the first an organizing scheme was imposed on the data, and in the second the categories were derived directly from the data. In both cases some procedures for validating the results were used, either independent reviewers or other researchers examining the same data, using the organizing scheme and applying it to the data. Validating the results is an important component of analyzing qualitative data because of the possible subjectivity associated with the analysis and interpretation of the results. (Chapter 8 deals with some of these issues. Also see LeCompte and Goetz (1982) for a comprehensive discussion and suggestions relating to the reliability and validity of qualitative research.)

In the next example, we will follow the specific steps the researcher took in analyzing qualitative data and establishing the reliability of the categories.

Example

A researcher (Gordon 1987) was conducting research in order to discover the strategies which test-takers use while doing a reading comprehension test. The qualitative verbal data were collected from 36 test-takers through the 'think aloud' technique where the test-takers reported to the researcher on the processes which they were engaged in while attempting to answer test questions. The interviews were audio recorded.

The data were analyzed through the procedure of protocol analysis (Newell and Simon 1972, Olshavsky 1977, Mann 1983). Here, the data determines the analysis rather than the analysis imposing predetermined categories on the data. The following is a description of the stages involved in analyzing those data:

1 Written transcriptions were made of the verbal protocols for each subject.
2 The protocols were carefully reviewed and notes made relating to processes involved in answering test questions.
3 A comprehensive list of all strategies, processes, and information relevant to the issue of test-taking strategies was compiled. This list was analyzed in an attempt to collapse and combine certain categories. A finite group of categories and sub-categories was

formulated. These categories then became the criteria by which each of the protocols was analyzed.

4 Each answer to each question in the test was analyzed according to the categories formulated.

5 Descriptive statistics (frequencies and percentages) were computed for each of the categories. (In this phase it is not always possible to observe or infer information in all cases. The researcher may often feel that intensive probing of a reluctant respondent would result in invalid information.)

6 In order to obtain some indication of the reliability of the analysis and the categories formulated, rater reliability was examined in the following ways:

Inter-rater reliability was judged by giving a random selection of four protocols to a judge who was a professional in the field of applied linguistics, and who was asked to analyze and categorize the responses. The results were compared with the researcher's analysis and categorization. A high degree of agreement was achieved between the judge's analysis and that of the researcher on all four of the protocols.

Intra-rater reliability was assessed by the researcher re-rating half of the sample of tapes after a period of time had elapsed from the initial categorization of the responses in the protocols, in order to compare the degree of agreement which existed between the first and second analyses. High agreement was obtained and this established an indication of the reliability of the analysis.

Once the data has been satisfactorily analyzed, the results need to be described and reported. Procedures for reporting the results of qualitative data analysis are discussed in Chapter 10.

We will conclude this section by listing a number of features reported by Tesch (1987) to be common to the different variations of qualitative analysis.

1 The analysis of qualitative data is systematic and orderly, but not rigid. It requires discipline, an organized mind, and perseverance.

2 The main tool used is comparison, a search for likenesses and differences. Commonalities or regularities and patterns play an important role.

3 In order to be compared and contrasted, the raw data usually need to be 'translated' in some way. These translations may consist of summaries or condensations of text segments.

4 These translations often become the 'names' of categories into which text segments can be sorted. These categories are viewed initially as tentative and preliminary, and then they are modified and refined as the analysis continues, although even then they remain flexible.

5 During the analysis, the connection to the whole, that is, the document from which the segment was extracted, is maintained.

6 The analysis is not simply the final phase of a research project. It begins as soon as the first data are available, and then analysis and collection run concurrently. The results of each round of analysis point to open questions that call for new data, and the return to the field enables the researcher to assess the validity of his analysis and, where necessary, refine the ordering system being used. The process ends when new data no longer bring new insights; the analytic procedure has 'exhausted' the data.

7 The result of the analysis is some type of higher-level synthesis.

8 The entire process is accompanied by a reflective activity on the part of the researcher, who is urged to record any idea that comes to mind in connection with the research project. Minimally, a chronicle of research events should be kept to help establish accountability. The type of information contained in such a second-level data document may help interpret the data, suggest how they could be analyzed, or give a specific direction to the data.

9 The researcher is an instrument in the research process. Although biases must be carefully kept in check, qualitative analysis grows out of the background and unique situation of the individual researcher, whose creative power and intuition are often the sources from which insights are derived. It often happens, for example, that during the analysis an important conclusion enters the researcher's mind. Qualitative analysis is a process that demands deep involvement on the part of the researcher and draws on a wide range of personal powers.

10 Finally, there is no one 'right way' of analyzing qualitative data, since it is possible to analyze any phenomenon in more than one way. Therefore the process should not become standardized and rigid.

In summary, qualitative analysis is the process used to reduce data obtained from qualitative research to its essentials. The process is not mechanical but rather involves skilled perceptions on the part of the researcher. The data still need to be analyzed systematically, since they must lead to results that others will accept as representative. If this is done the results of the analysis will provide a valid representation of the essential features of the data.

Further references on analyzing and reporting qualitative research data are presented at the end of the chapter, in the Appendix, and in Chapter 6.

Analyzing descriptive research data

Data obtained from descriptive research (see Chapter 6) are generally analyzed with the aid of *descriptive statistics*. These provide information such as *how often* certain language phenomena occur, the *typical* use of language elements by different language learners, how *different* and *varied* certain groups of language learners are with regard to certain linguistic phenomena, and the *relationship* among various variables.

Descriptive statistics refers to a set of procedures which are used to *describe* different aspects of the data. Such information can sometimes be the sole purpose of the research, or at other times, it may provide the researcher with basic insights and an initial impression of the data, information that will be useful for subsequent analysis phases of the research.

The types of descriptive statistics are *frequencies*, *central tendencies*, and *variabilities*. Correlations are also considered as descriptive statistical procedures and may be used in descriptive research studies. We will discuss correlations in their inferential use later in the chapter.

Frequencies (f) are used to indicate *how often* a phenomenon occurs and they are based on counting the number of occurrences. Such information is very useful in second language acquisition research, where the researcher is often interested in finding out how frequently certain language elements such as structures, lexicon, syntax, and speech acts are used by different types of language learners in different contexts. Frequencies also provide information on the performance of the subjects on tests and questionnaires before the results are used for analyzing the data of the whole study.

Example
In a study investigating how second language learners of different backgrounds use certain types of refusal statements, a researcher presents to two groups of subjects (40 natives and 40 non-natives) different

situations, each accompanied by four statements of ways of expressing refusal. The subjects are required to select the statement which they are most likely to use in the situations.

In analyzing the results of the above study, the researcher needs to compute the frequencies for the selection of each statement by each group and to compare the two groups. The frequency of responses to one of the situations is presented in Table 9.1. The table shows how often each of the statements was selected by the two groups for one situation.

Statement	Frequencies (natives) N = 40 f	Frequencies (non-natives) N = 40 f
1	20	10
2	15	15
3	5	3
4	0	12

Table 9.1   Frequencies of selecting refusal statements

Statement 1 was selected by 20 of the 40 native subjects, but only by 10 of the non-natives. Statement 4, on the other hand, was selected by 12 of the non-natives but by none of the natives. Clearly, it is possible, through an examination of the frequencies to see how common (how frequent) certain speech functions are among different language learners. (Whether the difference observed between the natives and the non-natives is meaningful statistically will have to be investigated by a different technique, the *Chi square*, which will be discussed later in the chapter.)

Frequencies can also be useful for obtaining insight into data of the research.

Example

A researcher is conducting a study of the length of residence of immigrants in the new country and their language proficiency, and so constructs a language proficiency test which is administered to three groups of learners: Group 1 consists of learners who have resided in the country between 1 and 3 years; group 2 have resided there between 4 and 7 years, and group 3, 8 years or more. The researcher wants to find out how frequently certain test scores occurred among the three types of subjects.

Table 9.2 shows these frequencies, that is, the number of subjects in each of the categories who obtained a specific score in each of the three groups, in a *frequency table*. These frequencies are expressed in *class intervals* which are a useful way of condensing, organizing, and summarizing the data when the score range is large. In this example, where scores ranged from 0 to 100, the researcher grouped them into intervals of fives and thus the data are condensed into smaller units.

It can be seen from the table that the three groups performed differently on the same test. By examining the frequencies, the researcher can see that for the third group the test was relatively easy, while it was much more difficult for the first group. The table also shows that while in the first group there was a wide range of levels of performance, the second and the third groups show similar distributions of scores.

Score	Group 1 (1–3 years) N = 30 Frequencies (f)	Group 2 (4–7 years) N = 30 Frequencies (f)	Group 3 (8 years and over) N =30 Frequencies (f)
95–100	2	5	10
90–94	1	3	8
85–89	1	4	6
80–84	4	8	3
75–79	5	3	2
70–74	3	2	1
65–69	6	2	0
60–64	0	0	0
55–59	2	2	0
50–54	3	0	0
45–49	1	1	0
40–44	2	0	0

Table 9.2   Frequency of scores of three groups of language learners on a language proficiency test

Frequencies can therefore provide the researcher with meaningful information on the measures used in the research even before the language proficiency of the three groups is compared. This can help the researcher obtain insights into and understanding of the data and the results.

Frequencies can be reported verbally by describing how frequently a phenomenon occurred among certain groups of learners, by quoting the frequencies raw or as percentages, or through a frequency table as shown above. Frequencies can also be reported on a *graph* where the values are taken from a frequency table. The scores are plotted along the baseline and the frequencies are plotted along the vertical axis. The height of each bar corresponds to the frequency of cases in that interval. Such graphs are *histograms*. Figure 9.3 is a histogram based on the frequencies of the scores of Group 1 in Table 9.2.

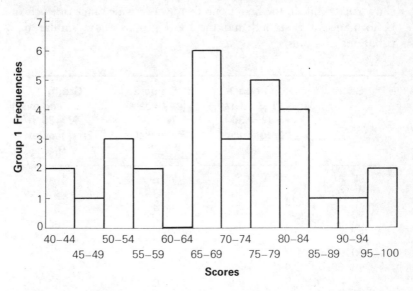

Figure 9.3   Presenting frequencies on a histogram

Frequency results can also be presented through a *crossbreak table*. This is a display of frequencies or percentages (or other types of data) that points out similarities and differences in sharp contrasts and is therefore useful in displaying trends and patterns.

The crossbreak table in Table 9.3 shows how the two groups 'monolinguals' and 'bilinguals' differ as to the frequencies of high or low scores on a metalinguistic test. A high metalinguistic score was obtained by 25 of the bilinguals but only by 8 of the monolinguals, while a low score was obtained by 19 of the monolinguals but by only 2 of the bilinguals. (In order to find out whether the difference between the gróups is statistically

Score Group	High score	Low score
Monolinguals	8	19
Bilinguals	25	2

Table 9.3   A crossbreak table for monolinguals and bilinguals in a metalinguistic test

significant, the researcher can use the *Chi square* test procedure which is discussed later in this chapter.)

In summary, *frequencies* provide the researcher with information about how frequent certain phenomena are, as well as initial insights, impressions, and understanding of the data. They can be reported through verbal description, tables, and graphs.

Central tendency measures

Central tendency measures, which are also part of descriptive statistics, provide information about the average and the typical behavior of subjects in respect of a specific phenomenon. The *mean* is the sum of all scores of all subjects in a group divided by the number of subjects. The *mode* is the score which has been obtained by the largest number of subjects, that is, the most frequent score in the group. The *median* is the score which divides the group into two in such a way that half of the scores are above it and half are below it. The mean ($\bar{X}$) is the measure which is most frequently used because of its stability in repeated sampling and its use in advanced statistical analysis procedures.

Example

A researcher conducts a study on the use of relative clauses by two groups of language learners, one of which has been exposed to formal instruction in the language, while the other has received no formal instruction. Each group consists of ten subjects. The researcher designs a task which requires the subjects to combine two single sentences into one, using the appropriate relative clause. Each correct use of the relative clause gets one point. There are ten pairs of sentences to combine.

Table 9.4 displays the scores that each of the ten subjects received on the task. The mean ($\bar{X}$) of each of the groups is the average score in each group and it is the summation of all the scores divided by the number of subjects. The X̄ was seven for each of the groups 70/7 = 10.

The mean, then, provides information on the average performance of a group on given tasks, and helps the researcher obtain insight by condensing large amounts of data. In the example above, the performance of each *individual* on the task does not provide meaningful information. However, the mean tells the researcher how the *group* as a whole performed, and that does provide more significant information.

Subject	Group A Formal instruction N = 10 score	Group B No formal instruction N = 10 score
1	6	10
2	6	8
3	7	5
4	8	10
5	7	9
6	8	8
7	7	7
8	8	6
9	6	4
10	7	3
Total	70	70
Mean (X̄) =	7	7

Table 9.4   Scores and means of two groups of learners on a task testing the use of the relative clause

Variability

While *frequencies* provide information on how common certain phenomena are and *central tendencies* provide information on the *average* behavior of the subjects on certain tasks, *variability* provides information on the spread of the behaviors or the phenomena among the subjects of the research. Specifically, it indicates how heterogeneous or homogeneous subjects are with regard to the behavior.

It is very possible, for example, that two groups will have the same mean, but the spread of scores will be different: while in one group all subjects obtained similar scores, in the other, there was a wider spread of scores and the group was more heterogeneous, that is, it had greater variability.

There are a number of variability measures. The most common one, which is therefore often used in subsequent analysis of the research data, is the *standard deviation* (S.D.).* It is the square root of the averaged square distance of the scores from the mean. The higher the standard deviation, the more varied and more hetero-geneous a group is on a given behavior, since the behavior is distributed more widely within the group.

If we return to the example presented in Table 9.4, it is clear that the group which received no formal instruction has higher variability, since the scores are more widely distributed among the different subjects. Some obtained higher scores, others obtained lower ones; in fact, most of the scores between 1 and 10 are represented in that group. On the other hand, the group that received formal instruction has lower variability since most of the scores were around the mean of 7. It is therefore a more homogeneous group. The S.D. for group A was actually .774 and for group B, 2.32; the more varied group having the higher standard deviation.

Another measure of variability used in statistical analyses is the variance, which is the standard deviation squared.

* Computing the standard deviation is performed as follows:

S.D. $= \sqrt{(\Sigma(X - \bar{X})^2)/N}$

where X = student's score; Σ = sum of; N = number of students; $\bar{X}$ = mean; $\sqrt{}$ = square root

Thus:

Group A		Group B	
$X - \bar{X}$	$(X - \bar{X})^2$	$X - \bar{X}$	$(X - X)^2$
$6 - 7 = -1$	$-1^2 = 1$	$10 - 7 = 3$	$3^2 = 9$
$6 - 7 = -1$	$-1^2 = 1$	$8 - 7 = 1$	$1^2 = 1$
$7 - 7 = 0$	$0^2 = 0$	$5 - 7 = -2$	$-2^2 = 4$
$8 - 7 = 1$	$1^2 = 1$	$10 - 7 = 3$	$3^2 = 9$
$7 - 7 = 0$	$0^2 = 0$	$9 - 7 = 2$	$2^2 = 4$
$8 - 7 = 1$	$1^2 = 1$	$8 - 7 = 1$	$1^2 = 1$
$7 - 7 = 0$	$0^2 = 0$	$7 - 7 = 0$	$0^2 = 0$
$8 - 7 = 1$	$1^2 = 1$	$6 - 7 = -1$	$-1^2 = 1$
$6 - 7 = -1$	$-1^2 = 1$	$4 - 7 = -3$	$-3^2 = 9$
$7 - 7 = 0$	$0^2 = 0$	$3 - 7 = -4$	$-4^2 = 16$
S.D. $\sqrt{(6/10)}$	$\Sigma = 6$	S.D. $= \sqrt{(54/10)}$	$\Sigma = 54$
S.D. $= .774$		S.D. $= 2.32$	

Measures of variability are very important in describing research data and most of the more complex analyses used in analyzing data from experimental as well as from multivariate research rely heavily on them.

In most research studies, the mean ($\bar{X}$), the standard deviation (S.D.), and the number of subjects (N), are reported together in a special descriptive statistics table, as in Table 9.5:

Group	N	$\bar{X}$	S.D.
Monolinguals	24	35	4.7
Bilinguals	20	45	7.2
Trilinguals	22	48	10.1

Table 9.5   Mean ($\bar{X}$), standard deviation (S.D.), and number of subjects (N) for test scores of three groups of language learners

There are, then, three common procedures for obtaining descriptive information about the data of a study: frequencies, central tendencies (principally the mean), and variabilities (the standard deviation and the variance). This type of information may be the main purpose of the research, that is, a description of the data; it is also required for more complex types of analysis, and can provide the researcher with a greater insight into and understanding of the data to be analyzed, as will be seen later in this chapter.

Analyzing correlational research data

Correlations

Correlational techniques are used for analyzing data obtained from descriptive research which, as described in Chapter 6, examines existing relationships between variables, with *no* manipulation of variables.

Consider a research project in which the relationship between a certain personality trait, such as outgoingness (extroversion/introversion), and second language proficiency is examined. When a *high positive* correlation is obtained between these two variables (outgoingness and proficiency) it means that there is a close relationship between the two variables. This means that the more outgoing (extroverted) the learners are, the better their language proficiency; the less outgoing (introverted), the poorer their language proficiency. A *low* correlation between the variables will mean that these two variables are not related to one another, that is, language proficiency is not related to the personality trait of being outgoing. A *negative* correlation between these two variables will imply that the less outgoing the subjects are (the more introverted), the higher their language proficiency or that the more outgoing they are, the lower their proficiency level. In this case, proficiency and outgoingness would be inversely related.

In order to compute correlations, the researcher will need to obtain scores of *two* sets of measurements on the *same* group of individuals. Thus, in examining the relationship between proficiency and outgoingness, each of the subjects in the research needs to have two measurements, one of language proficiency, and one of the degree of outgoingness. The first may be based on a language test and the other on some type of psychological measure.

Depending on the type of data (numerical, ordinal, and so on), different types of formulas will be applied to compute the correlation (r). The results are expressed in a *correlation coefficient* which ranges from −1.00, indicating perfect negative correlation, to 1.00 indicating perfect positive correlation.

Figure 9.4 shows different degrees of correlations, ranging from −.95 to +.90. The dots in each of the groups represent the intersection of the two sets of measurements for each subject.

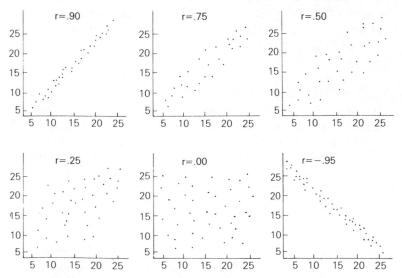

Figure 9.4   Graphs indicating degrees of correlations

If researchers want to make *inferences* from the correlations obtained in their study to the total population, they will have to examine their statistical significance. The statistical significance can be determined if the correlations have been obtained from a sample that has been randomly selected. Statistical significance relates to the confidence which the researchers can have in the correlations obtained. The significance of the correlation depends on the size of the correlation and the size of the sample from which it has been obtained. Thus while a correlation of .50 for example, may not be significant statistically if it was based on a small sample, the same correlation may be statistically significant when it is based on a larger sample.

The significance level is very important since it relates directly to whether the null hypothesis is rejected or not. That is, when a correlation is found to be significant statistically, the researcher can reject the null hypothesis that states that there are *no* significant correlations between the variables. The conventional level of rejecting the null hypothesis is $p \leq .05$ or $p \leq .01$, which means that, given the size of the sample of the study, a correlation of the magnitude found would have occurred by chance fewer than five times out of 100 for $p \leq .05$, and once out of 100 for $p \leq .01$. In other words, the correlation value can be assumed with more than 95 (or 99) per cent confidence to be different from 0.0.

For example, if a researcher has the null hypothesis stating that there will be no significant correlation between language aptitude and proficiency in L2 and obtains a correlation of $r = .70$ which is also found to be significant at the .01 level, the researcher can now reject the null hypothesis.

There may also be situations when the correlation is found to be significant *statistically*, but the researcher still needs to find out whether it is also significant from an educational or a linguistic point of view. Consider an example where a researcher obtains a correlation of .45 between two variables, and it is found to be statistically significant at the .01 level. The researcher is then faced with the question of determining whether a correlation of .45 is 'high enough' in spite of the fact that it is *statistically* significant.

The answer to this question is that 'it depends'. In some situations where there was no rationale and no theoretical basis which would lead the researcher to hypothesize a close relationship between two variables, then a correlation of .45 that was found incidentally to be statistically significant may be considered to be high, or at least interesting. On the other hand, when there were grounds for predicting a close relationship between variables and a relatively low (but significant) relationship was obtained, a correlation of .45 may not be high at all.

For example, if a number of studies in second language acquisition result in high correlations between proficiency in L1 and proficiency in L2 in a variety of contexts and with a variety of learners, a researcher investigating the relationship between the proficiency in L1 and L2 of immigrant children, for example, who obtains a correlation of .35, will not consider it to be high or important although, given the sample size of the study, such a correlation may be statistically significant. However, if in another study, a researcher obtains the same correlation between second language learning and knowledge of music, for example, it may be considered very important, since there was no real basis to predict that there would be a correlation between these two variables; thus obtaining such a correlation may be significant for exploring new variables and new relationships which researchers did not know existed.

Regardless of how high the correlations are, they do not imply *causation*. High correlations do not mean that one variable causes the other, but only that the two variables are related. In order to prove causality there is a need for an experimental research design, as in the case where one group receives a treatment to train students to achieve positive attitudes toward the language, and another group, the control, does not receive such a treatment. Following the treatment, the two groups take a proficiency test on the basis of which they are compared. If it is shown that the experimental group performs significantly better than the control on the proficiency test, there would be support for the hypothesis that attitude affected proficiency. Without using such a design, results for correlational research cannot be used to claim causality.

In a typical correlational study a number of variables are being correlated with one another and the coefficients are displayed in a *correlation matrix*, as shown in Table 9.6 over. (The correlation of 1.00 in this matrix represents the correlation of the variable with itself.)

In reporting correlations the researcher needs to specify the *sample size* (n) the correlations were based on, as well as the *level of significance* (p) since the size of the sample is related to the level of significance of the correlation. For example, the correlation between L1 and L2 for a group of second language learners might be reported as follows: $r=.37$ ($n=37$, $p \leq .01$), where 'r' is the size

Variable	Attitude	L1 Proficiency	L2 Proficiency	IQ
Attitude	1.00	.40	.50	.30
L1 Proficiency	.40	1.00	.65	.70
L2 Proficiency	.50	.65	1.00	.60
IQ	.30	.70	.60	1.00

Table 9.6   A correlation matrix of four variables

of the correlation, 'n' is the number of subjects, and 'p' is the level of significance.

A correlation is a statistical procedure which is very useful for different purposes in research and, apart from examining relationships between variables as a purpose in itself, it is also used for examining the reliability and validity of data collection procedures (see Chapter 8), and for subsequent types of more advanced statistical analysis. Correlational analysis is useful for analyzing data involving *two* variables. However, researchers often need to analyze data obtained from more than two variables, for example, L1, L2, *and* language aptitudes. The next section discusses data analysis techniques which can handle more than two variables at a time.

Analyzing multivariate research data

Data obtained from multivariate research, described in Chapter 6 as another form of descriptive research, can be analyzed through a set of techniques where a *number* of dependent variables and one or a *number* of independent variables are analyzed simultaneously. These techniques can be used for analyzing research where language aptitude, personality, and learner's background, for example, are examined for their contribution to acquiring the second language. The techniques can be used with different types of data, providing there is an acceptable sample size.

In this section we will discuss three multivariate procedures: *multiple regression*, *discriminant analysis*, and *factor analysis*.

Multiple regression

Through multiple regression analysis it is possible to examine the relationship and predictive power of one or more independent variables with the dependent variable. For example, in a study a researcher investigates the relationship between proficiency in L1 and proficiency in L2, and finds the correlation (r) to be .50. Computing the regression will indicate the *prediction* of L2 from L1, or how much of the learner's L2 proficiency can be accounted for by knowledge of L1.

Using *multiple regression*, the researcher can also predict and estimate the amount of variance in the dependent variable attributable to a number of independent variables. For example, how much of the variance in L2 (the dependent variable) can be accounted for by the independent variables 'age', 'IQ', 'language aptitude', and 'L1 proficiency'?

Multiple regression can also be used in experimental research for assessing *how much* influence the treatment has on the outcome, information that cannot be obtained through the analysis techniques used for experimental research, described in the next section of this chapter.

Multiple regression, therefore, has major advantages over simple correlational techniques in which the relationships of only two variables can be examined at a time. Such advantages are especially relevant for second language learning research, in which focusing on only two variables at a time represents too narrow a view. L2 learning is known to involve social, personal, situational, contextual, and cognitive variables, all operating simultaneously. The following example illustrates how focusing on more than two variables at a time can change the results.

Example

Researcher A is investigating the relationship between students' attitude toward learning English as a foreign language and proficiency in that language. The results of the study, expressed in correlations, found such a relationship to be r=.60; the regression coefficient, r^2, indicated that 36 per cent of the variance in L2 proficiency can be accounted for by the attitude of the learners toward learning the second language.

Researcher B is investigating the extent to which proficiency in L1 can predict proficiency in L2. The research is conducted with the same group of students used by researcher A. The results of the study indicate that r=.70, that is, r^2, the common variance between proficiency in L1 and in L2, is .49. This implies that 49 per cent of the proficiency in L2 can be explained by proficiency in L1.

Researcher C is investigating the extent to which the two independent variables, attitude (examined by researcher A) *and* L1 (examined by researcher B) *together*, explain L2 proficiency with the same sample of students. Using multiple regression, researcher C found that while 'L1' explained 40 per cent of the variance in L2 proficiency, 'attitude', the other independent variable, explained only 15 per cent.

The above example illustrates how, through a multiple regression analysis, the researcher can obtain a more realistic picture of the language learning phenomenon by simultaneously examining a number of variables believed to explain some aspects of second language learning (in this case attitude *and* L1). The analysis shows that while attitude correlates relatively highly with L2 proficiency when it is examined by itself, its contribution to the dependent variable of second language learning is much smaller when it is analyzed in conjunction with another variable, L1 proficiency. L1 proficiency turns out to be of greater importance in explaining L2, while the contribution of attitude is shown to be much smaller. Multiple regression, then, provides the researcher with a useful tool for examining the contribution of a number of independent variables to a dependent variable.

In analyzing data with this technique, the results provide information on the relative contribution of each of the independent variables to the dependent one. Each of the independent variables will then need to be tested for its *significance*, that is, whether the contribution to the dependent variable is statistically significant. Once a variable is found to be significant, it is important to see *how much* of the variance in the dependent variable is explained by this variable. Results of such an analysis show the amount of contribution of one independent variable, and how much *additional* variance is added by the second variable, the third, and so on. This is illustrated in the following example:

Example
A researcher (Kemp 1984) is interested in examining the contribution and prediction power of eleven variables, all sub-tests of academic proficiency in L1, as predictors of proficiency in L2. The question concerns the aspects in L1 academic proficiency which are relevant for learning a second language. The variables which are hypothesized to predict proficiency in L2 are listed in Table 9.7 which also displays the results of the multiple regression analysis performed on these independent variables in relation to scores obtained on the L2 test (the dependent variable).

(This example and those used for discriminant analysis and factor analysis are taken from Kemp: 'Native Language Knowledge as Predictor of Success in Learning a Foreign Language with Special Reference to a Disadvantaged Population.' Unpublished MA Thesis, Tel Aviv University, 1984.)

In analyzing data using multiple regression, the researcher needs to take into account the order of entry of the variable into the analysis, since the sequence of entry of the independent variables can influence the amount of contribution.

(1) Variables	(2) Significance level	(3) R^2 change	(4) R^2
1 Error correction (register)	.001	.37	.37
2 Innovative words (analysis)	.001	.07	.44
3 Cloze	.01	.02	.46
4 Completions	.03	.02	.48
5 Exceptions	.14	.005	.485
6 Register	.28	.003	.488
7 Correction (recognition)	.32	.002	.490
8 Nonsense words	.46	.0014	.490
9 Definitions	.51	.0011	.491
10 Innovative words	.71	.0003	.492
11 Synonyms	.87	.0000	.492

Table 9.7   Multiple regression of scores on the L2 test by sub-tests of L1 academic proficiency

The first column of Table 9.7 lists all eleven variables used in the multiple regression analysis. The line under the fourth variable (*completions*) indicates that once the first four variables were entered in the analysis, no other variables added significantly to the explained variance. (The remaining variables may have significant simple correlations with the dependent variable, but taken together as a set of independent variables they do not add any explanation after the four variables which were entered first.)

Regression analysis indicates to the researcher not only which variables are significant contributors to the dependent variable, but also *how much* of the variance in L2 can be accounted for by the four variables which were found to be significant. R^2 *change*, the third column in the table, indicates the *amount* of the contribution of each of the variables to the percentage of the explained variance. The table indicates that the first variable, *error correction (register)*, contributed most variance (37 per cent) to L2 proficiency. This was followed by the second variable, *innovative words (analysis)*, which accounted for an additional 7 per cent of the variance, followed by *cloze* which explained another 2 per cent, and a further 1 per cent was explained by *completions*.

The fourth column, R^2, indicates the cumulative variance. Thus, while *error correction (register)* by itself explained 37 per cent, when it was combined with *innovative words (analysis)*, together they explained 44 per cent (37 + 7). Since *cloze* explained an additional 2 per cent, together the cumulative variance of the three variables was 46 per cent (37 + 7 + 2). All together the four significant variables explained about half (48 per cent) of the variance in L2 proficiency as measured by the test used in this research.

In summary, from multiple regression analysis we can obtain results showing which variables are significant in their contribution to explaining the variance in the dependent variable *and* how much variance they contribute.

Discriminant analysis

Discriminant analysis is concerned with the prediction of membership in one of two (or more)' categories of a dependent variable from scores on two or more independent variables, in other words, which *combination* of independent variables distinguish between two or more categories of the dependent variable. Possible examples of categories may be males/females, monolingual/bilingual learners, or formal/informal contexts. A researcher may be interested in finding out which combination of variables, L1, attitude, aptitude, or type of instruction, for example, can best distinguish between two different types of second language learners.

The results of the analysis indicate the relative contribution made by the independent variables to the dependent variable, and these then need to be tested for their significance. The test of significance indicates whether the differences which exist among the groups of monolingual/bilingual, for example, as predicted by the independent variables, is significant. 'R^2' indicates the variance in the dependent variable which can be explained by the independent variables.

Example
A researcher (Kemp 1984) investigates which *combination* of sub-tests (variables), all believed to measure L1 academic proficiency, best discriminate between three groups of language learners of different socioeconomic (SES) backgrounds.

By using discriminant analysis, the best-discriminating variables were discovered in order of importance. Table 9.8 presents the results of such an analysis.

(1) Step	(2) Variables	(3) R^2*
1	Error correction (register)	.33
2	Synonyms	.40
3	Register	.44
4	Idioms	.47
5	Definitions	.49
6	Exceptions	.50
7	Completions	.51

$p \le .001$ *$R^2 = 1 - $ wilks

Table 9.8   Discriminant analysis among three different groups of SES learners on L1 academic proficiency

Table 9.8 indicates that the sub-test *error correction (register)* discriminates best among the three groups of second language learners, since $R^2 = .33$. This means that *error correction (register)* accounts for about 33 per cent of the variance among the three groups and *discriminated* best among the three groups of learners of different SES. The variable was then followed by the variable *synonyms* which added 7 per cent to the discriminating power of *error correction (register)* $(.40 - .33 = .07)$. Together they explain 40 per cent of the variance among the three groups. Similarly, *register* added another 4 per cent to the discriminating power of the first two. It was possible to apply the procedure through to step 7, the variable *completion*, the last sub-test to reach a level of statistical significance. The seven variables listed in the table account for 51 per cent of the variance in discriminating among the three groups of learners, as is shown in column (3).

This analysis leads the researcher to conclude that a combination of seven variables in L1 academic proficiency discriminated among the three groups of subjects of different SES. The technique of discriminant analysis then, can provide the researcher with useful information on which variables can best distinguish between different types of second language learners. This is an important issue in second language acquisition.

Factor analysis

Factor analysis helps the researcher make large sets of data more manageable by identifying a factor or factors that underlie the data. It is different from multiple regression and discriminant analysis in that it does not relate independent variables to a dependent one, but rather operates within a number of independent variables, without a need to have a dependent variable. In factor analysis, the interrelationships between and among the variables of the data are examined in[7] an attempt to find out how many independent dimensions (termed *factors*) can be identified in the data. It thus provides information on the underlying characteristics of the variables of the study. This type of analysis is based on the assumption that variables measuring the same factor will be highly related, while variables measuring *different* factors will have low correlations with one another.

For example, a researcher is constructing an instrument based on some theoretical notion of what aptitude consists of, in order to measure language aptitude. The researcher needs to confirm and validate that the measure used to investigate aptitude really does measure it. The technique of factor analysis will help the researcher identify the factor or factors underlying the data collected. Those aspects which do not come out as part of one factor may not be related to aptitude, or may constitute one or more independent factors. For example, it is possible that in examining the factors underlying aptitude, two factors are identified, one consisting of memory, sound coding, and rote memory, and the other consisting of recognition of grammatical structure and lexicon. These factors are obtained because, while the correlation within each of the factors is high, the correlation between the two factors is not high enough and therefore they remain two *separate* factors.

Factor analysis has been used extensively in second language learning in an attempt to validate and verify factors which are believed theoretically to underlie different language constructs, such as language proficiency, language aptitude, and attitude toward learning a second language. Factor analysis is also a procedure used extensively to validate language tests, for example, when a researcher constructs a test of reading comprehension and would like to find out whether all the items used on that test really measure reading comprehension.

In applying the procedure of factor analysis, different mathematical formulas are used to compute the correlations among the variables in a number of different ways. The *factor loadings* indicate the level of correlation between the factors and the different variables used in the analysis. Those variables which have the *highest* loadings with the factors are then used to define the factor. They are reported in the form of coefficients. After the variables with the highest loadings are identified, the researcher examines the factors with a view to interpreting them and understanding what feature they represent. Gardner and Lambert (1972), for example, interpreted the two factors they obtained in their factor analysis to mean 'integrative' motivation and 'instrumental' motivation.

Communality refers to the proportion of variance that the individual variable has in common with the other variables in the set. Thus it is similar to the R^2 obtained in multiple regression and in discriminant analysis discussed in the previous sections. R^2 indicates the amount of variance which is explained by the factor, that is, the relative importance of each of the factors in accounting for the variance measured by the total test, and it is possible to identify a statistically *significant* factor. These terms will become clearer with the following example.

Example

A researcher (Kemp 1984) developed a test for measuring L1 academic proficiency, that is, the knowledge in L1 which students need to have in order to succeed in school. The test consisted of a number of sub-tests each examining an aspect in L1 believed to be related to L1 academic knowledge. Some of the aspects included were: ability to correct errors in the use of registers, ability to define words accurately, use of idioms, and ability to identify errors. The researcher needed to find out whether all the sub-tests used as part of the test were related to academic language proficiency, and therefore needed to identify the factor, the construct, underlying this newly developed test and discover whether all the thirteen sub-tests warranted inclusion on the L1 academic proficiency test.

The researcher applied the procedure of factor analysis to find out whether all the sub-tests believed to measure L1 academic proficiency made a statistically significant contribution.

The results of the factor analysis identified only *one* factor which explained 55 per cent of the total variance. (See Table 9.9.)

Table 9.9 indicates that each of the thirteen sub-tests had significant loadings (above .50) on the one factor that was identified and thus each of them needed to be included in computing a learner's score of L1 academic proficiency. The researcher concluded, therefore, that all the sub-tests contributed to some

(1) Sub-test	(2) Loadings	(3) Communalities*
1 Cloze	.86	.73
2 Error correction (register)	.84	.71
3 Completions	.83	.66
4 Error correction (identifications)	.81	.65
5 Opposites	.75	.57
6 Definitions	.74	.57
7 Innovations (P)	.70	.49
8 Innovations (C)	.69	.47
9 Exceptions	.66	.43
10 Idioms	.65	.429
11 Nonsense words	.647	.42
12 Synonyms	.51	.26
13 Register	.50	.25

* Communalities (common variance) = loadings squared
$R^2 = .55$

Table 9.9   Factor matrix showing proportion of loadings and common variance among thirteen sub-tests of L1 academic proficiency

extent to the overall score of L1 academic proficiency. The sub-tests which had most in common with the general factor were *cloze* (communality =.73) *and correction* (.71). The sub-tests *synonym* and *register* had least in common (.26 and .25 respectively) with the entire test.

From the example above we can see that factor analysis helps the researcher identify the underlying features of a measurement tool (in this case one factor was identified), and the contribution of each of the sub-tests to that factor. In addition, the researcher can obtain information on how much of the total variance in the test was explained by the different sub-tests.

The three procedures described in this section, *multiple regression, discriminant analysis*, and *factor analysis*, are all used to analyze data obtained from multivariate studies, and are applicable to different types of research problems in second language acquisition. There are additional and equally useful multivariate procedures not discussed in this chapter, such as *path analysis, canonical analysis*, and *multivariate analysis of variance* (MANOVA). MANOVA, for example, can help the researcher estimate the effect of the treatment in experimental designs. These are very effective data analysis techniques. The major requirement, however, when using such techniques is that there be a sufficiently large sample. It is recommended that readers refer to the statistics books listed in the Appendix for detailed discussion on the use of the procedures, as well as their limitations (see especially Amick 1975, Kerlinger and Pedhazur 1973, Cohen and Cohen 1975, Thorndike 1978).

The procedures described up to this point concern what was referred to in Chapter 6 as descriptive research. The next section will focus on analyzing data obtained from experimental research.

Analyzing experimental research data

In this section we will discuss procedures for analyzing data obtained from different types of experimental designs. (See Chapter 7.) The different designs call for different methods of analysis. When two groups, for example, experimental and control, are being compared, the researcher will use the t-test which is capable of comparing two groups on a given measure. *One way analysis of variance* will be used to compare more than two groups, and *factorial analysis of variance* to analyze the more complex experimental designs such as factorial designs.

The t-test

The *t-test* is used to compare the means of *two* groups. It helps determine how confident the researcher can be that the differences found between two groups (experimental and control) as a result of a treatment are not due to chance. The results of applying the t-test provide the researcher with a *t-value*. That t value is then entered in a special table of t values included in most statistics books and which indicates whether, given the size of the sample in the research, the t-value is *statistically significant*.

Example
A researcher is comparing the performance of two randomly selected groups learning French by two different methods. The experimental group learns with the aid of the computer, that is, each frontal lesson is followed by a practice session with the computer. The control group is not exposed to the practice session with the computer, but has practice sessions with the teacher. The researcher investigates the effect of the computer practice sessions on students' achievements in French. At the end of the three-month experiment, both groups undergo an achievement test. The

researcher uses the t-test to examine whether there are differences in the achievement of the two groups.

The results indicate the t-value to be 1.786. The researcher enters this value in the table of t values and finds that, based on the size of the sample, that value is significant at the .05 level. The researcher reports the results as: t = 1.786; p≤.05, and therefore rejects the null hypothesis which states that the difference between the two groups is not significant.

In the example just described, the researcher uses the t-test procedure to examine the differences between the two groups where one is exposed to a certain treatment (computer practice sessions) and the other is not. The results of the analysis provide the researcher with information regarding the effect of using the computer on achievements in learning French.

It is advisable when presenting the t-test results, to precede them with a descriptive statistics table displaying the mean ($\bar{X}$), standard deviation (S.D.), and size of sample (N), in order to provide a better insight into the data. In the example just described, the descriptive statistics table should show the means of the experimental and control groups, as well as the spread of the scores in each.

The t-test described applied to two independent groups. A slightly different t-test formula is applied when the comparison is between the same group compared at two different times (such as pre- and post-tests).

One way analysis of variance (one way ANOVA)

One way analysis of variance is used to examine the differences in *more than two groups*. It specifically indicates how confident the researcher can be that the differences observed among, for example, two experimental groups and a control group as a result of a treatment are not due to chance. The analysis is performed on the *variance* of the groups, focusing on whether the variability *between* the different groups is greater than the variability *within* each of the groups. The F value is the ratio of the 'between' variance, over the 'within' variance, as indicated below:

$$F = \frac{\text{Between group variance}}{\text{Within group variance}}$$

Thus, a significant F will occur when the variability among the groups is greater than the variability within each group. When the reverse is true (the variability within each group is greater than the variability among or between the groups), the F is likely to be insignificant because that means that differences among the groups are not large enough to be significant.

A one way analysis of variance will result in an *F value*. That value is then entered into a special table of F values (found in most statistics books) to find out whether, given the sample size in the study, the F value is statistically significant. If F is found to be significant, the researcher rejects the null hypotheses. The researcher reports the F value in an *analysis of variance table*, which describes the process of arriving at the F value and its level of significance.

When F is significant, the researcher rejects the null hypothesis of no difference, but still does not know *where* the differences are, that is, between which of the groups. The researcher therefore needs to compare the pairs of groups (1 and 2, 2 and 3, and 3 and 1, for example), using certain procedures similar to the t-test, which are capable of examining *two* groups at a time. Here, too, descriptive statistics (mean, standard deviation) will provide an indication of where the differences are likely to be. However, these insights need to be examined by statistical procedures which specifically examine contrasts, and compare two groups at a time. Such procedures are discussed in the various statistics books listed at the end of this chapter.

Example
A researcher is examining the effect of different instructional treatments in learning French. Group A is exposed to peer teaching where students teach each other. Group B is exposed to individualized instruction, and group C is learning via traditional frontal teaching. The researcher is interested in finding out the effect of the two new approaches (peer teaching and individualized instruction) on students' achievements in learning French.

The researcher administers an achievement test to all three randomly assigned groups at the end of the experiment, and compares the results, using the one way analysis of variance, which compares the variability among the three groups in relation to the variability within each of the groups, and finds the F value. That value is then entered in the F table and, considering the number of subjects in this research, the F value turns out to be significant. This leads the researcher to reject the null hypothesis which states that no difference will be observed between the three groups. However, the researcher also wants to find out *where* the significant differences are, that is, between groups A and B, A and C, B and C, or between all of them. The *Scheffé* contrast test, which is commonly used to examine whether differences between *pairs* are significant is therefore used. The results of this analysis show that the differences between all the three pairs are significant. The researcher then examines descriptive statistics (mean and standard deviation), and finds that, although all the three groups differed from each other, the most pronounced difference is between group B, the one exposed to individualized instruction, and each of the other two groups. The descriptive statistics of that study are presented in Table 9.10.

Group	X̄	S.D.
Group A: Peer teaching	83.5	25.2
Group B: Individualized instruction	85.7	32.1
Group C: Frontal teaching	80.2	23.9

Table 9.10   Descriptive statistics of three types of instruction

Factorial analysis of variance (ANOVA)

The procedures described so far, the t-test and the one way analysis of variance, are capable of analyzing data obtained from experimental research comparing either two groups (the t-test) or more than two groups (one way ANOVA). *Factorial ANOVA* is capable of analyzing the effect of different treatments in more complex conditions, such as with different types of learners, or different proficiency levels, as in the examples given in Chapter 7. All these are expressed as independent variables which are considered in the analysis of variance. This is illustrated in Figure 9.5 below.

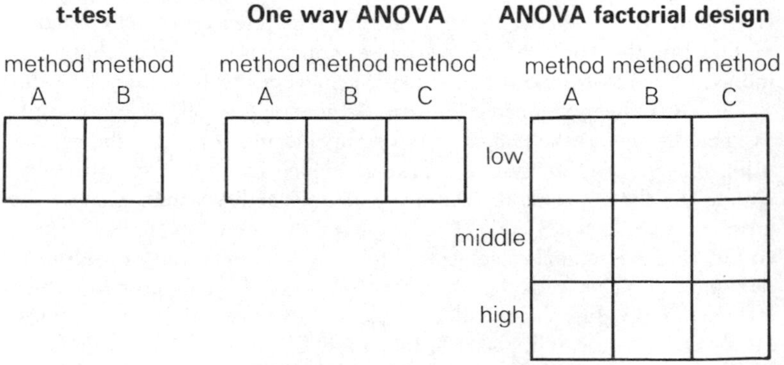

Figure 9.5   Types of designs appropriate for t-test, one way, and ANOVA

Figure 9.5 shows how factorial ANOVA can examine a question such as the effect of different treatments on three different types of learners, of low, middle, and high proficiency. It examines the effect of several variables studied simultaneously (termed *main effect*), as well as the *interaction* among the variables, or factors.

For example, when a researcher examines the effect of two different methods of teaching on learners of different proficiency levels, the *main effect* is the effect of the methods on all proficiency levels and the *interaction* is whether the methods act differently with students of different proficiency levels. One of the methods, for example, may work well with low-level students but not with high-level ones.

In ANOVA, the means of all the samples (groups as well as proficiency levels) are compared with one another. The results of such a comparison are expressed as an F value. That F value is entered into the F table (described in the section on one way ANOVA) to find out whether, given the size of the sample, F is statistically significant. If it is significant, the researcher can reject the null hypothesis. However, the researcher does not know *where*, in all these comparisons, the significant differences are. It may very well be that it is significant for all the groups relating to all the proficiency levels. It is also possible that there are significant differences only between certain groups and certain learners. As the ANOVA relates to all the samples simultaneously, when researchers obtain a significant F, they need to perform subsequent analyses to find out *where* in the data the significance occurs. Results obtained from the ANOVA are reported in an ANOVA summary table which shows the different calculations used to arrive at the F value.

ANOVA is an exploratory tool. It tells the researcher that somewhere in the data there are significant differences and that after subsequent analysis, information on where they may be can be obtained. However, there will still be no information about the *size* of the effect; the researcher merely knows that there is an effect or an interaction. (For further information, see the Appendix, as well as references in Chapter 7, and especially Winer 1971.)

It is possible, however, to apply multivariate analysis procedures, specifically the *multivariate analysis of variance* (MANOVA), not discussed in this book, to examine the size of the effect. The MANOVA procedure utilizes both analysis of variance and multivariate techniques. It can provide information on whether significant differences due to a treatment occur, and it can estimate the size and the magnitude of the effect as well.

Chi square

The *Chi square* (χ^2) is a data analysis procedure which helps the researcher address questions about relations between two *nominal* variables. In this procedure the researcher compares the *frequencies* observed in a sample with some *theoretical* or *expected* frequencies. The frequencies refer to categories used to classify the data, such as males/females, natives/non-natives, monolinguals/bilinguals, or high language learning achievers/low achievers.

Example

In a study on the use of certain speech acts, the researcher needs to find out whether there is a *significant* difference between natives and non-natives in using certain ways of requesting. The researcher selects a sample of natives and non-natives and finds out through a questionnaire how often they use specific requests in speech, and then counts the frequencies of these requests and applies the Chi square to examine whether there are statistically significant differences in the uses of these speech acts by natives and non-natives, based on these frequencies.

The researcher obtains a significant Chi square (χ^2). This indicates that there is a meaningful difference in the use of the different types of requests between native and non-native speakers of the language. The researcher can reject the null hypothesis of no difference.

It is possible to apply the technique to data involving more than two categories, such as monolinguals, bilinguals, and trilinguals, provided that it is used with frequency data. Scores obtained on tests can also be used in Chi square analysis if they are categorized as frequencies, that is, if the researcher creates categories such as *high*, *average*, and *low* frequency based on the test scores.

As was discussed earlier in the chapter in the section on frequencies, many of the problems in a second language acquisition call for the examination of frequencies of certain language behaviors by different language learners in different contexts. The Chi square procedure is therefore used extensively in analyzing data in second language acquisition research.

Summary of the different statistical procedures

In this section we have described a number of procedures which the researcher can use in analyzing data. The different analyses produce results which are used to arrive at the conclusions of the research. As we observed, different types of data analysis are appropriate for different types of research problems.

Data collected in qualitative (heuristic) research by data collection procedures of a low level of explicitness will be analyzed through qualitative techniques. In applying these techniques the researcher will identify certain patterns and categories in the data, or apply certain schemes to the data.

When the research is descriptive, the researcher will use the different types of descriptive statistics such as frequencies, central tendencies, and variabilities. Descriptive statistics is also useful for obtaining insights into, and a better understanding of, the data. For this reason it is often used for more complex statistical analysis.

When the research problem requires an examination of the relationships between variables, the researcher will use correlational analysis. Obtaining significant correlations will show whether the relationship between the variables is meaningful, but it will not indicate whether one variable caused the other; these kinds of problems call for experimental research design. When the researcher wants to examine the common variance between the two variables which have been correlated, that is, how much of the variance in one variable also exists in the other, or the extent to which one variable can predict the other, regression analysis will be used.

Multivariate procedures are used for examining more complex relationships than those examined through correlations, since they are capable of dealing with a number of variables at a time. We discussed three such procedures: multiple regression, which can examine the relationship and prediction power of a number of independent variables with a dependent variable; discriminant analysis, which is concerned with the prediction of membership in one of two (or three) categories of a dependent variable from scores on two or more independent variables; and factor analysis, which helps the researcher identify factors in the data, and thus makes the data more manageable.

In the last section we discussed a number of procedures for analyzing data obtained from experimental research. Specifically, we described three procedures: the t-test, which helps examine whether the differences between two samples are statistically significant; one way analysis of variance, which examines differences between more than two groups; and factorial analysis of variance which is capable of analyzing the effect of a treatment under more complex conditions such as with different types of instruction or learners. We also included in that section the Chi square which compares frequencies observed in a sample with some theoretically expected frequencies.

The procedures described here are obviously not the only procedures available to the researcher for analyzing the data. We have discussed the more commonly used ones, but other statistical procedures, mostly variations on the procedures discussed in this chapter, are also available. We did not discuss *how* to carry out the various procedures. For this, the researcher needs to refer to the statistics books listed in Appendix A to obtain more comprehensive information on the use of these procedures in research.

Most of the analyses discussed in this section can be performed with the computer, using prepared statistical packages. In the next section we will discuss computer analysis of data.

Using the computer for data analysis

Most of the data analysis techniques described in the previous section of this chapter can be performed with the computer. A number of statistical packages designed for this type of research are available. The computer is essential for the analysis of most quantitative research data, since it can handle complex analyses of large amounts of data in a very short time and at a very reasonable cost.

The most commonly used systems are the *Statistical Package for Social Science* (SPSS) (Nie *et al.* 1975) and its updated version, SPSS X (1986), which include programs for most types of data analyses. It is accompanied by a manual which not only describes in great detail how to perform the analyses but also offers comprehensive and thorough descriptions of the procedures. The researcher is advised to find out which packages are available when preparing the research proposal. Most universities offer intensive courses and assistance in using these packages for research data analysis.

In this section we will briefly describe the different phases involved in performing computer data analysis.

The computer analysis should be planned in advance so that when preparing the data collection tools, a coding system can be integrated into the procedure. When using a questionnaire, for example, it becomes very useful to have a coding system to facilitate the process of recording the data later.

After the data collection procedure has been administered, the data are transferred to coding sheets or directly to the computer database. Below is a sample of a coding sheet where each item is represented by a column on the coding sheet. Thus, column 1 represents the person whose data is being coded, columns 4 and 5

IBM FORTRAN CODING FORM

PROGRAM		PUNCHING INSTRUCTIONS	GRAPHIC					
PROGRAMMER	DATE		PUNCH					

COMM.	STATEMENT NUMBER				CONT.	FORTRAN STATEMENT																																																									
1	2	3	4	5	6	7	8	9	10	11	12	13	14	15	16	17	18	19	20	21	22	23	24	25	26	27	28	29	30	31	32	33	34	35	36	37	38	39	40	41	42	43	44	45	46	47	48	49	50	51	52	53	54	55	56	57	58	59	60	61	62	63
3	1		0	1		1		0	3		1		2		2		3		0	2																																										
3	1		0	2		2		0	4		1		2		2		3		0	2																																										
3	1		0	3		2		0	6		1		1		1		3		0	1																																										
3	2		0	1		1		0	6		1		1		1		3		1	6																																										
3	2		0	2		1		0	7		1		2		2		3		0	2																																										
3	2		0	3		1		1	1		1		2		2		3		0	2																																										
3	2		0	4		1		1	2		1		3		1		3		1	5																																										
3	3		0	1		1		0	2		1		2		2		3		0	7																																										
3	3		0	2		1		0	3		1		1		1		3		0	1																																										
3	3		0	3		1		1	0		1		1		1		3		1	5																																										
3	3		0	4		1		1	1		1		2		2		3		1	5																																										
3	3		0	5		1		1	1		2		2		2		4		1	4																																										

Figure 9.6 An example of a coding sheet

are the student number, column 7 is the person's sex (1 for male, 2 for female); columns 9 and 10 are the answers to the test questions, and so on. Each value is assigned an alpha-numerical value (letter or number).

After the data have been entered onto the coding sheets, they need to be transferred to the computer database. This can often be done with professional help, especially when there are large amounts of data to be entered. When the data are in the computer database, it is essential to check that the information has been entered accurately. It is possible to obtain a printout of the data and compare this with the coding sheets.

Once the data have been entered accurately into the computer database, an appropriate program for the analysis must be found. If a statistical package is not available, then a new program may have to be written, with the help of experts.

In preparing for the analysis, instructions should be formulated to guide the computer on the specific analysis that needs to be performed. It is common not to obtain meaningful results from the first analysis, as there may be various problems such as errors in coding or in the description of data. When working with the computer, attention must be given to the smallest details.

Once the results are obtained and printed out, the researcher reads the outputs to obtain the information needed. (Computer manuals give guidance on this.)

It is important for the researcher to have a 'feel' for the results and to use intuition. False results may be produced if there are any errors in the program, the database, or in the running of the program. The researcher needs to keep a close watch on the results to see if they seem sensible. It is important to *understand* the statistics used for the data analysis. The use of the computer for analysis often gives us the false impression that we do not need to understand the statistical procedures. However, we suggest that the researchers acquaint themselves with the specific statistical procedures used in a given piece of research; this, in turn, will lead to a more valid interpretation of the results.

Summary

In this chapter we first introduced the concept of analyzing data and differentiated between quantitative and qualitative types of data analysis. We then related data analysis to the different research designs introduced in Chapters 6 and 7, by describing the techniques used to analyze the data obtained from qualitative, descriptive, correlational, multivariate, and experimental research. The various techniques were described within the context of specific second language acquisition research problems. The chapter ended with a brief outline of the stages involved in using the computer for analyzing research data.

Activities

1 Select three articles in the journals on second language acquisition. For each of the articles, go over the description of the data analysis techniques and the tables, and hypothesize the research questions or problems for which these techniques are used to provide answers.

2 Select an area of research in second language acquisition. Now devise five research problems in that area, each lending itself to a different data analysis technique: a) qualitative, b) descriptive, c) correlational, d) multivariate, and e) experimental. Describe the kind of data you would collect for each analysis and the procedures you would use for the analyses.

References

Amick, D. J. and **Walberg, H. J.** 1975. *Introductory Multivariate Research.* Berkeley, CA.: McCuthan.

Cohen, J. and **Cohen, P.** 1975. *Applied Multiple Regression/Correlation Analysis for the Behavioral Sciences.* Hillsdale, N.J.: Lawrence Erlbaum Associates.

Hollander, M. and **Wolfe, A.** 1973. *Nonparametric Statistical Methods.* New York: J. Wiley.

Gardner, R. and **Lambert, W.** 1972. *Attitudes and Motivation in Second Language Learning.* Rowley, Mass.: Newbury House.

Gordon, C. 1987. 'The Effect of Testing Method on Achievement in Reading Comprehension Tests in English as a Foreign Language.' MA Thesis, Tel Aviv University.

Kemp, J. 1984. Native Language Knowledge as Predictor of Success in Learning a Foreign Language with Special Reference to a Disadvantaged Population. MA Thesis, Tel Aviv University.

Kerlinger, F. N. and **Pedhazur, E. J.** 1973. *Multiple Regression in Behavioral Research.* New York: Holt, Rinehart and Winston.

LeCompte, M. D. and **Goetz, J. P.** 1982. 'Problems of reliability and validity in ethnographic research.' *Review of Educational Research* 52:31–60.

Mann, S. 1983. 'Verbal reports as data: A focus on retrospection' in S. Dingwall, S. Mann, and F. Katamba (eds.): *Problems, Methods and Theory in Applied Linguistics.* Lancaster: Lancaster University.

Newell, A. and Simon, H. 1982. *Human Problem Solving.* Englewood Cliffs, N.J.: Prentice-Hall.

Nie, N. H., Hull, C. H., Jenkins, J. K., Steinbrenner, K., and Bent, D. H. 1975. SPSS: *Statistical Package for the Social Sciences* (second edition). New York: McGraw-Hill.

Olshavsky, J. 1977. 'Reading as problem solving.' *Reading Research Quarterly* 12/4:654–674.

Siegal, S. 1956. *Nonparametric Statistics for the Behavioral Sciences.* New York: McGraw-Hill.

SPSS X User's Guide (second edition). 1986. New York: McGraw-Hill.

Tesch, R. 1987. 'Comparing the Most Widely Used Methods of Qualitative Analysis: What Do they Have in Common?' Paper presented at the American Educational Research Association Convention, Washington, D.C.

Thorndike, R. M. 1978. *Correlational Procedures for Research.* New York: Gardner Press.

Winer, B. J. 1971. *Statistical Process in Experimental Design.* New York: McGraw-Hill.

10 Putting it all together

'It seems very pretty,' she said when she had finished it, 'but it's *rather* hard to understand!' (You see, she didn't like to confess even to herself, that she couldn't make it out at all.) 'Somehow it seems to fill my head with ideas – only I don't exactly know what they are!. . .'

(Lewis Carroll: *Alice in Wonderland*)

Reporting, summarizing, and interpreting the results

Once the data have been analyzed and the results obtained, the last phase in the research process is to *summarize* the results, *interpret* them, and then to *report* the research to the relevant audiences. It is at this stage that the researcher puts the results together and then attempts to understand their meaning within the general context of the research problem and topic. This is the point at which the researcher asks questions such as: What were the major findings of the research? What do these results mean? What can be learned from them? What are their implications? How can they contribute to existing knowledge in the research area? What recommendations can they lead to?

In order to minimize misinterpretation of the research results, it is customary to differentiate between *reporting* and *summarizing*, and *interpreting* the results; it is recommended that these be kept apart in the research report.

In the reporting and summarizing section the researchers report the results that were obtained from the analysis of the data, often using tables, graphs, charts, and category lists; they then synthesize the findings in a cohesive and clear way.

In the interpretation section the researchers go beyond the results toward conclusions, implications, and recommendations based on the results. In most research reports this part is referred to as the 'discussion'.

We will now consider each of these in turn.

Reporting and summarizing

Reporting research results in quantitative research is usually done through presentation of the statistical results obtained, illustrated by tables, graphs, and charts. Results obtained from qualitative analysis are reported through detailed descriptions of the processes which the researcher used in arriving at the categories and patterns of the research. These are often accompanied by examples, quotations, and anecdotes from the actual data.

The type of tables and graphs used in reporting *quantitative* research will depend on the specific data analysis technique that was performed. In descriptive research, for example, results will be displayed in tables which show the means, standard deviations, frequencies, and the sample sizes. Correlational research will be displayed in matrices which give the correlational coefficients obtained, the degrees of significance, and the sample size. The results of experimental research will be presented by giving the F or the t values, together with the degrees of freedom and the p value (level of significance), either in table form or through verbal descriptions, or a combination of the two. The process used to obtain the results is also described. ANOVA (analysis of variance) tables, where the steps which lead to the F value are described, are used to show results obtained from the various types of analysis of variance.

As was mentioned in Chapter 9, most analyses are preceded by tables of descriptive statistics, intended to provide initial insights into the data before the main statistical analyses are performed. These analyses are then followed by a summary which synthesizes the major findings of the research.

The method of reporting the results of *qualitative* research also depends on the specific type of analysis that was used. Thus, when categories were derived directly from the data, the report will explain the process used in deriving them, as well as providing a list or a description of the categories obtained. If the analysis was performed by applying an organizing scheme to the data, as discussed in Chapter 9, then a description of the frequencies obtained for each of the categories is provided, either in raw numbers, or in percentages. For both types of analyses, quotations and actual examples from the written or oral data, anecdotes, diagrams, and tables displaying the frequencies (if they are available), are provided to give supporting evidence for the patterns and categories obtained.

An important element in reporting any type of research is to include information about the reliability and validity of the procedures used to collect the data, so that another researcher attempting to replicate the research is able to do so. For this reason it is especially important in reporting results from qualitative research to include descriptions of the process of conducting the research, the different procedures used to collect the data, the research site, the exact conditions prevailing during data collection, and the validation procedures applied. While it is important to include such information in reporting both types of research, it is of special significance in qualitative research since there are no set procedures for conducting such research, and therefore documenting the process is essential for validating the results.

Below are examples taken from reports of the results of some studies.

Example 1
In a study comparing three different methods of teaching EFL (DG – Discussion Group; STADS – Student Teams and Achievement Divisions; and Whole-class), Bejarano (1987) reports the results by first providing a table of descriptive statistics in which the means, standard deviations, and sample sizes for each of the groups of the pre-tests and post-tests are displayed. These are then followed by a verbal description of the results of the analysis of variance, as follows:
Pupils in the DG classes registered greater improvement than their peers in the whole-class setting on both the total test, $F(1,265) = 4.23$, p<.05, and on the listening comprehension scale, $F(1,465) = 11.99$, p<.001. . . . the size of the change that occurred in the DG and the STAD classes from pre-test to post-test (4.49 and 4.34 respectively) was bigger than that in the whole-class setting (2.23). (Bejarano 1987, pp. 492–3)

Example 2
Pica, Young, and Doughty (1987) examine the impact of the type of interaction on comprehension. In reporting the results, the authors display them in a number of tables which compare the comprehension scores of the subjects in the two experimental situations. Each of the tables focuses on different features of the input and provides the means and the standard deviations, and shows whether the differences were significant in the t-test analyses performed on the data for each of the input features.

For reporting qualitative research we will refer back to the example described in Chapter 9 (p. 205), where a researcher analyzed the syntactic and morphological errors made by immigrant children and the reactions of native speakers to these errors.

Example 3

The results are reported by listing the types and categories of errors in relation to the organizational scheme that was implemented on the data. The categories include some numerical data in the form of frequencies of occurrence of the errors which are reported for each child individually. The lists are accompanied by specific examples, such as that a certain error was observed in 30 per cent of cases, and that it was produced only when the child answered a question, but never when he or she initiated one.

The reactions of the native speakers to these errors are treated in a similar way. Since they were derived directly from the data without an organizing scheme, the researcher describes the process used to derive them in sufficient detail for another researcher reviewing the data to be able to obtain identical categories. The descriptions of the reactions are also reported by presenting frequencies, such as that a certain reaction was observed in only 10 per cent of cases, while another reaction was observed in about 50 per cent; or that native speakers ignored errors in unfamiliar words in about 40 per cent of occurrences while in 10 per cent the native speakers asked the learner to explain what he or she meant. Here, too, the descriptions are accompanied by quotations of the actual responses made by the native speakers to certain types of errors, indicating particular speakers. For example: 'John, who is a shy child, almost always ignored the errors, while Ann, who is more open and outgoing, kept asking: "And what do you mean by that? Can you please say it again? I do not understand what you say."' These examples are very helpful in exemplifying and explaining the categories as well as in familiarizing the reader with the data.

Interpreting the results

Once the results have been reported and described, they must be interpreted. Interpretation occurs at a number of levels. Common to all these levels is that the research results are carried one step further toward an examination of their meaning in a broader context and toward possible recommendations. These different levels of interpretation are often put in the discussion section of the report.

The *conclusions* discuss the meaning of the research results and place them in a broader and more general context and perspective, often generalizing beyond the specific sample of the study.

Implications address the consequences of the results by relating them to the more general theoretical and conceptual framework of the research topic. It is here that the researchers add their own speculations and interpretation. Different researchers may, therefore, arrive at different implications from the same results, and this may lead to disagreement and discussion.

Recommendations are general or specific suggestions as to the use, applications, and utility of the research results. A recommendation may be made, for example, that a new teaching method which proved in the research to be advantageous should be adopted, or it may be that the teaching of foreign languages at an early age is not endorsed, since the research findings revealed that those who started early did not have an advantage compared to late starters. Recommendations can also be in the form of a call for the replication of a research study with different data collection procedures and a different research design, so as to obtain more convincing evidence for the results obtained. Recommendations from a piece of qualitative research may suggest that a quantitative research study should be conducted, using the findings obtained in the qualitative study as hypotheses; or, vice versa, the results of a piece of quantitative research may sometimes lead to a recommendation that a qualitative study be carried out to examine the problem in an in-depth manner, so as to explain the results obtained in the experimental research. In general, results obtained from quantitative research, often based on large, random samples, are more generalizable and may therefore lead to conclusions that recommend implementation of programs, curricula, or methods. However, since results of qualitative research are usually of an 'explanatory' nature, are often based on small samples, and are less generalizable, they do not often lead to recommendations for specific implementations.

It is important that the context for which the recommendations are made is the same as the one in which the research was conducted. For example, results obtained from research conducted in the classroom cannot usually lead to recommendations for learning languages out of the classroom, nor are results obtained in an informal language learning context applicable to a formal school learning context. Similarly, research conducted with one group of learners, such as children, cannot usually lead to recommendations for adult learners, since it is likely that a different set of variables affects learning in each of these settings.

We will now present some examples of interpretations of research results taken from the research studies referred to above. In Bejarano (1987) the conclusions are stated as follows:

These findings illustrate the greater effectiveness of the two group methods in developing listening comprehension skills and the greater effectiveness of the STAD techniques compared with the

DG and whole-class methods in teaching and learning discrete points (such as grammar and vocabulary) in the EFL classroom (p. 493).

In discussing the implications of these results, the researcher addresses the issue of 'what promoted higher language achievement in the classes utilizing small group techniques'. Here she relates the results of the study to the more general theoretical and conceptual framework of the research topic, that of the interaction of the social and communicative skills within the experimental context of the small-group setting.

This is in line with Taylor's (1983, p. 72) view of the features classroom instruction should incorporate. It is also in accordance with the communicative approach to language teaching, which assumes that language acquisition occurs with intensive engagement in extended discourse in real communicative contexts (Breen and Candlin 1980, Krashen 1981, Morrow 1981, Taylor 1983, Widdowson, 1978).

The researcher continues with the implications of the different parts of the results according to the stated social and linguistic theories. The same results could possibly have led another researcher to arrive at different implications.

Finally, the researcher provides specific recommendations for classroom teaching, based on the results:

Based on the theoretical principles underlying this research and the findings reported here, a cooperative small-group methodology in the language classroom is recommended. The different group techniques complement one another; they serve different teaching objectives in the language class and thus form the link between the teaching content (what) and the teaching process (how). Implementation of this approach requires intensive teaching training for use of the techniques, both in terms of operational procedures in the classroom and in terms of appropriate design of the learning tasks.

It is at this point that the researcher should ask questions as to whether the recommendations are warranted by the results and whether these recommendations are generalizable to all language learning contexts and to learners other than those participating in the research.

In the other study, Pica, Young, and Doughty (1987) present their conclusions as follows:

. . . redundancy in input was found to be an important factor in comprehension, whereas grammatical complexity of the input seemed to make little difference. The quantity of the input also appeared to be important, but primarily as a vehicle for redundancy (p. 753).

In placing the results in a broader context and a wider and more theoretical perspective, they report as follows:

. . . these results provide empirical support for what, up to now, have been only theoretical claims about the importance of interactional modifications in aiding comprehension of input. Interaction had a facilitating effect overall on comprehension, but when interaction had the greatest effect, this appeared to be accomplished through interactional modifications, in the form of confirmation and comprehension checks and clarification requests that brought about the greater number of repetitions necessary for comprehension (p. 753).

Some of the implications of the study lead to general recommendations and are presented as follows:

Our current findings suggest that it is possible for teachers to assist understanding of input through adjustments in quantity and redundancy of teacher talk, made without requests for clarifications or confirmation from their students, and that with certain kinds of input, these adjustments may be sufficient for learners' comprehension. However, our research results also indicate that an increase in the redundancy of teacher talk is not, in itself, enough to ensure comprehension, rather teachers should check on how well their students have understood and should constantly encourage them to initiate requests for clarification of meaning or to check with the teacher that they have understood (p. 753–4).

They go on to describe other implications of the results, such as the need for a special relationship to be established between teachers and students, different from the typical pattern of teacher elicitations taking place in the classroom, so that teachers check learners' understanding and not merely their spoken production.

The authors (Pica, Young, and Doughty) state their recommendations for classroom teaching, based on these results, as follows:

Perhaps the most significant pedagogical implication to be drawn is that any teacher or method that facilitates a realignment of the traditional roles of teacher and student, so that students can take greater initiative or assume more responsibility for their own learning, is likely to encourage in-class oral interaction, which in turn can increase comprehension of input (p. 754–5).

Thus, the results of the study lead to conclusions, to implications, and eventually to recommendations of a practical nature, that is, changing behavior within the classroom.

Reporting research

Once the research has been completed, from the initial phase of selecting the problem and determining the purpose of the study, to the last phase of interpreting its results, the research as a whole needs to be reported to the relevant audiences.

Types of reports

There are a number of formats for reporting research, such as articles to appear in journals, reports addressed to funding agencies, theses or dissertations as part of the requirements for university degrees, and papers to be presented at conferences. These formats differ from one another mostly in their purposes and the audiences which they address. We will now briefly describe them.

The *journal article* is a way of reporting research for professional journals or edited collections. The research is reported in a brief, yet informative way, focusing mostly on the main features of the research such as the purpose, review of the literature (often referred to as 'background'), procedures used for carrying out the research accompanied by tables, charts, and graphs, and interpretations of the results (often referred to as 'discussion').

The content and emphasis of the journal article will vary according to the intended readers (researchers or practitioners) and it is important for the researcher to be aware of the background and interest of the readers of the journal. Articles intended to be read by practitioners will emphasize the practical implications and recommendations of the research, while articles intended to be read by researchers will describe in detail the method used to collect the data, the construction of the data collection procedures, and the techniques used for analyzing the data. It is important for the novice researcher to be aware of the fact that articles submitted to journals go through a process of evaluation by experts who make a judgment and recommend whether they should be published or not.

The *thesis* or *dissertation* is a format for reporting research which graduate students write as part of fulfilling the requirements for an advanced academic degree. The student is expected to describe in great detail all the phases of the research so it can be examined and evaluated carefully by the reader. Thus the thesis or dissertation includes the purpose and significance of the study, the rationale, a thorough review of the literature, detailed information as to the research tools and the procedures involved in their development, a description of the process of data analysis and the results, and an interpretation of the results in the form of conclusions, implications, and recommendations. This detailed description of the process of the research is needed to provide the professors with an indication of the student's ability to carry out research.

Frequently, before conducting the research, the researcher writes a *research proposal*. This is a plan for research, usually written by graduate students, in order to obtain feedback on the proposed plan. Proposals are also required by funding agencies. Although different academic institutions and funding agencies have slightly different specifications as to the content and length of proposals, most call for a brief description of the research plan, emphasizing specifically the rationale and significance of the study, a survey of other work in the research area, a description of the procedures which the researcher is planning to use, and a discussion of the significance and intended contribution of the research.

The *research report* is another method of presentation. This term generally refers to the document which is required by agencies which support and fund research. Often such agencies will require *interim* or *progress* reports which describe the research process while it is going on, and a *final* report, once it is completed, which summarizes the research results, and includes conclusions and recommendations based on the whole study.

The *conference paper* is a way of reporting research at conferences, seminars, and colloquia. At such meetings research papers are usually presented orally. They are similar to the research article since research is reported in a concise, yet informative way, focusing on the most essential elements of the research. Hand-outs and transparencies can also accompany the presentations. As with the research article, here too, the content and emphasis of the oral report will depend to a large extent on the type of audience present at the meeting, and whether they are researchers or practitioners.

The components of the research report

In the previous section we described different ways of reporting research. While each form varies in the emphasis it puts on the different components of the research, in general, each will include elements of the following components: introduction and description of the problem or topic; review of the literature; design and methodology; data analysis and findings; and discussion of the results.

We will briefly describe each of these components. *Introduction and description of the problem or topic* is the section in which the researcher discusses the nature of the research. The introduction contains the background to the research problem or topic, the purpose of the research, the significance of the problem, and the questions to be addressed. Here the researcher may also state the hypotheses and research questions, but still in general terms. Definitions of important terminology should also be given. (See Chapters 1, 2, and 3 for further details of this component.)

In the *literature review* the researcher reports on the literature relevant to the problem: journal articles, research reports, and books that focus on different aspects of the problem, both in second language acquisition and in related areas. In the description of the literature the researcher focuses on the theoretical claims made in the research. A thorough survey of findings is made, particularly the major findings of the studies, with discussion of how they were obtained and what can be learned from them and applied to the specific research that is about to be conducted. Another important part of the literature survey is a critique of the research studies quoted, pointing to any problems in design, instrumentation, analysis, and conclusions. Thus the literature review is intended to provide a theoretical framework for the research as well as a description of how different studies contribute to the topic, leading to a statement of and a rationale for the study. (See Chapter 4.)

The *design and methodology* component generally begins with a clear and precise description of the research questions or hypotheses and of the different variables of the study. It then details the specific methods which the researcher selected to investigate the research problem or topic, and specifies the design of the study (whether it is qualitative (descriptive), experimental, or correlational, for example) and discusses the data collection procedures which will be used to investigate the different variables, how they were selected, developed, and used, and their reliability and validity. Then follows a description of the sample and subjects of the study, the procedures used to select them and, finally, the type and form of data collected. (See Chapters 5, 6, 7, and 8.)

In the *data analysis* component the researcher reports either on the statistical techniques used for analyzing the data or, in the case of qualitative analyses, on how the data were analyzed and the categories arrived at, together with a description of the ways in which the data were validated. (See Chapter 9 and the beginning of this chapter.)

The *discussion* component of the research report consists first of a summary statement of the research results as obtained from the previous component, and then a discussion of their meaning in a broader context, going beyond the results toward an interpretation in which the results are put in a broader perspective. This includes the contribution of the results to the general area of research, their implications, and whether they can lead to recommendations and suggestions for further research. (See the first part of this chapter.)

The last part of the research report consists of a bibliography and appendices. The *bibliography* contains the sources and references which the researcher used and consulted while conducting the research, and the *appendices* include additional material used, such as samples of data collection procedures, tests, raw data, copies of permission to use the instruments, or anything which may be of significance to the readers but is too detailed to be included in the body of the research report.

Closing the research cycle?

Research is cyclical; it is a recurring sequence of events. When we first began the research, we had a purpose for doing it: there was a topic, a problem, questions or hypotheses. (See Chapters 2 and 3.) We realized that different types of problems require different ways of seeking solutions. (See Chapter 3.) We reviewed the literature and contextualized the research problem within a larger body of knowledge. (See Chapter 4.) We designed and planned the research according to the type of problem. (See Chapters 5, 6, and 7.) We selected the appropriate procedures for collecting the research data (see Chapter 8), and then applied various techniques to analyzing the data and obtaining the research results. (See Chapter 9.) In the last phase of the research we summarized the results and interpreted them within the context of the problem as it was posed at the outset. Closing the research cycle means that the interpretation of the results leads the researcher back to the starting point. Figure 10.1 illustrates this notion of the research cycle.

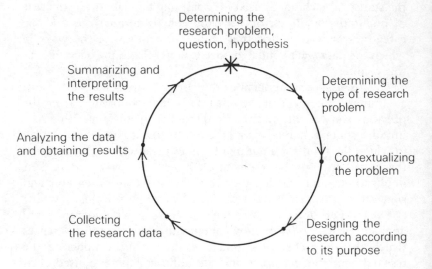

Determining the research problem, question, hypothesis

Summarizing and interpreting the results

Determining the type of research problem

Analyzing the data and obtaining results

Contextualizing the problem

Collecting the research data

Designing the research according to its purpose

Figure 10.1   The research cycle

However, the nature of research is such that the more answers are obtained, the more questions arise. Curiosity, in second language acquisition as in other disciplines, leads researchers to more problems, more questions, and more areas of research. Can we therefore ever consider that the research cycle is 'closed'?

For example, the results of a research study based on a group of learners can lead a researcher to conclude that a certain teaching method is preferable to another for teaching second languages. However, this very conclusion may lead to new questions, such as whether the method is also effective and appropriate for other types of learners, for different proficiency levels, for different backgrounds, in different contexts, and with different teachers. To take another example, a researcher who investigates the extent to which certain identified variables predict success in acquiring a second language may, in the process of carrying out the research, identify new variables which were not known to exist at the outset of the research. These new variables will now provide challenging questions for new research.

Furthermore, in social science research results need to be

replicated. Only when the same results come up time and again can the researcher have confidence in the findings. *Replication* of research is therefore a way of conducting research for the purpose of verifying and confirming research results. Here, too, the cycle does not end, but rather the results of one study lead to further research.

Another common phenomenon in research with human beings is that similar research problems generate conflicting and contradictory results. Such results have been found, for example, in research on age and second language acquisition, the order of morpheme acquisition, the effect of certain teaching methods on achievement, and the effect of bilingualism and bilingual education on learners. In such instances the researcher may have recourse to *meta analysis*. Meta analysis takes the results obtained from a number of research studies on the same problem, synthesizes, summarizes, and combines them in order to arrive at more conclusive answers about the problem (Hedges and Olkin 1985). Research studies require certain properties in order to be included in the analysis, that is, an acceptable sample size and similar research designs.

Although there are a number of areas in second language acquisition research that have produced conflicting results, there have as yet been few meta analysis studies. One such study, which has received major attention recently, is on the effectiveness of bilingual education (Willig 1985, Baker 1987, Willig 1987, Secada 1987). A number of studies that produced conflicting results on the impact of bilingual education were analyzed together in an attempt to arrive at more conclusive findings.

Secondary analysis is yet another way of continuing the research cycle. In this approach a researcher returns to the data that have already been analyzed and re-analyzes them in a different way. This analysis often leads to new and different findings from those obtained in the first analysis.

The procedures of replication, meta-analysis, and secondary analysis all show that the research cycle is an on-going and continuous process in which answers to questions may raise new ones.

This perpetual cycle is a result of the complexity of the phenomenon of language learning. As no simple solutions can be found, different and varied approaches to research are required, because no single approach can provide valid answers on its own. In order to capture the complexity and uniqueness of this area of research into second language acquisition phenomena, in Chapter 2 we introduced four parameters. The different research designs, the procedures for collecting the data, and the ways of analyzing these data as described in the subsequent chapters, were all a reflection of these parameters.

The parameters represent some underlying principles from which research approaches that capture the uniqueness and complexity of the discipline were developed. These four parameters, each presented on a continuum, provided the framework for second language research as presented in this book.

The first two parameters involved the conceptual levels and the other two the operational level. At the conceptual level, with the *first* parameter we focused on the approach. We differentiated between a synthetic and an analytic approach to research, the synthetic emphasizing the interdependence of the parts of the field, the analytic implying research focused on the role of the constituent parts that make up the total phenomenon. The first thus represents an approach which allows the researcher to view the separate parts as a coherent whole, and the second identifies a single factor or cluster of factors which are constituents of the major systems.

The *second* parameter related to the purpose of the research, and there we differentiated between heuristic and deductive objectives of second language research. *Heuristic* research has as its objective the discovery or description of patterns of relationships, yet to be identified, in some aspects of second language, while the *deductive* aims to test a specific hypothesis about second language learning. In the first, the objective may be limited to describing what happens or to gathering data and generating hypotheses about the phenomenon studied, while in deductive research the aim is to test hypotheses in order to make predictions or to develop theories about the phenomenon in question.

The *third* parameter was the degree of control and manipulation of the research context. In this parameter, on the one hand there is research which intentionally exerts little control, manipulation, or restriction on the research context, while at the other extreme there are research designs which methodologically manipulate and control various components in the research context, such as the experimental treatment, or the subjects who will participate in the study.

The *fourth* and last parameter concerned the degree of explicitness or specificity of the data and the data collection procedures. At one end of that continuum are data collection procedures of a high degree of explicitness, where the data collection tools specify in advance the data that will be elicited, while at the other end there are data collection procedures which do not specify the exact data that will be collected, the researchers themselves often being the tools who collect the data that seems relevant at the time of the study.

These four parameters (described in detail in Chapter 2) provide a general framework for second language acquisition research, since they allow a variety of combinations and approaches. These combinations lead to differentiation between qualitative and quantitative research designs, which imply a variety of methods for collecting and analyzing data and different ways of interpreting the results.

It is important to remember that there is on-going debate regarding the nature of the relationship between qualitative and quantitative research. One issue is whether they are based on complementary or entirely different and incompatible assumptions – quantitative on a positivist paradigm claiming that behavior can be explained through objective facts, and qualitative on the assumption of a phenomenological paradigm according to which there are multiple realities that are socially defined. A related issue concerns the nature of the relationship between quantitative and qualitative research *methods* and these paradigms. On the one hand there are those who believe that qualitative and quantitative methods are incompatible because they are based on paradigms that make different assumptions about the world and about the things which constitute valid research, and that there is a logical relationship between the principles inherent in the paradigm and the methods chosen (Smith and Heshusius 1986). On the other hand there are others who see a looser relationship between paradigms and methods, so that methods are a collection of techniques and the attributes of a paradigm are not inherently linked to either qualitative or quantitative methods; both method-types can be associated with the attributes of either the qualitative or quantitative paradigms, and it is possible to combine them (Reichardt and Cook 1979, Smith 1983, Firestone 1987, Atkinson, Delamont, and Hammersley 1988). In both cases the end result of either approach is a more comprehensive and elaborated under-standing of the phenomena under study.

Whatever approach and belief a researcher has, the use of a variety of methods, irrespective of the underlying assumptions, will lead to a better and more thorough understanding of the topic researched.

There are, then, many different approaches and directions for carrying out research in second language acquisition. No one method is preferable and no single approach will suffice; rather, in order to acquire more knowledge in this field we need to combine and blend different approaches. The result will be a broader perspective and a more comprehensive insight into the complex phenomenon of how people learn second languages.

Summary

In this concluding chapter we discussed the last phases of the research. First we described ways of reporting and summarizing research results, and differentiated between methods of reporting the results of quantitative and qualitative studies. Then we discussed ways of going beyond the results to the interpretation phase where the researcher discusses the meaning of the results within the general theory, proceeding from the specific study toward implications and recommendations. In this section we introduced different ways of reporting the research and differentiated between a variety of formats, the choice of format usually depending on the intended readership of the report. In the last section we discussed the cyclical nature of research, and introduced meta analysis and secondary analysis to point to the need for synthesis of different research findings on a given topic. We concluded the chapter by reviewing the four parameters and by discussing the major differences between quantitative and qualitative research calling for the combination of a variety of approaches in researching second language acquisition problems.

Activities

1 Select a general area or topic of research in second language acquisition (such as the learning of vocabulary, reading strategies, formal versus informal learning). Plan two research studies, one which will be heuristic/synthetic and the other deductive/ analytic. For each of the studies show how they will be different in terms of the following: research question, theoretical framework, research design (sample, type of data collected, data collection procedures, number of subjects, etc.), data analysis techniques, and expected conclusions and recommendations from the research.

2 Select two articles from a journal in the field of second language acquisition, and identify the parts in the discussion which focus on the conclusions, implications, and recommendations. Show how the same research results could lead to different implications or recommendations.

References

Atkinson, P., Delamount, S., and Hammersley, M. 1988. 'Qualitative research traditions: A British response to Jacob.' *Review of Educational Research* 58/2:231–250.

Baker, K. 1987. 'Comments on Willig's "A meta-analysis of selected studies on the effectiveness of bilingual education."' *Review of Educational Research* 57/3:351–362.

Bejarano, Y. 1987. 'A cooperative small-group methodology in the language classroom.' *TESOL Quarterly* 21/3:483–504.

Breen, M. P. and Candlin, C. N. 1980. 'The essentials of a communicative curriculum.' *Applied Linguistics*, 1:89–112.

Firestone, W. 1987. 'Meaning in method: The rhetoric of quantitative and qualitative research.' *Educational Researcher* 16/7:16–21.

Hedges, L. V. and Olkin, I. 1985. *Statistical Methods for Meta Analysis*. Orlando, FA: Academic Press.

Krashen, S. 1981. *Second Language Acquisition and Second Language Learning*. New York: Pergamon Press.

Morrow, K. 1981. 'Principles of communicative methodology' in K. Johnson and K. Morrow (eds.): *Communication in the Classroom*. London: Longman.

Pica, T., Young, R., and Doughty, C. 1987. 'The impact of interaction on comprehension.' *TESOL Quarterly* 21/4:737–758.

Reichardt, C. S. and Cook, T. D. 1979. 'Beyond qualitative versus quantitative methods' in T. D. Cook and C. S. Reichardt (eds.): *Qualitative and Quantitative Methods in Evaluation Research*. Beverly Hills, CA.: Sage.

Secada, W. G. 1987. 'This is 1987, not 1980: A comment on a comment.' *Review of Educational Research* 57/3:377–384.

Smith, J. K. 1983. 'Quantitative versus qualitative research: An attempt to clarify the issue.' *Educational Researcher* 12/3:6–13.

Smith, J. K. and Heshusius, L. 1986. 'Closing down the conversation: The end of the quantitative-qualitative debate among educational inquiries.' *Educational Researcher* 15/1:4–12.

Taylor, B. P. 1983. 'Teaching ESL: Incorporating a communicative student-centered component.' *TESOL Quarterly* 17:69–88.

Widdowson, H. G. 1978. *Teaching Language as Communication*. London: Oxford University Press.

Willig, A. C. 1985. 'A meta-analysis of selected studies on the effectiveness of bilingual education.' *Review of Educational Research* 55/3:269–317.
Willig, A. C. 1987. 'Examining bilingual education research through meta-analysis and narrative review: A response to Baker.' *Review of Educational Research* 57/3:377–384.

Appendix
References for further reading

Research methodology

Babbie, E. R. 1973. *Survey Research Methods*. Belmont, CA.: Wadsworth.

Borg, W. R. and Gall, M. D. 1979. *Educational Research: An Introduction* (third edition). New York: Longman.

Campbell, D. T. and Stanley, J. C. 1966. *Experimental and Quasi-experimental Designs for Research*. Chicago: Rand McNally.

Cook. T. D. and Campbell, D. T. 1979. *Quasi-experimentation: Design and Analysis for Field Settings*. Chicago: Rand McNally.

Gay, L. R. 1981. *Educational Research*. Columbus, Ohio: Merrill.

Hatch, E. and Farhady, H. 1982. *Research Design and Statistics for Applied Linguistics*. Rowley, Mass.: Newbury House.

Isaac, S. and William, B. M. 1983. *Handbook in Research and Evaluation*. EDITS.

Kamil, M., Langer, J., and Shanahan, T. 1985. *Understanding Reading and Writing Research*. Boston: Allyn and Bacon.

Kaplan, M. A. 1984. *The Conduct of Inquiry: Methodology for the Behavioral Sciences*. New York: Harper and Row.

Kerlinger, F. 1973. *Foundations of Behavioral Research* (second edition). New York: Holt, Rinehardt and Winston.

Kuhn, T. S. 1970. *The Structure of Scientific Revolutions* (second edition). Chicago: University of Chicago Press.

Shulman, L. S. 1981. 'Discipline of inquiry in education: An overview.' *Educational Researcher* 10/6:5–12.

Thorndike, R. L. and Hagen, E. 1969. *Measurement and Evaluation in Psychology and Education* (third edition). New York: Wiley.

Thorndike, R. L. 1971. *Educational Measurement*. Washington, D.C.: Council on Education.

Travers, R. M. W. 1964. *An Introduction to Educational Research*. New York: Macmillan.

Vockell, E. L. 1983. *Educational Research*. New York: Macmillan.

Van Dalen, D. B. 1979. *Understanding Educational Research*. New York: McGraw-Hill.

Wiersma, W. 1985. *Research Methods in Education*. Boston: Allyn and Bacon.

Statistics

Amick, D. J. and Walberg, H. J. 1975. *Introductory Multivariate Research*. Berkeley, CA.: McCuthan.

Cohen, J. and Cohen, P. 1975. *Applied Multiple Regression/Correlation Analysis for the Behavioral Sciences.* Hillsdale, N.J.: Lawrence Erlbaum.

Cochran, W. G. 1977. *Sampling Techniques* (third edition). New York: Wiley.

Cochran, W. G. 1981 *Statistical Analysis in Psychology and Education.* New York: McGraw-Hill.

Guilford, J. P. and Fruchter, B. 1973. *Fundamental Statistics in Psychology and Education* (sixth edition). New York: McGraw-Hill.

Hays, W. 1973. *Statistics for the Social Sciences.* New York: Holt, Rinehart and Winston.

Hedges, L. V. and Olkin, I. 1985. *Statistical Methods for Meta Analysis.* Orlando, FA.: Academic Press.

Hollander, M. and Wolfe, A. 1973. *Nonparametric Statistical Methods.* New York: J. Wiley.

Kerlinger, F. N. and Pedhazur, E. J. 1973. *Multiple Regression in Behavioral Research.* New York: Holt, Rinehart and Winston.

Nie, N. H., Hull, C. H., Jenkins, J. K., Steinbrenner, K., and Bent, D. H. 1975. *SPSS: Statistical Package for the Social Sciences* (second edition). New York: McGraw-Hill.

Shavelson, R. 1981. *Statistical Reasoning for the Behavioral Sciences.* Boston: Allyn and Bacon.

Siegal, S. 1956. *Nonparametric Statistics for the Behavioral Sciences.* New York: McGraw-Hill.

Thorndike, R. M. 1978. *Correlational Procedures for Research.* New York: Gardner Press.

Winer, B. J. 1971 *Statistical Process in Experimental Design.* New York: McGraw-Hill.

Woods, A., Fletcher, P., and Hughes, A. 1986. *Statistics in Language Studies.* Cambridge: Cambridge University Press.

Qualitative research

Atkinson, P., Delamount, S., and Hammersley, M. 1988. 'Qualitative research traditions: A British response to Jacob.' *Review of Educational Research* 58/2:231–250.

Chilcott, J. H. 1987. 'Where are you coming from and where are you going? The reporting of ethnographic research.' *American Educational Research Journal* 24/2:199–218.

Eisner, E. 1981. 'On the difference between scientific and artistic approaches to qualitative research.' *Educational Researcher* 10/4:5–9.

Erickson, F. 1984. 'What makes ethnography "ethnographic"?' *Anthropology and Education Quarterly* 15/1:51–56.

Ericsson, K. and Simon, H. A. 1980. 'Verbal reports as data.' *Psychological Review* 87:215–251.

Firestone, W. 1987. 'Meaning in method: The rhetoric of quantitative and qualitative research.' *Educational Researcher* 16/7:16–21.

Jacob, E. 1987. 'Qualitative research traditions: A review.' *Review of Educational Research* 57/1:1–50.

Miles, M. B. and Huberman, A. M. 1984a. 'Drawing valid meaning from qualitative data: Toward a shared craft.' *Educational Researcher* 13/5:20–30.

Miles, M. B. and Huberman, A. M. 1984b. '*Qualitative Data Analysis: A Sourcebook of New Methods.*' Beverly Hills, CA.: Sage.

Patton, M. Q. 1980. '*Qualitative Evaluation Methods.*' Beverly Hills, CA.: Sage.

Reichardt, C. S. and Cook, T. D. 1979. 'Beyond qualitative versus quantitative methods' in T. D. Cook and C. S. Reichardt (eds.): *Qualitative and Quantitative Methods in Evaluation Research.* Beverly Hills, CA.: Sage.

Rossman, G. B. and Wilson, B. L. 1985. 'Numbers and words: Combining quantitative and qualitative methods in a single large-scale evaluation study.' *Evaluation Review* 9/5:627–43.

Smith, J. K. 1983. 'Quantitative versus qualitative research: An attempt to clarify the issue.' *Educational Researcher* 12/3:6–13.

Smith, M. L. 1987. 'Publishing qualitative research.' *American Educational Research Journal* 24/2:173–183.

Smith, J. K. and Heshusius, L. 1986. 'Closing down the conversation: The end of the quantitative-qualitative debate among educational inquirers.' *Educational Researcher* 15/1:4–13.

Tesch, R. 1987. 'Comparing the Most Widely Used Methods of Qualitative Analysis: What do they have in Common?' Paper presented at the American Educational Research Association Convention, Washington, D.C.

Van Maanen, J. 1983. *Qualitative Methods.* Beverly Hills, CA.: Sage.

Data collection procedures

Allwright, R. 1988. *Observation in the Language Classroom.* New York: Longman.

Buros, O. K. (ed.) 1978. *The Eighth Mental Measurement Yearbook.* Highland Park, N.J.: Gryphon Press.

Guilford, J. P. 1954. *Psychometric Methods* (second edition). New York.

Guttmann, L. 1950. 'The basis for scaleogram analysis' in S. Stouffer *et al.* (eds.): *Measurement and Prediction.* Princeton: Princeton University Press/McGraw-Hill.

House, E. R. 1980. *Evaluating with Validity.* Beverly Hills, Ca.: Sage.

Isaac, S. and William, B. M. 1983. *Handbook in Research and Evaluation.* EDITS.

LeCompte, M. D. and Goetz, J. P. 1982. 'Problems of reliability and validity in ethnographic research.' *Review of Educational Research* 52:31–60.

Levy, P. and Goldstein, H. 1984. *Tests in Education*. London: Academic Press.

Likert, R. A. 1932. 'A technique for the measurement of attitudes.' *Archives of Psychology* No. 40.

Mathison, S. 1988. 'Why triangulate?' *Educational Researcher* 17/2: 12–23.

Mehrens, W. A. and Lehmann, I. J. 1969. *Measurement and Evaluation in Education and Psychology*. New York: Holt, Rinehart and Winston.

Nunnally, J. C. 1967. *Psychometric Theory*. New York: McGraw-Hill.

Osgood, C. E., Suci, G. J., and Tannenbaum, P. H. 1957. *The Measurement of Meaning*. Urbana: University of Illinois Press.

Schuman, H. and Presser, S. 1981. *Questions and Answers in Attitude Surveys*. New York: Academic Press.

Snider, J. G. and Osgood, C. E. 1969. *Semantic Differential Technique: A Sourcebook*. Chicago: Aldine.

Spraeley, J. P. 1980. *Participant Observation*. New York: Holt, Rinehart and Winston.

SPSS X User's Guide (second edition). 1986. New York: McGraw-Hill.

Thurstone, L. L. and Chave, E. J. 1929. *The Measurement of Attitude*. Chicago: University of Chicago Press.

Wiersman, E. and Jurs, S. G. 1985. *Educational Measurement and Testing*. Boston: Allyn and Bacon.

Webb, E. J., Campbell, D. T., Schwatz, R. D., and Sechrest, L. 1966. *Unobtrusive Measures*. Chicago: Rand McNally.

Language testing

Carroll, B. 1980. *Testing Communicative Performance*. Oxford: Pergamon Press.

Cohen, A. 1980. *Testing Language Ability in the Classroom*. Rowley, Mass.: Newbury House.

Cohen, A. and Hosenfeld, C. 1981. 'Some uses of mentalistic data in second language research.' *Language Learning* 31/2:285–313.

Henning, G. 1987. *A Guide to Language Testing*. Rowley, Mass.: Newbury House.

Madsen, H. S. 1982. *Techniques in Testing*. London: Oxford University Press.

Oller, J. W. 1983. *Issues in Language Testing Research*. Rowley, Mass.: Newbury House.

Shohamy, E. 1985. *A Practical Handbook in Language Testing for the Second Language Teacher* (experimental edition). Tel Aviv University.

Underhill, N. 1987. *Testing Spoken Language*. Cambridge: Cambridge University Press.

MAJOR JOURNALS IN SECOND
LANGUAGE ACQUISITION

Applied Psycholinguistics
Applied Linguistics
Canadian Modern Language Review
ELT Documents
ELT Journal
English Teaching Forum
Foreign Language Annals
Interlanguage Studies Bulletin
IRAL (International Review of Applied Linguistics)
Language Testing
Language Acquisition
Language Learning
Modern Language Journal
Second Language Acquisition Research
Studies in Second Language Acquisition
System
TESOL Quarterly

MAJOR JOURNALS IN RELATED
DISCIPLINES

Linguistics and language

Child Development
Discourse Processes
Journal of Research in Reading
Journal of Reading
Journal of Reading Behavior
Journal of Multilingual and Multicultural Development
Language
Language Problems and Language Planning
Language in Society
Language Speech
Linguistic Inquiry
Reading Research Quarterly
Reading Education
Reading
Studies in Language
Written Communication

Education

American Educational Research Journal
American Journal of Education
British Journal of Educational Studies
Education
Education and Psychological Measurement
Educational Research
Educational Research Quarterly
Educational Researcher
Educational Review
English Education
Journal of Communication
Journal of Educational Measurement
Journal of Educational Research
Journal of Teacher Education
Journal of Verbal Learning and Verbal Behavior
Research in Teaching English
Review of Education
Review of Educational Research

Sociology and psychology

American Educational Research Journal
American Journal of Psychology
American Journal of Sociology
American Psychologist
Applied Psycholinguistics
Behavioral Science Research
British Journal of Sociology of Education
British Journal of Psychology
Child Development
Cognition
Cognitive Psychology
Developmental Psychology
Educational Psychologist
Journal of Experimental Psychology
Journal of Psycholinguistic Research
Journal of General Psychology
Memory and Cognition
Psychological Review
Reading Psychology

Index